BREWOOD GRAMMAR SCHOOL
HEADMASTERS MAKING HISTORY
1547–1875

Margaret Heath

Grosvenor House
Publishing Limited

The right of Margaret Heath to be identified as the author of this
work has been asserted in accordance with Section 78
of the Copyright, Designs and Patents Act 1988

The book cover is copyright to Margaret Heath

This book is published by
Grosvenor House Publishing Ltd
Link House
140 The Broadway, Tolworth, Surrey, KT6 7HT.
www.grosvenorhousepublishing.co.uk

A CIP record for this book
is available from the British Library

Paperback ISBN 978-1-80381-748-4
Hardback ISBN 978-1-80381-749-1

Dedication

To Elliot and Ella,
May you love Brewood as much as I do.

Contents

Preface

I have used original sources, mainly from Staffordshire Record Office and the William Salt Library, but also from other archives. I have supplemented the material from newspaper reports of the time and books written about Brewood, and Brewood Grammar School.

I chose to research the biographies of the headmasters of Brewood because, surprisingly, their life stories had either not been covered in the books about Brewood Grammar School or, for certain headmasters, only briefly. As I researched each headmaster, I was impressed by their very interesting lives. Brewood Grammar School was certainly no ordinary school, and Dr Matthew Knightley, one of the founders of the school, was no ordinary person either. His ancestry was linked to some very well-known names in history.

The majority of the headmasters appointed had active interests outside the school, such as Reverend Feilde who researched a comprehensive history of Staffordshire which left him almost bankrupt. Reverend Henry Brookland Mason was an advocate of adult education, horticulture and railways. He believed in the need for the standardisation of time in Britain, particularly useful for railway timetables, and helped to ensure its introduction. Also of note for their teaching methods were Reverend William Budworth, Reverend George Croft, whose name has been linked to the Birmingham riots of the eighteenth century, and Reverend Richard Wall, all very successful teachers at the school.

It was a requirement by the Trustees that the headmaster had to live at the school. It was preferable for the headmaster to be married, but not essential. It was necessary though for any successful applicant within the period covered by this book, to have attended either the University of Oxford or the University of Cambridge, and be in holy orders. Ideally, the candidate would have obtained a Master of Arts degree.

The headmasters at Brewood Grammar School were limited in what they could teach and how they could improve both the school and the curriculum. This was partly because Brewood Grammar School was an Endowed Grammar School and the Trustees were under the jurisdiction of the Charity Commissioners. Reverend Kempson, who bequeathed a substantial amount of money to Brewood schools, tried to find a solution to raise the status of Brewood Grammar School by introducing another Classical School in Brewood, which would provide more teachers and accommodation than was allowed by the Charity Commissioners.

The headmasters and ushers were controlled by both the Trustees and the estate manager, the latter having some control over their finances. This was particularly the case during the headmastership of Reverend Brown when the sale of land at Willenhall for mining purposes left both Brown and his usher, Reverend Rushton, financially very weak. The residents of Brewood parish and the parents of the pupils also wanted to influence the curriculum at the school and the standard of teaching. If they had any problems with the headmaster or usher, public meetings were held to try and find a suitable solution.

In a decree of Chancery for 1630, the six Trustees of the school were named as John Lane of the Hyde, Edward Giffard of Brewood, Matthew Moreton of Engleton, Roger Fowke of Gunston, Geoffrey Somerford of Somerford and Richard Warton, vicar of Brewood. In later years this expanded to include the most respected members of the clergy and landed gentry in the area. The list of Trustees for 1780 embraced forty names of the landed gentry and clergyman of Staffordshire, and nearby areas, but excluded the Giffard family, who had re-founded the school in the sixteenth century along with relative Reverend Dr Matthew Knightley. The exclusion of the Giffards as Trustees, it is safe to assume, was because of their Catholic faith. The pupils at the school were expected to attend St Mary and St Chad's Church of England parish church, opposite the school where headmaster, usher and pupils all had their allocated seats and pews. In 1850, Mr T. W. Giffard and Mr W. P. Giffard were again listed as Trustees of Brewood Grammar School.

I have tried not to get side-tracked too much with important issues in Brewood, particularly the measures put in place by Brewood residents to prevent a cholera epidemic during the nineteenth century, or the sending away of some young Brewood children to the cotton mills of Lancashire, but the headmasters of Brewood were, undoubtedly, central members of the community.

The book finishes at 1875 as this is the year that the school is restructured under the Endowed Schools Act of 1869 and a new curriculum is officially embraced. In this year, Reverend Rushton, the last usher of Brewood Grammar School dies and the headmaster, James Heber Taylor, leaves the school. The autumn of 1875 is a new beginning for the school under the leadership of the new headmaster Thomas England Rhodes.

Acknowledgements

This book was researched and written for more than a decade, and it could not have been achieved without the help and support of so many people.

I should firstly like to thank Paul Anderton, of the *North Staffordshire Historians Guild*, who has edited my book with so much encouragement, patience and tactfulness. His knowledge, enthusiasm and expertise have been unwavering. I am also indebted to Rebecca Jackson who has also cheerfully given so much help and advice with the final proof-reading. Any mistakes now are entirely my own.

I am extremely grateful and honoured to receive a grant towards the publication of this book by the *North Staffordshire Historians Guild*. I feel extremely humbled to receive it from a group of local historians for whom I have so much respect.

I should also like to thank all my former colleagues at the Staffordshire Record Office and William Salt Library who have been untiring in their support and encouragement, providing documents and the reproduction of the illustrations so quickly and efficiently. I am also grateful to the Trustees of the William Salt Library for permission to reproduce the Staffordshire Views.

There are other people who have helped me in so many different ways, in particular Catherine Nichols but also Nigel Tringham, Randle Knight, James Sutton, David Horovitz and Richard Nichols, who have all provided information and so much help and support at different times.

I should like to express my gratitude to Sharon Pitt and Cathy Knight at Brewood Library but also to Graham Bailey of Brewood Civic Society for kindly providing the illustrations from the Brewood Civic Society Archives. I am indebted to the Old Boys' Association of Brewood Grammar School, in particular David Evans and Sallie Cormes for allowing me access to the school museum, but also to Roy Wright, President of the Old Boys' Association for permission to reproduce the colour engraving of the school by Richard Paddy, dated 1799. Credit and sincere thanks for the enhancement of this old engraving goes to John Lambert who has brought it back to its former glory.

I thank my family for their encouragement whilst writing this book but I am particularly grateful to my husband, Maurice, who has provided advice and help on so many occasions.

My apologies to anyone whose name I have inadvertently omitted.

Margaret Heath, Brewood, 2023

Abbreviations

LRO   Lichfield Record Office

ODNB   *Oxford Dictionary of National Biography*

SHC   *Collections for a History of Staffordshire*

SRO   Staffordshire Record Office

VCH   *Victoria County History*

WSL   William Salt Library

The Lichfield Record Office, Staffordshire Record Office and William Salt Library are currently being amalgamated on one site and will, in future, be known as the Staffordshire History Centre.

List of Illustrations

Chapter One

The origins of Brewood Free Grammar School

In January 1546/47 the school in Brewood was an empty building. The schoolmaster had left, or died, and without him there were no pupils. Henry, Lord Stafford, of Stafford Castle, was not happy with the situation. He was an influential man, learned and eager to promote the education of children. He wrote to Sir John Giffard of Chillington Hall, requesting that Giffard and the other parishioners of Brewood, rectified the situation.[1]

Giffard and Stafford knew each other. They had both attended Henry VIII at the Field of the Cloth of Gold in 1520 and Sir John Giffard had held key positions in Henry VIII's household as well as being Sheriff of Staffordshire at various times between 1518 and 1542. Lord Stafford wanted the school at Brewood in use again and he had the perfect candidate, the bearer of the letter, Sir Raufe Blowre, who had taught Lord Stafford's own children. Stafford gave Blowre a glowing report, describing him as very diligent and very honest.[2] No records survive to confirm if Blowre ever taught at Brewood, but this was the very first move leading to the foundation in 1547 of what was to become Brewood Free Grammar School.[3]

The empty school was likely to have been a chantry school and was almost certainly located at The Chantry, now a house, opposite Brewood parish church. Chantry priests were attached to a parish church and appointed for the sole purpose of regularly singing mass for the souls of deceased benefactors, who had bequeathed land, goods or money for that purpose. The priests taught their pupils not only to sing but also to read and write, but in Latin rather than English. The schools then expanded to provide an education for boarders too, which provided welcome extra income, as the priests were expected to provide food for any visitors including carpenters, masons and other church workmen.[4]

The earliest record of mass being said for the souls in Brewood is a bequest from Robert Papagy. In approximately 1294 Papagy gave two selions of land in Whete croft, between the land of John and William of Bromehale [Broom Hall], as payment for a priest to regularly pray and sing mass for his soul in Brewood church on the Lord's days.[5] Broom Hall was owned by the Knightley family, ancestors of Matthew Knightley one of the founders of the new Brewood Free Grammar School, from at least the early fifteenth century.[6] Matthew Knightley and his family later lived at nearby Engleton.

In 1545 an Act was passed by parliament for the dissolution of Colleges, Chantries and Free Chapels. The purpose of the Act was to ensure that any bequests remained as the benefactors intended and were not improving the personal finances of one or more trustees. King Henry VIII used this Act to survey the chantries and confiscated all chantry endowments which had been misappropriated. This conveniently helped to finance his military activities in France. Henry VIII died on 28 January 1546/7, ten days after Stafford's letter to Giffard, and his son and heir, Edward, succeeded Henry as king and during his reign, in 1547, parliament passed the Act for the Dissolution of Chantries. It has been estimated that there were 145 chantry priests in Staffordshire at the beginning of the sixteenth century, being reduced to 74 by 1548, and the number of schools in Staffordshire reduced from ten schools to five.[7] Tong Collegiate School, Shropshire, five miles from Brewood, was dissolved by Henry VIII in September 1546, but there is no record of Brewood School having been forced to close too, but as many papers have not survived, this may have happened.[8] However, it was not unknown for the early schools to have stood empty from time to time.[9]

The beginnings of Brewood Free Grammar School

Sir John Giffard followed the request of Henry, Lord Stafford and enlisted the aid of his son, Thomas Giffard, and a relative, Matthew Knightley, clerk and Doctor of Divinity, to help reinstate the school. There has been much written about the Giffard family, but who was Dr Matthew Knightley?[10] At the time that Dr Knightley was approached for help from John Giffard, he was rector of All Saint's church, Cossington in Leicestershire, and rector of St. Mary's church, Fowlmere, Cambridgeshire, but he had been born at Brewood and attended school there. More detail about Matthew Knightley can be found in the addendum in this book, but briefly, Knightley was related to the Knightley families of Staffordshire, and the Moreton family of Engleton, Brewood. However, Matthew Knightley was also related to both John Howard, Duke of Norfolk, who had acquired Fowlmere in Cambridgeshire, and to the Danyell/ Daniel families of Rathwire and Messing.

The school at Brewood that John Giffard, Thomas Giffard, and Matthew Knightley helped to re-establish was to continue for centuries as their legacy for the education of the "youth" in the parish of Brewood and other towns, villages and hamlets nearby, and for the "commonwealth of the whole country". The Giffards and Matthew Knightley probably asked their friends, relatives, and local people, to donate land and houses for the benefit of the education of the young. These gifts were then put in trust to pay for the salary of "one honest discreet man sufficiently learned in grammar to keep a Free Grammar School in Brewood" and instruct all manner of children and young men at the school, free of charge. It is generally thought that Matthew Knightley made a large financial contribution to the cost of the school. He certainly left money in his will to the school at Brewood, the vicar, and the poor people of the town and parish of "Bruyde", where he was born.[11] The school property was located in Brewood, Chillington, Gunston, Willenhall, Wheaton Aston, Lapley, Bushbury, Hartley Green, Gayton and Coven, all within the historic county of Staffordshire.[12]

Brewood Free Grammar School is likely to have been re-established at The Chantry and moved at some time to its present site after the Civil War but the documentary evidence is unclear. The *Victoria County History* states that a coloured pen drawing of the school, possibly done in 1799 by Richard Paddy, shows the school to have been built in the late seventeenth century. In this drawing it can be seen that the school is at its current location.[13]

There is an indenture written in 1715, during the reign of George I confirming that the School House was in the same place that it had been in 1667-1668.[14] This would support the theory that the school had moved after the Civil War. The Chantry received renovations in the early eighteenth century.

Another indenture of 1727 at Staffordshire Record Office, relates to the premises and hereditaments of Brewood Free Grammar School from the time of Elizabeth I, and refers to the School House. It mentions clearly the messuage commonly called the School House where the school was "then and now" is kept, together with the garden etc.[15] In other words, it was on the same site as it had been during the seventeenth century. However, a transcript of the abstract of title of the Trustees of Brewood Free Grammar School within the Giffard Collection at the Staffordshire Record Office, implies that the school had moved by 1726/7. It omits the words "and now".[16]

Notes

1 For further information *see* SHC 4th *Series, Volume 25,* pp. 11-14.
2 Ralph Blower/Blowre/Blore became rector of All Saints' Church, Worthen, Shropshire from 1558–1570 and rector of Tysoe, Warwickshire from 1561–1562. On 16 May 1652, Ralph Blore, clerk, bought the advowson of the rectory of Church Eaton for £40 from Henry, Lord Stafford. Henry, Lord Stafford was buried at Worthen church on 8 May 1563, and Sir Raufe Blowre, rector of Worthen, was buried at the church seven years later in 1570. 'Sir' was used as a title for clergymen who had taken the Bachelor of Art degree.
3 *SHC 4th series, Volume 25, Letter 125,* p. 150.
4 Household accounts kept from 1453–60 by a chantry priest at Bridport. W.A. Pantin in *"Chantry Priests' Houses and other Medieval Lodgings"*.
5 VCH and WSL, S.MS 201 (1) p. 356. A 'selion' is a strip of land used in the open cultivation system.
6 John de Knightley owned Broom Hall [Bremhale] in 1410 before he, his son Richard, and John Porcell leased it to Hugh and Edith Parker of Patshull *see* Northampton Archives *catalogue reference* K (C)142, 1st November 1410; Richard Knightley sued several people from Brewood and Horsebrook for letting their cattle graze on his land at Broom Hall in 1422 *in* David Horovitz, *Brewood: Some notes on the history of Brewood in Staffordshire, with an account of the escape of Charles II after the Battle of Worcester on 3rd September 1651,* (David Horovitz, 1992), p. 94.
7 *SHC 1915,* p. xxxiii.
8 Robert Jeffrey, *Discovering Tong, Its History, Myths and Curiosities,* (Robert Jeffrey for Tong Parochial Church Council, 2007), p.78.
9 Nicholas Carlisle, *A Concise Description of the Endowed Grammar Schools in England and Wales, Volume 2,* (Baldwin, Cradock and Joy, 1818), p. 487.

10 For information about the Giffard family _see_ *Volume V New Series*, 1902: Honourable George Wrottesley: *The Giffards from the Conquest to the present time*, pp. 1-232; _and_ Patrick Joseph Doyle: *The Giffards of Chillington, a Catholic landed family 1642–1861,* M.A. thesis, Durham University, 1968.

11 Will of Matthew Knightley, written 21 June 1560 and proved 19 July 1561, held at Leicestershire, Leicester and Rutland Record Office.

12 *SHC 1931: Chancery Proceedings, Bundle 118, No 57, to Sir Nicholas Bacon, Knight.* pp. 188–189.

13 *VCH Staffordshire, Brewood, Volume V, p. 23*; WSL, R. Paddy, *Staffordshire Views II 135 and 137.*

14 SRO, 545.

15 SRO, 475/M/1, Indenture on parchment.

16 SRO, 590/297/12, Abstract of Title on paper.

Chapter Two

Brewood Grammar School: late sixteenth and early eighteenth centuries

The new Brewood Grammar School had been thriving since its re-establishment in 1547. However, less than 30 years later, after the deaths of John and Thomas Giffard and Matthew Knightley, there was unrest in the local community about school funds and lands being misused by two new Trustees: John Giffard of Chillington, son of the now deceased Thomas Giffard, and John Lane of the Hyde, Chillington. Feelings ran so high that the case was heard in Chancery by Nicholas Bacon, Lord Keeper of the Privy Seal.

The plaintiffs for the case were Matthew Moreton of Engleton, a relative of Matthew Knightley, and Thomas Lane, son of the defendant John Lane. The actual date of the case has not survived but it was between 1561 and 1576, the dates of the decease of Matthew Knightley and John Lane.[1] Matthew Moreton and Thomas Lane believed that as John Giffard was lord of the manor of Brewood he had too many influential friends, relatives and allies in Staffordshire for a hearing in the common court to be fair.[2]

The plaintiffs accused John Giffard of converting part of the school premises for his own use and using the funds for his own private profit, as a result the school was not as prosperous as it had been in earlier years. They also wanted more transparency. They wanted a list of new Trustees to the school with the lands and property legally conveyed to the school trust, so that it was not absorbed into private hands to the detriment of the school.[3] The income from this estate was intended to be used to provide a teacher at the Free Grammar School, honest, discreet and "sufficiently learned in grammar" who would instruct "all manner of children and young men". The income would also finance repairs to the school. The "all manner of children" does not include girls, but means boys from all backgrounds.

John Giffard replied that the bill against him was raised "in malice and evil" by Matthew Moreton because of "other causes and controversies" that had happened between them, but he did not elaborate. Giffard did not believe that the inhabitants of Brewood wanted this court case, and that Matthew Moreton had "unlawfully" used the name of Thomas Lane in the bill, to "sow discord" between John Lane and his son. As Thomas Lane no longer lived or owned a house in Brewood, Giffard believed that Thomas Lane had no say in matters relating to the case, and no subpoena had been served on John Lane "as he was prayed for in the bill".[4] It is likely, from this statement, that a subpoena had been served on Giffard.

Giffard denied all accusations from the plaintiffs. He claimed that the school was well maintained, pupil numbers were constant and the profits of the premises were paid to the schoolmaster on a regular basis and had been an almost constant annual amount. Any queries or disputes about the conveyancing of school property, Giffard said, should be directed to John Lane and not himself.

Thomas Lane and Matthew Moreton repeated that the majority of Brewood had agreed to the suit and that the school was not as prosperous as it had been. John Giffard had converted part of the premises for his own use, and because of the negligence of the Trustees this suit was brought for the benefit of Brewood and "the other towns adjoining".[5]

Matthew Moreton may have been using the opportunity of the court case to gain power in the area. King Henry VIII's split with the Roman Catholic Church had caused a religious rift in the country. John Giffard, lord of the manor of Chillington from 1560 until his death in August 1613, was a loyal Royalist but he also remained a Roman Catholic. Matthew Moreton was a Protestant and England was ruled by the Protestant Queen Elizabeth I.

On 11 August 1575 Queen Elizabeth stayed with John Giffard at Chillington Hall. There are no records of the preparations that were put in place for the royal visit. However, after Brewood the Queen proceeded to Hartlebury Castle, Worcester. The Chamber Order book for Worcester reveals that great efforts were made to welcome the Queen and gifts carefully organised. All houses in the city were expected to be freshly limed and painted in "comely" colours, and all dung hills cleared away.[6] Whilst the Queen was staying at Hartlebury, as guest of the Bishop of Worcester, she took the opportunity to send out a writ to all Catholics who did not regularly attend the Church of England service, which included Sir John Giffard. These Catholics were put under arrest until they "reformed". After a delay, Giffard eventually promised to attend Brewood parish church on Sundays and Holy Days but as the distance was too far, he would not always be able to do so.[7] The distance is less than three miles today by road, and even less across fields and footpaths.

The outcome of the Chancery suit is not recorded, although on later documents there is a list of Trustees with a list of lands owned by the school.

Schoolmasters

Sir Raufe Blowre was the first possible master of the school since its re-instatement in 1547. This was the master recommended by Sir Henry Stafford who held Sir Raufe Blowre in high regard. The Stafford family held the patronage of All Saints' church, Worthen, Shropshire, so it was almost certainly the same Ralph Blower who was rector of the church there from 1558-1570. He was also rector of Tysoe, Warwickshire, from 1561–1562, and then, on 16 May 1562, he bought the advowson of the rectory of Church Eaton for £40 from Henry, Lord Stafford.[8] Stafford died at Caus Castle, Shropshire, but was buried at Worthen on 6 May 1562.[9] Sir Raufe Blowre, [Radulphus Blowr] was buried at Worthen on 11 August 1570.[10]

Harry Duncalf was the next known master of Brewood Grammar School but he was employed as the second master of the school, known as the usher. Harry Duncalf, was curate or reader of divine service at Stretton chapel, Penkridge. He became ill at Brewood, on Tuesday 7 April 1607, which was Easter week and then "departed out of this wretched worlde" the following Monday. He was buried at Brewood on the same day. A week later Francis Poole was appointed as the new reader at Stretton but there is no record of him being appointed as the replacement usher.[11]

John Hilton

John Hilton the new schoolmaster of Brewood is mentioned in the "Book of Events" written by Thomas Congreve of Stretton on 13 April 1611. Congreve was related to the Knightley, Moreton and Giffard families, Edward Moreton being his cousin. Hilton stood guarantor for Congreve's daughter, Isabel Benyon, as she had a debt of £20 which she owed her brother-in-law, Thomas Benyon of London.[12]

A few years later, on 23 May 1617, Walter Giffard of Chillington, rented Woolley Farm to John Hilton, schoolmaster of Brewood Grammar School and to his wife Elizabeth. It was in consideration of the care, diligence, pains and industry that John Hilton had taken with the Grammar School, and also in consideration of the great expense that John Hilton had incurred in repairing the school building. There was an orchard next to the School House, which in future could be used by the schoolmasters and ushers to study there, or walk for recreation, as long as they did not damage it.[13] Elizabeth Hilton was buried at Brewood parish church on 21 January 1622/23.

On 18 August 1624 the same John Hilton married Ellen Anston at the church of St Editha, Church Eaton. They remained at Woolley Farm and bought it on 20 October 1624 from Walter Giffard for £180.[14] Elnor Hilton was buried on 21 February 1627 at Brewood churchyard and a few weeks later, on 10 April 1627, John married Christian Smyth at Brewood church.[15] Hilton remained at Woolley Farm and had a family. His daughter Elnor was baptised 20 February 1627/8 at Brewood but did not survive and was buried the next day. His other children were John, christened on 28 May 1629, Ann christened 30 November 1630 and Mary christened 29 January 1633/4. John Hilton's daughter Elizabeth was buried 21 June 1637, and John Hilton's wife, Christian, was buried 1 July 1638.

Although John Hilton was now a farmer, he continued in the role of churchwarden for Brewood, from at least 1637 until 1646 and again in 1653.[16]

John Hilton wrote his will on 18 June 1652, proved on 20 November 1654. John Hilton of Woolley Farm, "sometime Schoolmaster of

Brewood", left to his married son John Hilton, some land, three oxen, three kine or cows, and half the corn and grain that he gave him on his marriage. John Hilton also bequeathed his son a little coffer in the day chamber over the buttery, all of the books and also his "birding piece and steele bowe". John hoped that his son would be a kind and loving brother to both his sisters, Ann and Mary, who were left the excess money from the estate. The sisters, as well as the son, John, were also to be the executors. The overseers of the will were Walter Giffard of High Onn, Staffordshire, John Hilton's cousin the Reverend Robert Hilton of nearby Tong and John's "obedient son John Hilton".[17]

John Huntbach in his manuscripts, held at the William Salt Library, noted the memorial to John Hilton in Brewood parish church. He wrote that an inscription could be found "Upon a little table upon the south wall of the south aisle" where the words were inscribed: "Not farre beneath this place do lie interred 4 of the cheildren of John Hilton and of Xtian his wife". Huntbach confirmed that this "John Hilton was Schoolmaster of Brewood the space of 20 yeares".[18]

It is not clear who replaced John Hilton when he resigned as headmaster, or the exact date of the resignation, but it was probably between 1617 and 1624 which is when Hilton took over Woolley Farm. One possibility for his replacement, is Reverend Hamlet Bourne, also written as Hamblett Bourne. He was born in 1595 and had been a pupil Wolverhampton Grammar School, before obtaining his B.A. in 1616 from Queen's College Oxford, and his M.A. in 1619 from St Edmund Hall, Oxford. Reverend Bourne was ordained a priest in 1620, became a curate at Darlaston, and in 1631 vicar of Bushbury. He was also vicar of Kingsbury, Warwickshire, near Tamworth.[19] A "History of Bushbury Parish" written in 1936, states that at some time Hamblett Bourne was schoolmaster of Brewood but there is no other evidence found to substantiate this claim.[20] If the information is correct, then Bourne is likely to have been schoolmaster of Brewood School at some time between 1620 and 1631.[21]

Edward Davis

The next known schoolmaster was Edward Davis, also known as Edward Davies. He is listed as usher of the Free School at Brewood Grammar

School, and was appointed to read the public prayers in the parish church at Bushbury on 13 January 1626.[22] The only other known reference to this schoolmaster is in the Quarter Sessions records where, in July 1629, there is a memorandum of Recognisance for his good behaviour of £10, and sureties are given by Clement Careless, blacksmith [£5] and Walter Gough, skinner, [£5].[23]

Bill of complaint against the Giffard family

There was another bill of complaint taken out against the Giffard family between 1628-1630. This time it was Francis More, one of the Trustees of the school, who was claiming that Walter Giffard had misappropriated the school funds or estates for his own use. More believed that the estates produced £37 6s 2d annually but that the master only received £18 per year, and the usher £6 13s 4d, leaving a deficit in funds of £12 12s 10d per annum in Walter Giffard's favour, a substantial amount of money at that time. Francis More also believed that the rents charged to the tenants were too low and that the tenancy agreements were in the name of Walter Giffard and should, instead, be in the name of the school. In addition, More believed that the masters were "unfit and unlearned" and had been appointed to the great evil of the "King's Majesty's subjects inhabiting thereabouts, being a place where many Popish recusants or such other as are addicted to Popery do dwell". In other words, it was a quarrel which again had its roots in religion as Walter Giffard was a Catholic.[24]

When the Chancery suit concluded, Walter Giffard did not have to repay any money but it was made clear that the Trustees should be running the estate and not one person. It was also confirmed that sufficient provision should be made for a schoolmaster and usher. However, Francis More was still not happy and so there was another Chancery suit on 21 October 1631. This related to the insufficient rent being paid, in More's opinion, by Thomas Goldsmith and Margaret Fenyhouse for school property and land in Wheaton Aston. Walter Giffard died in 1632 and Francis More in 1640. The court case was abandoned until 1674 due to the turbulent times of the reign of Charles I and the Civil War but finally the court ruled that the school lands should be supervised by a number of local landowners: John Lane of the Hyde, Matthew Moreton of Engleton, Roger Fowke of Gunstone, Geoffrey Somerford of Somerford, Richard Warton, vicar of

Brewood and Edward Giffard of Whiteladies, near Brewood. These men were all Protestants and now Trustees of the school and its land.[25]

Abraham Barwick[e]

The next reference to a schoolmaster is in the Brewood parish register where Abraham Barwicke is mentioned as schoolmaster during the period 1641 until 1644. He had been educated at Trinity College, Cambridge, where he obtained his M.A. degree and received his fellowship from Emmanuel College, Cambridge, in 1634.[26] He was curate of Stretton chapel, Penkridge, from 1651-1652.[27]

On 18 March 1640/41, Abraham Barwicke's son, John, was baptised at Brewood parish church but Abraham's wife, Jane, was buried a few weeks later on 15 July 1641. Barwicke remarried, as another son, Richard, was baptised in Brewood on 21 November 1644. There is no record of the marriage in the Brewood parish registers, or those of surrounding localities, but the Civil War was taking place, and records may be incomplete. The church at Brewood, opposite the school, had been used as a Royalist defence point, and Chillington Hall was a Royal garrison until it was defeated by the Parliamentarians. There was also fighting at nearby Tong, Lapley and Whiteladies Priory.[28]

Charles, trying to claim his right to be King, had been defeated at the Battle of Worcester in September 1651. He made his escape with the help of friends and supporters, including many people local to Brewood: Charles Giffard of Chillington, Jane Lane of Bentley Hall, Colonel William Carless of Broom Hall and the Penderel family. Charles' route to safety took him close to Brewood and it was at Boscobel House, that the future King Charles II took refuge from the Parliamentarian troops in an oak tree.[29]

Reverend Richard Emery

Richard Emery became schoolmaster after Abraham Barwicke. He was christened on 6 January 1621/22 at Stone, Staffordshire, the son of Thomas Emery, a yeoman. Richard Emery attended Shrewsbury Grammar School for one year, before proceeding to St John's College, Cambridge, in 1639 aged 17.[30] Richard Emery was a conforming Commonwealth

13

minister at Shareshill church from 1651 until 1652 and was schoolmaster at Brewood Free Grammar School from at least 1662, when he signed the Act of Uniformity. At this time, he became curate of Boningale chapel, near Albrighton. He was ordained deacon and priest at Lichfield, in 1663 and became vicar of Brewood, in 1664.[31]

Richard Emery's children were christened at Brewood parish church but there is no name given for his wife. She is possibly the Mary Emery, widow, who was buried on 26 June 1682 at Brewood churchyard. Richard's son, Edward, was christened on 18 June 1657 but died when he was 15 years old. His other children were Mary, Richard and Thomas. Reverend Richard Emery died on 1 January 1677/78 and was buried at Brewood parish church a week later. One known Brewood Grammar School pupil during these years was John, son of John Carter of Brewood. who was admitted to St John's College, Cambridge, in 1666 and gained his degree in 1669-70.[32]

Rowland Cooke

On 26 September 1662 Rowland Cooke, like Richard Emery, signed the "Subscription Book" for the Act of Uniformity being a person already in office as a schoolmaster at Brewood School. Cooke was probably the usher, as that is his description in a document of 1679 when the School House was listed as being in the occupation of Hugh Dickenson, Rowland Cooke, usher of the school, and afterwards in possession of William Cooke, who was his son.[33] There is no other documentary evidence to confirm that the Hugh Dickenson mentioned was ever schoolmaster.

Rowland Cooke was married to Joyce and had a family of seven children. He was probably teaching at the school from at least 1646/47 when his daughter Elizabeth was christened. He took part in church activities, for example as churchwarden and signing the memorandum of lewns. In 1671 he received payment for writing the "ould churchwarden's presentment twice over" being as it was very large.

Joyce was buried at Brewood churchyard on 12 January 1679/80 and her husband, Rowland, was buried almost a year later, on 31 December 1681.

The will and inventory for Rowland Cooke have survived which, along with the Hearth Tax, gives an idea of the house in which he and his family were living, there being only sixty houses listed in Brewood at the time. Cooke's house had one chimney. There were four rooms in the house being used as bedrooms, some described as being over the house and some over the parlour. Rowland's daughter Anne was bequeathed the feather bed with curtains, the largest brass pan and forty shillings. Mary, another daughter, was bequeathed Rowland's own feather bed, along with the chest and all the clothes that had belonged to her mother. Mary was also bequeathed the yarn in the house to make herself a new ticke,[34] two pairs of sheets, the "white Rugg and Coverlid" which came from Treesle [Trysull], and 40 shillings. His other children Elizabeth, Thomas, John and William each received 40 shillings but Richard, his eldest son who was overseas, was only to receive 20 shillings when he returned home.

Rowland Cooke kept his clothes in a chest which his son John inherited, along with a lexicon and his school books. Rowland's children William and Anne were executors, as well as his cousin, Francis Cooke. After Rowland Cooke's death, William continued to occupy the School House.

From the inventory of Rowland Cooke's belongings taken on 9 February 1681/2 it is clear that he also occupied himself with farming, which was usual for the schoolmaster at the time. Rowland Cooke owned, amongst other things, a horse which was two years old, a colt, two cows and two calves, a pig and 12 sheep. There was corn and malt in the house, hay and straw in the barn and amongst his cooking utensils there were four brass pots and six brass kettles.

Rowland Cooke's books were valued at £1, but he also had a glass case and a looking glass. There was also a cradle, three spinning wheels and as well as the yarn there was unspun wool, hemp and flax.

William Cooke

William Cooke, Rowland's son, became the new usher at the school, after Rowland's death. He had been christened at Brewood parish church in 1659. A school cottage with a barn, garden and an adjoining croft along with one acre of land in Shargreave Hill field and one acre of land in

Hargreave field was leased to him on 15 March 1688 for 99 years. These lands were near the parish church.[35] William Cooke was buried at Brewood churchyard on 23 February 1705/6. Little else is known about him or his family, except that he was married to Susannah and his wife was allowed the use of the school cottage until 13 January 1727/8 when it was leased to a Thomas Hand, mason. Susannah, his widow, is probably the same person that was buried at Brewood parish church on 24 June 1731.

Reverend Matthew Drakeford

Matthew Drakeford was schoolmaster at the Grammar School from September 1679. He was the son of Richard Drakeford, attorney, who lived at Forebridge Hall, Stafford and his wife, Ann née Babington. Matthew was born on 31 December 1653 and christened at the church of St Chad's, Stafford. He attended school in Stafford and was admitted to St John's College Cambridge, at the early age of 15 years. He obtained his B.A. degree in 1672/3 and received his M.A. in 1676 when he immediately became a curate at St Chad's, Stafford, until he was appointed schoolmaster at Brewood Grammar School. He remained at Brewood until 1682, when he became rector of Colton for one year before becoming rector of St Mary's church, Stafford in 1683, a position he retained until his death. Drakeford also took on additional duties as rector of Tixall church, Staffordshire, in 1698.[36]

Matthew Drakeford married Anne Astley, daughter of Jonas and Anne Astley of Wood Eaton, Staffordshire on 14 May 1689 at the church of St Mary's, Stafford. Ann's sister was Lucretia Wilkes, mother of Richard Wilkes the physician, antiquarian and diarist from Willenhall, a Trustee of Brewood Grammar School named in a document dated 1715, along with some other of Anne's relatives.[37] The couple had one daughter, Anne, born in December 1690.

Reverend Drakeford was buried at St Mary's church, Stafford, on 5 November 1703. In his will he bequeathed everything to his wife Anne, who died just over a year later. She in turn bequeathed her inheritance for the maintenance and education of her daughter Anne Drakeford. Anne lived at Willenhall in her later years and was buried at St Giles church,

Willenhall on Thursday 24 March 1742/3. She asked for gold rings to be bought for Dr Wilkes and his wife Rachel, and also John Wilkes, surgeon.

Thomas Russell

Thomas Russell replaced Matthew Drakeford as schoolmaster. This may be the Thomas Russell, son of John Russell of Wolverhampton, who matriculated at Magdalen Hall, Oxford in 1674 aged 15. Although very little is known about this Thomas Russell, he seems to have taught at the school until 1706 when Thomas Hillman was elected as the new headmaster. In an indenture relating to the school dated 1715 there is mention of a cottage which was in the possession of Thomas Russell and now is in the possession of Elizabeth Russell. It could be assumed that this was his widow, but it is not certain.[38]

Thomas Hillman

Thomas Hillman was appointed as schoolmaster at Brewood on 11 April 1706. He was christened at St Peter's church, Kinver on 16 April 1666, the son of farmer and parish clerk, John Hillman, and his wife Elizabeth of Kinver. He was ill in 1707, and wrote his will on 20 May, stating that he was Thomas Hillman, late of Kinfare but now of Brewood, schoolmaster. He was buried at St Peter's church, Kinver, on 8 July 1707.

In his will, Thomas asks his brothers Edward and Jonathan to act as executors and guardians of his three children Thomas, John and Edward. Thomas Hillman gave Edward and Jonathan the power to sell his houses and use the money for the care of his children. There is no mention of his wife. Thomas Hillman requested that his other brothers, John Hillman of Wolverhampton, clerk, and James Hillman of Brewood, clerk, should oversee his will. This same James Hillman was elected as the new schoolmaster for Brewood Grammar School.

Reverend James Hillman

Reverend James Hillman, was born at Kinver and christened there on 12 December 1676. He was the brother of the previous schoolmaster, Thomas Hillman. James Hillman attended Pembroke College, Oxford, and matriculated 10 October 1693 aged 16, gaining his degree in 1698.

His father, John Hillman of Kinver, bequeathed his son James his great bible and 5 shillings in consideration of his being at university.

On 23 March 1703/4 James Hillman married Marrabella Rocke, daughter of George Rocke of Horsebrook, at the parish church of St Mary and St Chad, Brewood.[39] Their children were John, Thomas, James, George, Benjamin and Sarah.

Reverend James Hillman had become curate of Boningale chapel, near Albrighton, by 26 April 1706. He also had duties at Brewood parish church, signing the church register in 1715 and in 1720/1. In addition, he received 12/6d for writing the births and burials in the church register, at the time that prayers were being said for protection against the plague.[40]

Marrabella Hillman was buried at Brewood parish church in 1724/5 but her husband was buried at Kinver church on 12 May 1731.

James Hillman taught Richard Hurd, later Bishop of Worcester, who wrote that he had been taught at a "good Grammar School at Brewood" first by Reverend Mr Hillman and, after his death, by his successor, Reverend Mr Budworth. Hurd states that both were well qualified for their office and both were very kind to him.[41] James Hillman was also likely to have taught Benjamin Blake and William Finch, later Reverend Finch, who both became ushers of the school.

Benjamin Blake

Benjamin Blake was appointed usher at the school on 2 September 1707, but also taught English within the Free School of Brewood.[42] He was probably the youngest son of John and Susannah Blake, baptised at Brewood parish church on 17 January 1687/8. His ancestors had lived in Brewood for centuries, so it is likely that he had attended Brewood Free Grammar School. Benjamin Blake became blind in his old age. There was no state pension in Great Britain at this time, so in order that Mr Blake received some extra money, there was an "optional charge" for writing lessons, the proceeds being received by Mr Blake. He was buried at Brewood churchyard on 15 March 1760 aged 72 years.

Reverend William Finch

William Finch was the son of a local Brewood farmer, Henry Finch, and his second wife, Margaret Sansome. He attended Brewood School and was appointed usher at the school on 16 July 1713, under Mr James Hillman.[43] On 4 April 1716 Finch was admitted to St John's College, Cambridge, as sizar for Mr Fenwick, and tutored by Dr Anstey. He was awarded his B.A. at St John's Cambridge, and became a deacon on 3 June 1721 and a priest 1722. He became a curate of Leigh parish church near Uttoxeter, but was buried at Brewood church on 28 June 1724 only 25 years of age.[44]

William Godfree or Godfrey

William Godfree was appointed to teach at the school on 17 July 1724 soon after the death of Mr Finch.[45] As usher, he helped Mr James Hillman in the teaching duties, but there is no other detail about him.

A new era

When James Hillman died in 1731, William Budworth from Rugeley succeeded him as headmaster. Budworth felt that the school had been left in a very bad state of repair by the "aged, sickly and infirm" Reverend Hillman.[46] It took two years before Budworth and his wife, Lucia, moved to Brewood as Budworth had extensive work done on the School House, but he was a very successful and much respected headmaster.

Notes

1 *SHC New Series v,* pp. 122-123; *SHC 1931*, pp. 88–193: *Chancery proceeding, during Elizabeth I reign, between 1558–1579, Bundle 118, number 57*, To Sir Nicholas Bacon, Knight. John Giffard died 12 November 1556, [born 1466]. Thomas Giffard died 27 May 1560, and Matthew Knightley died on 9 June 1561.
2 John Giffard was Sheriff of Staffordshire in 1573.
3 *SHC 1931,* pp. 188-192, *Chancery Proceedings Bundle 118 No 57.*
4 *SHC 1931,* p. 190, *Chancery Proceedings Bundle 118 No 57.*
5 *SHC 1931,* pp.188-192, including will of Matthew Knightley.
6 John Nicholls, *The Progresses and Public Processions of Queen Elizabeth.* Volume 1, (John Nichols, 1823), pp. 533-541.

7 *SHC New Series V, pp. 127-31;* Michael Greenslade, *Catholic Staffordshire,* p.45.

8 John Lancelot Lee, *Notes on the Parish of Worthen and Caus Castle* in *Transactions of Shropshire Archaeological Society, 3rd Series, Volume VI,* pp. 97,101 and pp.113–114.

9 *Worthen parish registers, Shropshire.* The year of death is often given as 1563, but the register clearly gives the date of burial as 6 May 1562.

10 *Worthen parish registers, Shropshire.*

11 SRO, D1057/O/1 A-B *Commonplace book of Thomas Congreve 1585–1611,* folio 78 [p.45 transcript] typed 1937 by Miss L. Jevons of Penkridge.

12 SRO, D1057/O/1 A-B *Commonplace book,* folio 48, pp. 31 and 62 of transcript.

13 SRO, D5827/4/6/1.

14 SRO, D590/460.

15 A Christian Smithe and Robert Smithe were baptised at Brewood parish church on 17 September 1601.

16 SRO, D932/5, *Memorandum book of lewns* levied in the parish of Brewood for the churchwardens, overseers and constables 1600–1663.

17 Robert Hilton had attended Brasenose College, Oxford, and obtained his B.A. in 1630. He became vicar of Lapley church in 1638 but was ejected from there in 1647 during the Civil War. His daughter Martha was buried at Brewood church on 23 July 1643, and his daughter Margaret was baptised at Brewood church in March 1647/8. Robert Hilton was appointed vicar of Tong in 1650 and also became the schoolmaster there. In 1660, Robert Hilton returned to Lapley as vicar. He died in in October 1667. *Clergy of the Church of England database* and *Brasenose College registers*; Foster's *Alumni Oxonienses 1500–1714*; Robert Jeffrey, *Discovering Tong,* p. 113.

18 WSL, S.MS. 201 (i), p.392. The Huntbach manuscripts were transcribed in 1833 by Thomas Fernyhough (1777-1844). John Huntbach (1639-1705) lived at Featherstone, Staffordshire, six miles from Brewood.

19 SRO/ LRO, B/A/4/18 *Lichfield Subscription Book* 1631, and *Clergy of the Church of England Database.*

20 WSL, CB/BUSHBURY/1 *History of Bushbury Parish* [1936/37].

21 www.historywebsite.co.uk/articles/bushbury/churchrectors.htm

22 *Clergy of the Church of England database*; SRO/ LRO, B/A/4/18.

23 SRO, Roll No. Q-SR/192, Translation 1629. Thank you to James Sutton for bringing this information to my attention.

24 Douglas Thompson, *A History of Brewood Grammar School 1553–1953,* (Brewood Grammar School, 1953), pp. 5-6; SRO, CEG/2/1; SRO, 545/1.

25 Douglas Thompson, *A History of Brewood Grammar School 1553–1953,* (Brewood Grammar School, 1953), p. 7.

26 John Venn, *The book of Matriculations and degrees 1544–1659,* p. 47.

27 John Venn, *Alumini Cantabrigienses*; *S.H.C. 1915,* pp. 208 and 211.

28 Patrick Joseph Doyle, *The Giffards of Chillington, a Catholic Landed Family 1642-1861*; *SHC 1915,* pp. 174–177.

29 Further information about Charles II and Brewood can be found in David Horovitz, *Brewood. Some notes on the history of Brewood in Staffordshire, with an account of the escape of Charles II after the Battle of Worcester on 3rd September 1651.* (David Horovitz, 2nd edition, 1998), pp.122-137.

30 *Admissions to the College of St John the Evangelist, Cambridge,* 1629/30–1715, pp. 50-51, line 16, 1882.

31 *Clergy of the Church of England database*: Brewood Free Grammar School and SRO, D30/1/2/62 previously held at LRO. This is a "Subscription Book" which Richard Emery has signed. The school is not stated but it is logically Brewood Grammar School as his children were christened at Brewood church.

32 venn.lib.cam.ac.uk

33 SRO, 475/M/5/1.

34 Bolster or mattress covering*: S.H.C. Fourth series, V.*

35 University of Nottingham, www.staffordshireplacenames.esdm.co.uk Shurgreave Hill Field is listed as Shorgreave Hill ffield. Hargreave Field Piece is located at Deansfield. SRO, D(W)1813/23.

36 *Alumni Cantabrigienses* and *Clergy of the Church of England database.*

37 SRO, 545/1.

38 SRO, 545.

39 George Rocke was buried at Brewood parish church on 6 November 1703. In his will George Rock stated that Marrabella was to receive an additional inheritance of £500 bequeathed to her by her grandfather William Mansell, and her uncle Walter Mansell. *Will of George Rock, Gentleman of Horsebrook, Staffordshire, 11 February 1704;* National Archives, PROB 11/475/71.

40 SRO, D932/1/1/35.

41 Leonard Whibley (ed.), *Dates of some occurrences in my own life* in *The Correspondence of Richard Hurd and William Mason*, with an introduction by Ernest Pearce, 1932, cited Sarah Brewer (ed.), *The Early Letters of Bishop Richard Hurd 1739–1762* p. x.

42 SRO/LRO, D/30/1/2/62 *Subscription Book.*

43 SRO/LRO, D30/1/2/62 *Subscription Book.*

44 Brewood parish registers.

45 SRO/LRO, D30/1/2/62 *Subscription Book.*

46 William Parke, *Notes and Collections relating to Brewood,* (William Parke,1858), pp. 44, 47, 105 quoted in Aleyn Lyell Reade, *Johnsonian Gleanings* p. 47.

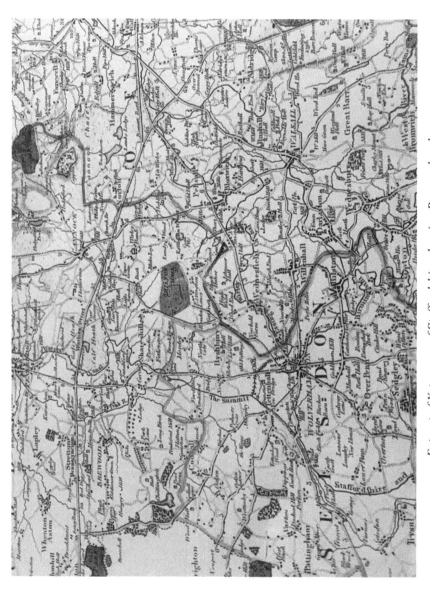

Extract of Yates map of Staffordshire showing Brewood and surrounding area, 1795.

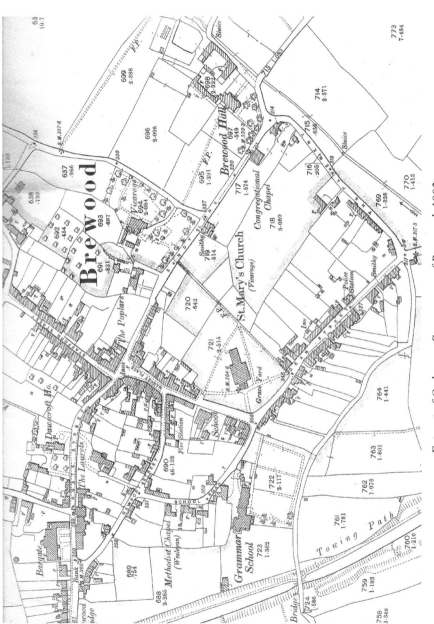

Extract of Ordnance Survey map of Brewood, 1902.

Chapter Three

Reverend William Budworth

Reverend William Budworth was one of the most popular and successful headmasters at Brewood Free Grammar School. His marriage was happy, tragic and full of drama, his death sudden and unexpected.

William Budworth, son of Reverend Luke Budworth and his wife Elizabeth, was christened on 8 July 1700 at St Giles church, Marston Montgomery, Derbyshire. William had eight or more siblings, and was educated at Derby Grammar School by the highly respected headmaster, author and classicist Reverend Anthony Blackwall. Budworth attended Christ's College, Cambridge, where he obtained his B.A. in 1721, and his M.A. in 1726 but was appointed deacon to Barton Blount church, Derbyshire, in 1723. This was close to his home and also the Staffordshire borders.[1] Budworth was ambitious and in 1728 was successful in his application to be headmaster of Rugeley Grammar School.[2]

In the summer of that same year, Budworth married Lucia, the youngest daughter of Obadiah and Ann Lane. The wedding took place at St Augustine's church, Rugeley, just before his mother-in-law's death in August 1728. Obadiah Lane had been a wealthy and influential ironmaster who had died 20 years before, and had been well known in the Midlands. Lucia should have received a substantial inheritance from both her father and her mother which, along with an expected dowry, would have left the Budworths very wealthy. However, a family dispute, intrigue and deceit resulted in a lengthy and stressful legal battle, the details of which are dealt with later. The couple were very happy together but the court case, and several miscarriages overshadowed their lives.

Three years after their wedding, Budworth was appointed vicar of St. Peter's church at Hope, in the Derbyshire Peak District. He still retained his teaching post, but this gave him some extra income, as he had received neither dowry nor money from his wife's inheritance.

He remained vicar at Hope church for just over a year.[3] At that same time, several of the inhabitants of Rugeley showed their dislike of the subjects being taught at the school by taking out a Chancery suit against Budworth and the Trustees of Rugeley Grammar School. The people were unhappy that the headmaster was not teaching English at the school, unlike his predecessor Mr Deakin. The parents wanted a useful education for their sons that would include English and accounts, but to obtain a place at a university an education in the classics was a necessity and this was the priority for Budworth.[4] Budworth refused to comply with the wishes of the community, perhaps thinking that English could be taught through other subjects, or maybe just to be stubborn, as it was reported in *The Gentleman's Magazine* that Budworth hated to be told that he was wrong in any capacity.[5] The result was the Chancery case.

One of the people that opposed William Budworth's teaching was John Bamford, a cooper, who later bequeathed money in his will for a new school in Rugeley so that poor children in the town could be taught to read and write in English. Bamford's bequest began the English School, alternatively known as the Writing School, in Rugeley.[6] Another adversary was Warine Falkner, Budworth's brother-in-law. Falkner had been living at Hagley Hall, Rugeley, with his wife Priscilla and their children since 1709, and continued to live there after Ann Lane's death. Falkner, son of a schoolmaster, may have genuinely believed that English should be taught to all schoolchildren but he was extremely ambitious, confirmed by his appointment in 1732 as Sheriff of Staffordshire. Lucia and the sisters who had continued to live at Hagley Hall since their childhood, had different views on Falkner's integrity. Falkner may have seen this court case as an opportunity to oust Budworth out of Rugeley. In this he was, in part, successful.

William and Lucia Budworth move to Brewood

Reverend Budworth was appointed to Brewood Grammar School for the post of headmaster in 1731, but he continued to teach at Rugeley School whilst Brewood School House was either newly built or received extensive repairs and renovations, which lasted for about two years.[7] Whilst this was happening, some of Budworth's Brewood pupils travelled to him. Richard Hurd, later Bishop of Worcester and a generous Trustee of Brewood Free Grammar School, was one such pupil.[8] As the distance to Rugeley from Brewood is about 14 miles, it is likely that the younger pupils and the day scholars that did not want to travel that distance, or did not want to board at Rugeley, were taught by the usher, Mr Blake at Brewood.

The exact date of the move is unknown, but Elizabeth Lane, Lucia's sister, refers to Budworth in her will, written on 21 October 1732, as Reverend William Budworth of Rugeley, clerk, and he was officially sworn into the position of headmaster at Brewood Free Grammar School in June 1733.[9]

William Budworth and his wife, Lucia, had certainly moved to Brewood by 26 January 1733/4 which is confirmed by the address given by Lucia in a letter to sibling Penelope who lived at Holme Lacy, Herefordshire. Penelope was working there in some personal capacity for Frances Scudamore, Duchess of Beaufort. The Budworths probably made Brewood their home during the Christmas school holidays as Lucia in a letter to her sister, apologised for not writing sooner as she had been busy with the move.

William Budworth and his teaching skills

The new school at Brewood had both an Upper and Lower School, separated by doors which folded back. Mr Blake, the usher or undermaster, taught the Lower School boys, whilst Mr Budworth taught the Upper School pupils. At the beginning and end of the school day, the doors dividing the two schools were opened and Reverend Budworth brought the pupils together for an assembly of prayers.

William Budworth was held in very high esteem at Brewood and was a very capable teacher. There were substantial articles written about him in *The Gentleman's Magazine* for August 1792 and *Literary Anecdotes of the Eighteenth Century*, both published by John Nichols of Red Lion Passage, Fleet Street, London.[10] Budworth was described as a very "neat" person of above average height and was the perfect gentleman. He was a very energetic, enthusiastic and inspiring teacher, who commanded respect. He never needed to raise his voice, but could terrify children with a look, if it was needed.

Budworth adopted his teaching style to the needs of the different classes at the school and the individual abilities of the children. He varied the pupils exercises so that it would stimulate their learning, and he found ways to reinforce his lessons. He would read the children's work publicly in the school and make remarks about it to his captive audience. It encouraged hard work from his pupils. Budworth was kind, but he did not like his authority being questioned. He never allowed a child to answer him back and once commented: "I would not suffer it, even if I was in the wrong, no, not to the first Nobleman's son in the kingdom".[11]

Budworth was an excellent classicist, particularly excelling in Latin. The Upper School boys were taught grammar with translations of Latin and Greek texts, including Ovid and Vergil. He also ensured that his pupils had knowledge of the developing scientific subjects which were known collectively as natural philosophy. His pupils attended public lectures given by experts such as Mr Griffith of Pembroke College, Oxford. The boys had to write an essay about what they had learnt and present their work to the headmaster outlining their own observations and thoughts on different subjects.

On Saturdays, the pupils heard extracts from *Mr Nelson's Companion for the Festivals and Fasts of the Church of England* which enhanced their religious understanding and, during Lent, the pupils were expected to repeat the catechism to Mr Budworth. They attended the parish church of St Mary and St Chad, Brewood on a regular basis.

Mr Budworth enjoyed music and singing, and Barnabus Gunn, a successful composer and organist at both St Philip's church, now cathedral, and St Martin in the Bull Ring church in Birmingham, was sometimes a guest at the school. Reverend Hurd remarked that Budworth had a melodious voice which he compared to the "sweetness of the Awolian harp" and sometimes sang with James Lyndon, the accomplished organist at St Peter's church, Wolverhampton, who was also invited to the school to perform.

Mr Budworth was reputed to have hated comedies, allegedly because they generated too much laughter, so instead he encouraged his pupils to watch tragedies at the theatre. When they returned to school the pupils had to write about the play and the principal characters. It is not certain where they would have seen these plays. The first theatrical performances listed in Wolverhampton were at the Town Hall in 1751 so it is more likely that the plays were seen at Moor Street Theatre, Birmingham, which had opened in 1740. Budworth would have regularly travelled to Birmingham to listen to Mr Gunn's music, and Gunn also sold tickets for performances at Moor Street Theatre. One of the productions at this theatre was Shakespeare's *The Tempest*, performed on 20 August 1744 by the Warwickshire Company of Comedians. The performance was to begin punctually at 7 o'clock. There was a choice of where to sit: boxes and stages cost 2/6d, pit 2/-, balconies 2/-, first gallery 1/-, end gallery 6d. The play could be seen on Wednesday, Thursday and Friday, until Friday 7 September.[12]

The Gentleman's Magazine reported that whilst Reverend Budworth was good company at times when he needed peace and quiet, he could appear sullen and bad tempered. In these moments, according to the article, the people of Brewood took pains to avoid him. He did suffer from many hardships as Lucia suffered many miscarriages and Budworth suffered from the gout, which Lucia described as being so bad that at times he was bedridden from it.

Samuel Johnson and Brewood

In 1736 Samuel Johnson applied for a job at Brewood Grammar School. Budworth had an immense respect for Samuel Johnson, recognising his intelligence and ability. In many ways he would have been an ideal candidate for teaching at this prestigious school. Johnson's knowledge and ability was extensive but he may not have had the desire nor personality to be a schoolmaster. It may have been Johnson's wife, Elizabeth or Tetty as she was also known, who persuaded Samuel Johnson to approach William Budworth for a position at Brewood Grammar School, as his own school at Ediall, Lichfield, was failing. Ediall School was also close to Freeford Hall, home of Richard and Mary Dyott. Mary, was Lucia Budworth's sister.

It is also reputed that Reverend Budworth declined Samuel Johnson as a master at the school believing that the children would make fun of the convulsive afflictions from which Samuel Johnson suffered.[13] However,

Budworth already had an usher, Mr Adams, and a curate, Reverend Bromley, who both taught at the school and he was highly unlikely to have been able to afford an extra teacher of Samuel Johnson's ability out of his limited funds. Dr Johnson had been employed as usher at Market Bosworth School for a few months, March–June 1732, by its patron Sir Wolstan Dixie, 4th Baronet, but had left after an argument. William Budworth knew the eccentric Sir Wolstan Dixie and may have met him when he visited his former headmaster, Blackwall, who had taught at Dixie's school after leaving Derby. Lady Anna Dixie gave Lucia Budworth a potion to help her through her pregnancy.

William Budworth's nephew, Joseph Budworth, thought that Budworth should have employed Johnson, as he would have been more practically minded than his uncle and he thought that he could have persuaded William Budworth to publish some books which would have shown William Budworth's genius and philanthropy as well as protecting his memory from obscurity.[14]

William Budworth, recreation and society

William Budworth liked to take exercise. He had enjoyed archery in his younger days and kept some bows and arrows in the parlour of the school, he also liked ringing the hand bells.

William and Lucia Budworth were sociable and had a wide circle of friends. Sir Edward Littleton and Richard Hurd were firm friends with their teacher, but the list also included many others such as Peter and Helena Giffard of Chillington. William and Lucia were not averse to travelling and visited Lucia's sister, Penelope, at Holme Lacy, Herefordshire. They also visited William's brother, Joseph Budworth, landlord of the Palace Inn, Market Street, Manchester. He, in return, came to Brewood. Joseph was also a singer, and the pair would often perform together. Joseph's son, also named Joseph and mentioned earlier, was born after Budworth's death. He wrote some details about his uncle in the *Gentleman's Magazine* under the authorship of A. Rambler.

William Budworth knew William Cunningham, 13th Earl of Glencairn, and received a present of a very grand scarf from him.

He may have been a pupil at the school, or have been taught by Budworth elsewhere.

In the autumn of 1734, September until October, Lucia and William Budworth were busy entertaining or, as Lucia wrote to Penelope, they had the "constant hurry of company". Mr Payne had just left them. This was possibly Thomas Payne of Badminton, Gloucestershire and later of Holme Lacy, Herefordshire, both homes of the Duke and Duchess of Beaufort. The Budworths had enjoyed his company, but Lucia was extremely ill in the morning because she had eaten four oysters which had disagreed with her so much that she thought she was going to die. In spite of the ill effects, Lucia was very pleased to have experienced the oysters. She asked Penelope to visit them in Brewood in the spring when the roads were better, and to stay for at least a week.[15]

During the same period, Lucia had met Mr Barbor, who she described as "an old acquaintance" who "gives his honorable service" to Penelope, implying that he knew both sisters. He offered to help Lucia and Penelope by providing legal advice to their lawyers. This related to their ongoing fight in the courts about their due inheritance from their parents, which they had still not received. Lucia spoke about Mr Robin Barbor, but it is likely to have been Robert Barbor who had bought Somerford Hall, Brewood, and was a lawyer at Inner Temple. He was also chief agent to Lord Gower at Lilleshall and Trentham from 1742–1758 but had worked at Lilleshall since 1722 assisting the then chief agent for Lord Gower, William Plaxton.[16] Lucia was so tired that Mr Budworth copied the letters for her relating to the court case so that they could be sent to Penelope.[17]

Lucia and the court case

Lucia had been born in 1701/2 at Normacot Grange, Longton, Staffordshire, once the home of the Giffards of Chillington. Her parents, Obadiah and Ann Lane, had moved there from Longton Hall, Stoke-upon-Trent, which Obadiah had improved and expanded and then sold to his son Nathaniel, who further improved the property.[18] Obadiah and his family continued to reside at Normacot Grange, but bought the additional property of Hagley Hall, also known as Bank Top, near Rugeley. This would have been convenient for his ironworks of Rugeley Slitting Mill and Cannock Wood Forges.

Obadiah Lane died on 27 March 1708 and was buried at Rugeley on 1 April, but the church records give his home as Normacot Grange. He had written his will two years earlier whilst at Bath, bequeathing his son Nathaniel Lane of Longton Hall only one broad piece of gold as he had already received his inheritance, but to each of his other nine children, including Lucia, he bequeathed £100 over and above what her mother decided to give them individually from the estate.[19] This was a substantial inheritance for Lucia, even if she only received the £100, but she was also expecting a dowry to be paid, due at the time of her marriage to William Budworth.

Obadiah wanted his wife, Ann, to use the estate for the comfortable maintenance of herself and the "prudent education" of the children. He wanted Ann to be the sole executor but the trustees were to be his partners and friends Thomas Hall of the Hermitage, Cheshire and his younger brother Edward Hall of the Cranage, Cheshire. One of the witnesses of the will was Warine Falkner, an apprentice clerk to Obadiah, recommended by Thomas Hall. Warine Falkner's father, Thomas Falkner, had been curate at Over, Cheshire and both schoolmaster and vicar at Middlewich, Cheshire, close to the home of Thomas Hall. Later, the Lane children wrote that they believed Thomas Falkner had lost his living at Middlewich in the early 1700s and moved away leaving his family in poverty.[20]

Three weeks after the marriage of William and Lucia Budworth, Ann Lane died.[21] She had written her will in February, and bequeathed nearly all her stock and land in the lucrative iron industry to her three youngest children, Elizabeth, Penelope, and Lucia. The executors, Edward Hall of Cranage, Chester, and John Greatbatch, of Cocknage, Staffordshire, were instructed to obtain the best price for the estate. As a result, Lucia and William were expecting to receive a substantial inheritance, especially as no dowry had been paid on Lucia's marriage to Budworth. Ann bequeathed a piece of broad gold to the value of £1 3s 0d to her married daughters Ann Walsh, who had married Captain Henry Walsh at Sandon; Priscilla Falkner, who had married Warine Falkner, and Mary, wife of Richard Dyott of Freeford Hall. Thomas, a married son, was to receive £20. The other sons, Nathanial and Obadiah, had both died. If there was any money left after the funeral expenses it was to be shared amongst the three youngest daughters: Elizabeth, Penelope and Lucia.

It was known by Lucia and her siblings that at some time before their father's death, probably between 1706-1707, Warine Falkner had started a clandestine love affair with their sister Priscilla. This was at about the same time that Obadiah's will had been written, and witnessed by Warine Falkner. Lucia's sister, Penelope, was in the house when her father found out about the affair. She described her father as being furious, calling Warine Falkner "the greatest villain alive for seducing his child" and refused to see either of them again, immediately terminating Falkner's employment, and giving Priscilla three days to leave the house.

The couple left on 2 or 3 December 1707, and were married at All Saint's church, Madeley, on 24 March 1707/8 by virtue of a banns letter from the Archbishop of Canterbury, the entry referring to the marriage of Mrs Priscilla Low and Warine Falkner both of Stoke. The reference to "Mrs" in the parish register would have been an indication of respect for a genteel lady, but the reason for the surname "Low" is less easy to explain unless it was a copy error. Correspondence exists at Staffordshire Record Office to show that Lucia, Penelope and their siblings were unaware that the couple had ever married.[22]

Budworth's teaching career was flourishing in Brewood, but the school continually needed an input of finances to keep it fresh and up to date. No inheritance or money of any sort had been distributed by the executors of Ann Lane's estate to Elizabeth, Penelope and Lucia. In 1732 with the help of William Budworth, the ladies filed a bill at the Court of Chancery against Warine Falkner and Edward Hall as the youngest sisters were entitled to their inheritance from Obadiah Lane's will of 1708 and from their mother's will of 1728.

Edward Hall of Cranage, an ironmaster and one of the trustees of Obadiah's will, who was used to running a business, had provided no accounts for the period 1710–1731. Instead, the family were told that Ann Lane had greatly overdrawn her stock and actually owed Hall money, but no proof was ever provided. In fact, Elizabeth claimed to have seen Hall take the books and papers belonging to the Lane estate and burn them. Elizabeth died in April 1733 and the inheritance that she would have received she bequeathed to be divided between Penelope and Lucia.[23]

Warine Falkner was very angry when a subpoena was served on him to appear in court, especially as he was coming towards the end of his term as Sheriff of Staffordshire. He sent a message to Budworth saying that he would charge Lucia for board and lodging for all the time that she had lived at Hagley Hall. This was in contrast to the free board and lodging that he and his family were alleged to have received from his mother-in-law.

A few months later, on 14 September 1734, Lucia Budworth wrote to Penelope that she was trying to meet with Mr Spateman and Mr Rider, lawyers who were helping with the court case. She wanted to hire a sedan chair at Four Crosses, near Brewood, rather than ride on horseback to meet them as she was pregnant.[24] Lucia had already been poorly early in September and now there was a threat of catching distemper, which was prevalent, a fever that she described to her sister that "lies in ye face and teeth".[25]

The court case was a topic of discussion in the locality. When Lucia had been invited by the Giffards to Chillington Hall, she had been introduced to a priest, who she described as a very sensible man. He appeared to know about the law and advised her not to let the court appoint Commissioners as he believed that they could be bribed.[26]

The court case was very expensive, and had already persisted for several years. There is no evidence that it impacted on Budworth's teaching, but it must have had some impact on his health and well-being, as well as that of Lucia. Budworth always wanted to improve the school, but his plans were expensive. Now both Penelope Lane and William Budworth needed to borrow money for the court case and in one instance it was as much as £200. Frances, Duchess of Beaufort, tried to help Penelope by offering to lend her money without interest and also supporting her with legal advice from Charles Cotes of Middle Temple. The Duchess also advised her to compromise whenever she had the opportunity as "there were so many tricks in the Law and so much Roguery amongst the Lawyers that the right side of the Cause is not always the surest".[27]

In October 1736 Penelope travelled the long distance from Holme Lacey to Staffordshire for one of the court case hearings. A few months later, in

January, there was another hearing which Lucia attended, afterwards dining at Freeford Hall with her sister, Mary. Lucia informed Penelope that Mr Rider, the lawyer, thought the case was going well. He had a son at Brewood Grammar School so it is likely that the payment of Mr Rider's fees would have been offset by the payment of the school fees. This was a common practice at the time, only children in the parish of Brewood being entitled to free schooling. In March 1736/7 the number of pupils at Brewood Grammar School had fallen to 14, as children were seeking employment rather than staying at the school.

In early 1737 Lucia was pregnant again, but as yet no baby had survived. Lucia declined an invitation to visit Penelope at Holme Lacy at Whitsuntide as the distance was too long for her on horseback, given the situation of her health.[28] A few weeks later, on 3 April 1737, Lucia wrote again to Penelope, reassuring her that she was feeling much better, but this was the time that she usually miscarried. She was taking Lady Dixie's medicine and felt hopeful that if she could manage another fortnight, she would be fine. Lucia was determined not to confine herself as she usually did and if Penelope wanted to come and visit them, Mr Budworth would send a horse to her. Lucia again commented on the awful state of the roads which she hoped would be better when Penelope came to stay. She added that Richard Dyott was delighted with the trees that Penelope had sent from Holme Lacy to Freeford Hall.

Two months later, on 4 June 1737, Penelope wrote to Ann Walsh at her lodgings in London describing Warine Falkner as swaggering that he had always been a rich fine gentleman. Ann had married Captain Walsh at Sandon parish church, and whilst her husband was stationed away from home, Ann had stayed with her mother at Hagley Hall. When Captain Walsh returned to Rugeley he and Falkner quarrelled and the couple moved out of the house.[29]

Warine Falkner was claiming that it had been an advantageous marriage for Priscilla and that he had given the partnership £7000, which Penelope and Lucia believed to be completely untrue. Penelope wanted him to prove this in court and also explain how her mother Ann had lost that exact same amount of money. Budworth wanted Warine and Priscilla to prove that they were married, but both Penelope and Ann were against this, believing that the affair would bring shame on Priscilla and the family. They were unaware that Warine and Priscilla had married at Madeley church and this lack of knowledge was why Warine Falkner had so much power over them.[30]

The death of Lucia

Lucia managed an almost full term with this pregnancy delivering her 10th or 11th child about five weeks prematurely on 20 September 1737. Sadly, the baby did not live long enough to even be baptised and Lucia died on 26 September 1737, aged 35 years old. She was buried at Shareshill parish church three days later. Dr Wilkes, friend, Trustee of the school, antiquarian and diarist, wrote about Lucia's miscarriages and her death in his diaries.[31]

Lucia had written her will a few weeks earlier, on 30 August 1737, bequeathing her real estate inheritance to her eldest child with her husband "enjoying" all her estate for his natural life. She gave William Budworth the "authority" to dispose of her personal estate as he thought fit but to remember the love and affection that she has always had for her sister Penelope Lane.[32]

Budworth was now mourning the loss of both wife and baby. He was paying for a lengthy court case, had received neither dowry nor expected money from his wife's due inheritance, and school numbers were declining. He wanted to enlarge and improve the school and make the accommodation for the headmaster and usher more comfortable, but lack of money was a problem, although it did not deter him from achieving his aim.

A few weeks after the death of Lucia Budworth, the elderly Reverend John Moss, vicar of Brewood, died and Reverend Budworth was appointed in his place which gave him some extra income.[33] He also copied up the parish registers in his neat handwriting which provided him a little more money.

In the meanwhile, Warine Falkner had continued to develop his financial interest and standing in the iron industry and had also renovated Hagley Hall to make it a grand house.

The initial court ruling, 1739

Finally, on 10 May 1739, there was a ruling in the court case in favour of Penelope Lane and William Budworth. Philip Yorke, the first Earl of Hardwicke and Lord Chancellor, ruled that the estate had been left by Obadiah Lane in trust for his children and must be paid. Any improvements that Warine Falkner had made to the estate he had done "with his eyes open, knowing of the trust". If the executors had done their job there would have been an inheritance from Ann Lane's estate of £1500 each for Elizabeth, Penelope and Lucia. As Elizabeth had died, this meant that Penelope and Lucia should have received £2250 each. Lord Chancellor Hardwicke, who in later years was responsible for an *Act for Better Preventing of Clandestine Marriage* ordered the defendants to find all Obadiah Lane's stock in the iron trade and have it made good to the plaintiffs, except for the £500 paid to Richard Dyott and the same to sister Priscilla, as dowries for their marriage. The money owed to the family had to be found from the Falkner's estate and Hagley Hall should, if necessary, be sold. Hardwicke also ordered financial accounts to be produced for the personal estate of Obadiah Lane and all expenditure.

The final court ruling, 1742

The accounts were duly provided in court to Lord Hardwicke on 29 April 1742. It was ruled that the personal estate of Obadiah Lane was £9225 16s 4d and that debts and expenses amounted to £5590 13s 1d leaving £3635 3s 3d plus a share of the ironworks, but with other debts the amount was reduced to £2481. It was not ruled that any part of the personal estate of Obadiah Lane had "come into the hands of the defendant Edward Hall" although Hall did admit that on the death of Ann Lane, he had taken goods, plate, books and furniture to the value of £257 16s 0d from the estate and had been employed by Ann Lane at a salary of £100 per annum to manage her ironworks and stock.

However, Hardwicke now changed his mind in court. He ruled that the will of Obadiah Lane was made by an "ignorant man", and Penelope Lane's council had misconducted the case. As Warine Falkner had married into the family it was unfair of him to have the purchase impeached after so many years, even though no accounts were produced for the purchase of Hagley Hall by Warine Falkner. The case was dismissed. Penelope

Lane was offered only £200 and she had to sign the releases, or they could go through the accounts for the iron stock over 30 years and try to recover the legacy of £100 which would likely incur costs. The court was in uproar, and Lord Hardwicke demanded that Penelope gave an immediate answer so, distraught, she chose the £200.

A few weeks later, when Penelope Lane had time to reflect on the court decision, she was still very angry and on 28 July 1742 wrote to William Budworth that she was prepared to take out another law suit against Edward Hall and Warine Falkner to contest and recover the inheritance. Penelope Lane was willing to bear half the cost, as long as she received an equal share of whatever was recovered. This did not happen and Warine Falkner continued to live a comfortable life at Hagley Hall whilst the bequests from the wills of Obadiah and Ann Lane had not been honoured, leaving Budworth and Penelope Lane in a financially weak position.

Sir Edward Littleton, Budworth's ex-pupil and a Trustee of the school, tried to help Budworth financially. In 1743, he gave him the living of Shareshill, after the church of St Mary and St Luke was rebuilt, and also appointed him to the office of Official Principal of the Collegiate Church of Penkridge.[34]

However, whilst Warine Falkner did retain the house at Hagley, it was ransacked on the night of 30 November 1745 by the Duke of Cumberland's men. The 1st Battalion of the Coldstream Guards had camped at Rugeley on their way to quell the Jacobite uprising and believing that Warine Falkner was a Jacobite sympathiser they threatened to blow his house up if he did not surrender. He let the troops into his house, and the house was pillaged.[35] Falkner died at Rugeley on 14 June 1748. In his will he bequeathed money in trust for two daughters, the other three children were only left one shilling each as they had been disobedient to him. Priscilla, his wife, was not mentioned although she did not die until 1750, being buried at St Augustine's church, Rugeley. Sir Nathaniel Curzon, 4th Baronet of Kedleston, Derbyshire and his youngest son Assheton later 1st Viscount Curzon, bought Hagley Hall from Falkner's representatives after Priscilla's death.[36] Assheton Curzon became a Trustee of Brewood Grammar School.

Mrs Vaughan, her daughter and the school in decline

After Lucia's death, Budworth is reputed to have had a relationship with an unnamed rich lady who lived in or near Brewood. This did not last and he then employed a genteel lady at the school, Mrs Vaughan, a widow with a young pretty daughter known as the Honourable Elizabeth Vaughan.

Mrs Vaughan and her daughter had lived at Elmshurst, Lichfield, with Lady Carew Biddulph and her husband Sir Theophilus Biddulph, another Trustee of Brewood Grammar School. Mrs Vaughan had married John Vaughan, 2nd Viscount Lisburne, unaware that this was a bigamous marriage until she read about the death of his wife on 31 July 1723.[37] John Vaughan had a reputation as a womaniser, a heavy drinker and gambler, and also had excessive debts. There is no record of Mrs Vaughan's maiden name, but she was buried at Brewood churchyard on 26 October 1742. Her friend, Lady Carew, was buried at Brewood a few months earlier, in April 1741.[38] The Honourable Elizabeth Vaughan, married firstly Watson Hand then, after his death, Bishop Newton.[39] Bishop Newton, wrote about his wife and her childhood in his autobiography.[40]

After Mrs Vaughan's death, Mr Budworth had a short relationship with a lady from nearby Shareshill. In what were to be the final years of Budworth's life, he became quieter and more introvert. It is reported that his congregation complained that his sermons were too highbrow and so to remedy the situation, Reverend Budworth said the prayers at the church and encouraged different people to deliver the sermons, but only those who could give a really boring sermon were eligible for the task.[41]

The economic impact on Brewood of a thriving school

Pupil numbers had begun to decline whilst Mrs Vaughan and her young daughter were living at the school. The parents were not happy with the situation, of two attractive ladies at the school, and soon began sending their sons elsewhere. The lack of pupils impacted on both the excellent reputation of the school and the income that Reverend Budworth received from the boarders. The shops and trade in Brewood also suffered. An idea of the economic impact that a thriving school could have on local businesses can be seen by the meticulous accounting of Mrs Frances Littleton, mother of Sir Edward Littleton.

In November 1740, Edward Littleton caught small pox at the school and his mother billed him for her visit and his medicines. Simpson Blakemore made wigs for Edward Littleton, and Richard Banister cut his hair. Richard Talbot made his shoes and pumps, and John Barber made his "Dantswick" shoes. Mr Salt made his hats, but Mrs Holmes mended his shirts. John Howle made his gloves, and William Hearn[s], John Southall and Richard Lyon were his tailors, although William Emery made Edward Littleton some doeskin breaches. Mr Rock and Mr Francis were his apothecaries, Mr Ford was his writing master.[42]

In April 1744 Edward Littleton was accepted for a place at Emmanuel College, Cambridge where, at the suggestion of William Budworth, Richard Hurd became Littleton's tutor. He was Richard Hurd's first and only pupil for some years and they became good friends, both maintaining contact with their former headmaster.[43] On the death of Reverend Budworth, Richard Hurd was offered the living of Shareshill by Edward Littleton but refused it and from then the post was usually presented to the headmaster of Brewood Grammar School to provide him with extra income. It was not an automatic right, as some headmasters thought. Littleton and Hurd both made a great contribution to the school in future years.

Mr Budworth's teaching staff

During Mr Budworth's headship, and after the death of Lucia Budworth, the usher, Mr Adams, and the curate, Reverend Mr Bromley, who also had some teaching duties, both resigned their positions at the school. Budworth was particularly upset when Mr Bromley left because he respected him both as a friend and colleague. However, both Adams and Bromley were well liked and respected by the pupils at the school. The new usher, was not such a success with the pupils but Mr Budworth admonished the pupils about their behaviour and daring to challenge his choice of a member of staff.

This usher may have been Watson Hand who was the first husband of Honourable Elizabeth Vaughan. In 1748, Elizabeth and Reverend Watson

Hand of Mavesyn Ridware buried two of their young children at Brewood: Charles Wilmot who was buried on 13 July and Elizabeth who was buried on 17 September. Reverend Watson Hand was buried at Brewood churchyard, a year later, on 5 August 1749.[44]

The death of Mr Budworth

Reverend Budworth enjoyed walking in the large garden adjoining the school and it was here, whilst waiting for his friends Sir Edward Littleton and Bishop Hurd to arrive, and whilst talking with an acquaintance he received a letter and died from "a fit of apoplexy". He was buried on 3 September 1745 at the church of St Mary and St Luke, Shareshill. Dr Richard Wilkes of Willenhall, and Trustee of the school, was the executor, principal creditor and administrator of William Budworth's estate, which was proved on 28 October 1745 but no will survives.[45]

Dr Hurd described Reverend Budworth as possessing "every talent of a perfect institutor of youth, in a degree, which he believed, had been rarely found in any of that profession since the days of Quinctilian".[46] Sir Edward Littleton and Richard Hurd erected a monument to Mr Budworth's memory in the chancel of the church at Shareshill. John Michael Rysbrack, the most renowned sculptor in London was chosen for the work. He had worked on Houghton Hall, Norfolk, for Sir Robert Walpole, first Lord of Treasury and carved the sculpture of Sir Isaac Newton in Westminster Abbey. It took Edward Littleton until 1750 to find the right piece of marble. Sir Edward Littleton wanted to "vindicate" Mr Budworth's character and reflect his warm friendship and affection for his memory. Bishop Hurd wanted a plain text in marble, of an elegant form.

It is believed that Bishop Hurd wrote the inscription to be carved into the stone. It was written in Latin but transcribed it reads: "To the Memory of WILLIAM BUDWORTH, Master of Arts, Late Pastor of this Chapel, and Vicar of Brewood, And Head Master of the Free Grammar School there, For the discharge of these respective duties, most highly gifted, By the purity of his life, - by the affability of his manners; By his literary attainments, - and by his unaffected eloquence, To all ease of access, and possessing benevolence of heart. To his friends zealous in the performance of every duty; at the same time a stranger to servility of every kind;

And particularly disdaining to cultivate, by mean compliances, the favours of the Great. To record the endowments of such a Man, First his most distinguished Master, and moreover his most affectionate Friend, This Monument, As a small token of his regard and gratitude, was erected by, Sir Edward Littleton, Baronet. 1748".[47]

Reverend Mr Budworth was an outstanding educationalist, who was an iconic figure in the history of the school.

Notes

1 *Clergy of the Church of England database.*
2 WSL, *Landor Misc 168, History of Rugeley,* Volume 2; *Johnsonian Gleanings*: Part IV, p. 47; *Clergy of the Church of England database.*
3 *Clergy of the Church of England database.*
4 SRO, D(W)1792/20; Letter from Isaac Cope of Leek to Mr Weston of Rugeley, 26 November 1793; *VCH, Staffordshire: Rugeley.*
5 *Gentleman's Magazine,* Volume 62, Part 2, August 1792, pp. 683–686, 785-788, 1001 and John Nichols, *Literary anecdotes of the Eighteenth-century,* Volume III, pp. 332-355.
6 *VCH Rugeley.*
7 John Nichols, *Literary anecdotes of the eighteenth-century,* Volume III, p. 332.
8 *Clergy of the Church of England database*; William Parke, *Notes and Collections relating to Brewood,* pp. 45, 47 and 105; *Johnsonian Gleanings,* part IV, p. 47.
9 SRO, D661/3/2/2; *Clergy of the Church of England database.*
10 John Nichols was editor and printer of *The Gentleman's Magazine* from 1777 when he inherited the printing business from William Bowyer, to whom he had been apprentice. *The Gentleman's Magazine* was considered a scholarly periodical, but Bowyer and Nichols collected memoirs and manuscripts, some of which were published in *Literary Anecdotes*. There were six volumes of anecdotes and the article about Budworth is in Volume III, pp. 332-355.
11 *Gentleman's Magazine,* Volume 62, part 2, August 1792, pp. 683–686, 785, 788.
12 *Aris's Birmingham Gazette or the General Correspondent*, 20 August 1744.
13 Peter Martin, *Samuel Johnson, a biography,* (Weidenfeld and Nicholson, 2012), pp. 116-117.
14 John Nichols, *Literary Anecdotes of the eighteenth century,* Volume III, p. 337.

15 SRO, D661/3/2, Letter from Lucia Budworth to Penelope Lane, 24 October 1734.

16 J.R. Wordie, *Estate Management in eighteenth-century England. The building of the Leveson-Gower Fortune*, (Royal Historical Society, 1982), pp. 41-42.

17 In 1733, Mr Barbor tried to sell the ground chamber at Sir Robert Sawyers buildings at Inner Temple because the view of the best chamber was impaired by the iron girders put up for support. His London address was Castle Yard, Holborn.

18 *VCH Staffordshire: Longton* regarding lease of 1702 at Normacot Grange. Longton. Lucia was christened at Caverswall church on 30 March 1701/2, daughter of Obadiah Lane of Normacot Grange. *See also SRO, D661/3/2.*

19 Obadiah and Ann Lane's children: Nathaniel, Obadiah Priscilla, Mary, Isabella, Ann, Elizabeth, Penelope, Thomas and Lucia.

20 Thomas Faulkner had attended Brasenose College, Oxford where he obtained his degree. He may have been the same Thomas Faulkner who was headmaster of Wheaton Aston Grammar School in 1703 *see* Mary Weate, *Three centuries of Schooling in Lapley and Wheaton Aston, Staffordshire, 1703-1996*, (Fritillary Press, 1995), p.1.

21 Mrs Lane was buried on 15 August 1728 at St Augustine church, Rugeley.

22 SRO, D661/3/2.

23 SRO, D661/3/2, Letter from Lucia Budworth to Penelope Lane, 16 January 1733/4.

24 SRO, D661/3/2.

25 SRO, D661/3/2, Letter from Lucia Budworth to Penelope Lane at the Beauforts, 14 September 1734.

26 SRO, D661/3/2, Letter from Lucia Budworth to Penelope Lane at the Beauforts, 14 September 1734.

27 SRO, D661/3/3, Letter from Frances Beaufort to Penelope Lane 6 December 1735.

28 SRO, D661/3/2, Letter from Lucia Budworth to Penelope Lane, 13 March 1736/7.

29 Walsh died in Minorca. Ann, widowed, eventually moved to Hampton Court.

30 SRO, D661/3/2, Letter from Penelope Lane to Ann Walsh, 17 June 1737.

31 SRO, 5350, Wilkes' Diary.

32 Will of Lucia Budworth SRO P/C/11 27 January 1738/9.

33 SRO/LRO, D30/1/2/62; *Clergy of the Church of England database*.

34 SRO, D260/M/F/5/89.

35 S.A.H. Burne, *Staffordshire campaign of 1745, Trans NSFC LX,* pp. 50–76. Further reading on the raid can be found in Landor Misc. 168, p.246, at WSL and in the Rugeley Parish Registers.

36 WSL, *Landor Misc. 168.*

37 John Vaughan had married Anne Bennett, daughter of Sir John Bennett, lawyer and politician.

38 Lady Carew Biddulph was the daughter of Charles and Anne Lyttleton of Frankley, Worcestershire. Charles Lyttleton had been Governor of Jamaica and a member of Parliament and his wife Anne Temple had been maid of honour to Queen Catherine, wife of King Charles II. When Lady Carew died, she had been living at Kiddemore Green, Brewood.

39 Elizabeth Hand, née Vaughan, married Reverend Thomas Newton, Bishop of Bristol on 5 September 1761 at Stiffkey, Norfolk. They were married by their mutual friend Theophilus Lowe, Canon of Windsor, friend of both Dr Newton and Mrs Hand. Dr Newton became Dean of St Paul's Cathedral where he was buried in 1782. Elizabeth Newton did not inherit any money from her father, 2nd Viscount Lisburne, but she did have a substantial inheritance from Dr Newton. She wanted a memorial to her husband at St Paul's Cathedral. This was not allowed by the cathedral authorities, so she commissioned a smaller sculpture by the renowned Thomas Banks which was completed and put on the west wall at St Mary Le Bow church in 1786. Banks' father was a surveyor at Badminton, Gloucestershire for the Duke and Duchess of Beaufort. The sculpture was destroyed when St Mary-le-Bow church received war damage during the blitz and all that is left is a print of the work. Elizabeth died on Sunday 16 February 1794 at Charles Street, Berkeley Square, London. *See also European Magazine 1790. XVIII*, p. 24.

40 WSL, Thomas Newton, *The works of the Right Reverend Thomas Newton, late Lord Bishop of Bristol and Dean of St Paul's London with some account of his life and anecdotes of several of his friends. Volume 1,* pp. 62-3.

41 *Nichols Literary Anecdotes of the eighteenth century,* Volume III, p. 351.

42 SRO, D260/M/T/5/107.

43 Sarah Brewer (ed.), *The Early Letters of Richard Hurd, 1739 to 1762* (Church of England Record Society, 1995), p. xxv.

44 Watson and Elizabeth Hand had married in 1745/6. Their third son, George Watson Hand was to become vicar of St Giles without Cricklegate church, London.

45 Will of William Budworth SRO P/C/11 28 October 1745.

46 John Nichol, *Literary Anecdotes of the eighteenth century,* Volume III, p 333.

47 *Gentleman's Magazine and Historical Review,* Volume 62, Part 2, August 1792, p. 785.

Chapter Four

Reverend Roger Bromley

Mr Budworth's unexpected death in 1745 was felt very keenly by the Trustees, particularly by Sir Edward Littleton and Dr Richard Hurd, who were close friends with the headmaster. However, there was a quick and unanimous decision from the Trustees of the school to ask Reverend Roger Bromley if he would accept the vacant position.

Reverend Roger Bromley had been a popular teacher, good humoured with a pleasant personality and had also been curate at Brewood church. He had left the school during Mr Budworth's difficult years in the 1740s, when student numbers were declining. *The Gentleman's Magazine* cited the reason for Bromley's departure as an argument between Budworth and Bromley but Budworth liked the teacher and had been upset when Bromley left.[1]

Roger Bromley was the son of Richard Bromley and his wife Ann Starkey from Castle Church, Stafford. The family lived at Rule Hall, Bradley, and Roger had been baptised at St Mary and All Saints' church, Bradley, on 20 April 1715. He had both elder and younger siblings but his mother died soon after the birth of his youngest brother Edward, who was christened in April 1717. His father, with a young family to raise, then married True Waltho, the widow of Walter Forrester of the borough of Stafford.[2]

Roger Bromley attended Magdalen College, Oxford, obtaining his B.A. on 22 March 1736/7, a few days after the death of his father. Roger Bromley became a commissioner for probate at the Cathedral church of Lichfield and on 27 January 1738/39, he was the person who gave permission for William Budworth to be lawfully granted probate of his wife's estate. In the same year, Reverend Bromley became a curate at the parish church of St. Mary and St Chad, Brewood and also taught at the Grammar School, Brewood.

When Bromley returned as headmaster, Sir Edward Littleton offered him the position of incumbent at the church of St Mary and St Luke, Shareshill, which he accepted. With an improved income, Bromley married Mary Bracegirdle at Shareshill church on 14 September 1746. Mary was the daughter of Henry Bracegirdle of Aspley Manor, Coven. Four years later, in 1750, Mary's sister Ann married Thomas Watson Perks of Great Saredon, attorney at law for the Trustees of Brewood Grammar School.

Reverend Bromley and his wife Mary, settled down in Brewood and enjoyed family life with their children: Henry, Mary, Ann, William and Susannah, although Henry did not survive infancy.

Reverend Bromley continued with his successful teaching using the same methods and material as Reverend Budworth. It was noted by several students in their later years that Mr Bromley was particularly proficient in Greek. His pupils included Thomas Pendrell Rock who had lived at what is now known as Speedwell Castle, and Richard Talbot, cordwainer, a man described as being of good character and a day scholar at the school.[3] Other pupils included Fisher Littleton, brother of Sir Edward Littleton, Moreton Walhouse of Hatherton and Robert, son of Robert Brown of Bradley, all of whom attended Emmanuel College, Cambridge.

In 1752, Reverend Bromley took on additional duties as rector of St. Andrew's church, Ryton, Shropshire.[4] He appears to have led a peaceful life in Brewood, maintaining a successful school, with the aid of his usher, Mr Careless.[5] On 15 March 1760 Benjamin Blake, for many years usher at the school, was buried in Brewood churchyard.

Roger Bromley remained as headmaster until his sudden death on 13 December 1761. He was only 46 years old when he was taken ill. He wrote his will in November and died a few weeks later. He bequeathed everything to his wife Mary.

Advertising for a new headmaster

It had been such a long time since the post for headmaster had been advertised that the Trustees were not clear of the correct procedure. On 19 December 1761, five days after the burial of Reverend Bromley, a Thomas Moss of Wolverhampton wrote to Mr Perks, the Trustees attorney at law, that the Trustees wanted the election of a new headmaster to take place as quickly as possible, and had given a date and time: Tuesday 5 January at 11.00 a.m. It is unclear who was employing Thomas Moss. He could have worked for Mr Perks, as an apprentice attorney, or for a Trustee. On Boxing Day, Sir Edward Littleton complained to Perks that the proposed date was insufficient time for suitable candidates to have their applications ready. Littleton put the blame on Thomas Moss for being in such a hurry when he visited him, or he would have thought of that problem earlier. Littleton believed that Lord Ward, chairman of the Trustees, would raise no objections and, as the date of the appointment was not in the papers, it would not inconvenience any of the candidates. Littleton wanted Moss to go to Lord Ward, and propose that the election of headmaster would be set for a week later.[6]

The Trustees were to have lunch at the Red Lion, Brewood, on the day of the appointment of the headmaster, which remained 5 January. Every Trustee was to be sent a letter requesting them to attend the election and the meal, with the name of the inn specifically mentioned. Moss was unacquainted with either where the Trustees regularly met, or the Red Lion, it is not clear in his correspondence, but the initial newspaper advertisement requested all Trustees to meet at the King's Arms, Brewood, which did not exist.[7] This was changed by the following week to the Red Lion. William Rippon was then the proprietor.[8] Now known as the Lion Hotel and Staffordshire Grill, it is in a prime position in the centre of the village, facing the village square and opposite the Swan Inn.

The notice that appeared in *Aris's Birmingham Gazette* of 28 December 1761, was dated 17 December 1761 and stated that Reverend Bromley, minister of Shareshill and headmaster of the Free Grammar School at Brewood had died last Sunday. This left vacant "an extraordinary good House capable of containing very commodiously upwards of Fifty Boarders, in a fine, pleasant, healthful Country, together with a salary of Sixty Pounds per Annum". The advertisement continued that it was "hoped that in a Thing of great Importance to the Country, the Gentlemen who are Trustees of the said School, will not promise their Votes and Interest to serve any particular Person, but keep themselves perfectly disengaged till the Time of Election, that they may pay a due Regard to the Merit and Abilities of such Gentlemen as at the Time may think proper to offer themselves as Candidates". There would be notice of the date of the election, but any candidate wishing to apply immediately could do so and enquiries would be made into his character. A list of Trustees could be obtained from Mr Perks at Shareshill, near Wolverhampton, as they were too numerous to list in the newspaper.[9]

The appointment of a new headmaster was made at the beginning of January 1762, without the candidates attending. Applications were received from all over the country and to even be considered the applicant needed to have a university degree and also be a clergyman.

There is no complete list of candidates within the Staffordshire Archives. However, one of the candidates for the post was Thomas Moss, who had attended Emmanuel College, Cambridge and graduated in 1761.[10] This is almost certainly the same person who was trying to sort out the interviews for the post of headmaster, and who was in such a hurry when visiting Sir Edward Littleton in 1761. He appears to have only worked for the Trustees for a short period of time, and it coincides with the dates for leaving university. This Moss became a curate at Uttoxeter in 1762.[11] He had little teaching experience, having just graduated. Reverend Richard Hurd had some recollection of Moss, the candidate, at Emmanuel College and wrote to Sir Edward Littleton, that this person "had behaved himself well at College, but that is all I can say".[12] This same Thomas Moss became a successful minister of the church. He was noted for his poetry, in particular the very popular *Beggars Petition*, which was learnt by schoolchildren, and even referred to in the fiction of Jane Austin and Charles Dickens.[13]

On 4 January 1762, Thomas Moss, B.A, put a notice in *Aris's Birmingham Gazette*, directly under the advertisement for the vacancy of headmaster of Brewood Grammar School, thanking the Trustees who have indicated their support of him and humbly hoping that the others would do so too.[14] He was not the only one to advertise his intention of being considered for the post of headmaster. Underneath the advertisement posted by Moss was another application from Reverend Mr John Stubb, M.A. of Queen's College, Oxford, who would have signified his intentions to the Trustees before, if notice of the vacancy had come earlier to his attention. All was set for the election of the next headmaster.

Notes

1 *Gentleman's Magazine,* Volume 62, Part 2, August 1792, p. 684.

2 Walter Foster had married True Waltho of Bradely on 24 August 1704 at St Mary's church, Castle Church, Stafford, they lived in the borough of Stafford. The widowed Richard Bromley married True Foster on 29 January 1717/1718 at Lichfield Cathedral.

3 SRO D1416/5/1, *Teaching at Brewood School* 1801.

4 *Clergy of the Church of England database.*

5 SRO, D1416/5/1.

6 SRO, D1416/4/2/1.

7 The Red Lion had been sold in 1760 following the death of Thomas Marygold, the proprietor. *Aris's Gazette,* 24 March 1760, p. 4; The Trustees were requested to meet at the King's Arms, Brewood, *Aris's Gazette* 26 December 1761, p. 3 and then a new notice placed lunch for the Trustees at the Red Lion, *Aris's Gazette* 4 January 1762, p. 3.

8 SRO, D1416/4/2/1.

9 *Aris's Birmingham Gazette,* 28 December 1761, p.4.

10 Sarah Brewer (ed.), *The Early Letters of Richard Hurd, 1739 to 1762* (Church of England Record Society, 1995), Note 3, Letter 253. Brewer believes that John Moss, who had been a vicar at the church of St Mary and St Chad, Brewood, and died in 1737 aged 85, may have been a relative.

11 *Clergy of the Church of England database.*

12 Brewer, Letter 253.

13 Thomas Moss, son of Francis Moss of Wolverhampton, at this time had just finished a university degree at Cambridge. He later went on to become a minister at Trentham, Oldbury and Brierley Hill.

14 *Aris' Birmingham Gazette,* 4 January 1762, p. 3.

The Lion Hotel, where the Trustees often met for lunch when electing
a new headmaster, is at the forefront of the photograph.

The Angel Inn is shown on the left-hand side of the photograph,
at the corner of Stafford Street.

The Fleur-de-Lys, which featured prominently in the history of Brewood,
would have stood opposite the post office and shop seen in the top
right-hand section of the image. The presence of the post office
helps date the photograph as having been taken after 1901.
It was a private house before that date. _See_ Horovitz, page 188.

Reproduced courtesy of Brewood Civic Society.

Chapter Five

Reverend Thomas Feilde

The Trustees met at the Red Lion, Brewood, at 11.00 a.m. on 5 January 1762 to select the new headmaster, before having lunch there, supplied by William Rippon, the proprietor.[1] The elected candidate was Reverend Feilde. He had been a curate at St John the Baptist church, Boyleston, Derbyshire from 18 March 1753, and was also curate of All Saints' church, Loughborough. When applying for the post of headmaster, Feilde had requested a written reference from Reverend Richard Hurd who was an incumbent at nearby All Saints' church, Thurcaston, Leicester, and then personally delivered it to Sir Edward Littleton at Teddesley Hall. This was a shrewd move as both Hurd and Littleton were influential Trustees who worked hard to ensure that Brewood Grammar School had an excellent reputation throughout the country.

Hurd admitted to Littleton that he had not known Feilde for very long but felt that he was extremely well qualified for the post and his character was "in all respects, unexceptionable".[2] A week later Hurd clarified his reference saying that he believed Feilde to be a very decent worthy man, and did not disagree with the "favourable representation" which Dr Erasmus Darwin had made of him.[3] Hurd thought that Feilde would be "a very creditable Master" but not to expect a second Mr Budworth.[4]

Feilde had been born in North Wingfield, Derbyshire, the son of rector Thomas Feilde, and his young wife Rebeckah.[5] The young Thomas was christened on 2 June 1730, just before his mother's death a fortnight later. Rebeckah's sister, Ellen, moved into the lodging room at the rectory to help care for the young baby. Nine years later Reverend Feilde died and the comforts of his home, where the young Thomas lived, were revealed in an inventory of the estate. The rectory was a large building containing a substantial library with several clocks and comfortable home furnishings as well as the usual brewhouse and the facilities to make butter and cheese. The named horses were Dragon, Robin, Boss and Starr but there were also four asses, two pigs and two cows.[6]

Fielde, the elder, wanted his curate and good friend, John Edwards, M.A., to be responsible for the care and education of his son. There is some confusion as to where young Thomas went to school. It may have been that he received his education from Reverend Edwards who was vicar of nearby Tibshelf church from 1736 until his death in 1753.[7] However, it is also possible that Thomas Feilde was educated at the local Chesterfield Free Grammar School whose headmaster was William Burrow. Under his headship, Chesterfield Grammar School had gained an excellent reputation, and amongst the pupils were Erasmus Darwin and his brother Robert, the same Erasmus Darwin who gave Feilde a reference for the post of headmaster at Brewood.[8] Wherever he spent his schooldays, in 1747 Feilde continued his education at St John's College Cambridge, like his father, obtaining his B.A. in 1750-1751 and his M.A. in 1754.

On 10 January 1753 Thomas Feilde married Elizabeth Fletcher, the eldest daughter of Reverend Henry Fletcher of Boylestone and Spondon, Derbyshire. They chose to marry at All Saints' church, Mackworth, Derbyshire, and the service was conducted by Reverend John Pickering, whose son was later to become another headmaster at Brewood School. On 18 March 1753, Thomas Feilde was licensed to the curacy of Boylestone and ordained a priest on 22 September 1754.[9]

Thomas and Elizabeth had five children whilst in Derbyshire, but only Martha, William Henry and Edmund survived infancy. The couple had another two children whilst at Loughborough, Elizabeth and Samuel and then moved to Brewood. Here, John was baptised on 25 July 1763; Paule, who it is believed had severe visual and hearing impediments, was baptised on 1 December 1764;[10] Thomas on 20 March 1766 and Jane on 8 September 1768 but she sadly died two days later and was buried in Brewood churchyard.

Reverend Thomas Feilde and his family move to Brewood

Following Reverend Feilde's election to the headmastership of Brewood Grammar School on 4 January 1762, Feilde lost no time by advertising in the newspapers the next day that he would be ready to take boarders at the school during the first week of March.[11] In spite of being new to the post of headmaster, Thomas Feilde also happily took on the duties of vicar at the parish church after the death of Reverend Mr Richard Fowler in March 1762. Feilde managed to juggle the duties of both vicar and headmaster at Brewood until Reverend Thomas Muchall took over as vicar in 1767. During this time Feilde recorded in the parish registers the number of people baptised and buried in his church, and their gender. Happily, from 1763 until 1766, there were more christenings than burials. Feilde also officiated at marriages, including the marriage of the usher of Brewood Grammar School, Thomas Careless, to Mary Muchall in 1764.

Feilde was also in regular contact with his father's relations, who were eminent citizens of Hertfordshire. In particular he was close to his aunt, Martha Paule Feilde of Stanstead Abbots, Hertfordshire, widow of Edmund Feilde, a barrister.

With the family growing, so had the financial commitments and, in addition to his work at Brewood, Feilde accepted the offer of two Hertfordshire livings from his family. The first was in 1765 at St Botolph's church, Eastwick, near Stanstead. The appointment was made after the death of Reverend John Allen, who had been rector of the church from 1726 until 1765.[12] It was here that Thomas and Elizabeth Feilde's youngest child was baptised on 11 October 1769. Feilde's great aunt, Martha Paule Feilde had died a few days earlier and was buried at Stanstead Abbots churchyard on 7 October, aged 89 years.[13] Feilde was also officially presented as vicar of St James church, Stanstead Abbots in 1767, by his cousin Paul Feilde, Martha's son. It is very unlikely that Reverend Thomas Feilde would have been able to preach regularly at either of these churches, and would have needed to employ a curate.[14]

Feilde and his history of Staffordshire

During his time as headmaster of Brewood Grammar School, Thomas Feilde was keen to write an authoritative history of Staffordshire. He may have been inspired whilst at St John's College, Cambridge. Here he had been taught by Dr Thomas Rutherforth whose father had collected material for a County History of Cambridgeshire.

Reverend Feilde wanted his history of Staffordshire to include the immense research that Dr Wilkes, the physician and antiquarian of Willenhall and Trustee of Brewood Grammar School, had already achieved and written as notes, but never published. Feilde wanted to add his own research as well as illustrations and a map of Staffordshire. It was to be truly comprehensive and Feilde was in a good position to achieve his dream as he was in regular contact with the Trustees of the Grammar School. These were the landed gentry of Staffordshire with their own archives and local knowledge of the county, and many of Feilde's pupils would have had similar backgrounds.

The initial problem though was to locate Dr Wilkes' research notes some of which he had gathered when he visited people in his capacity as doctor or friend. There was a fear that Dr Wilkes' wife, Frances, had burnt many of her husband's papers before she moved to Hampshire.[15] Frances Wilkes was the sister of Trustee Reverend Richard Wrottesley of Wrottesley Hall, near Codsall.

In October 1767, Reverend Feilde wrote to Reverend Mr Thomas Unett, assistant minister at St Mary's church, Stafford, and a relative of Wilkes, asking him if he had any idea as to the whereabouts of the material.[16] Reverend Unett had been educated at Brewood Grammar School whilst Mr Budworth was headmaster.[17] Unett was able to reply that he had the papers but wanted to publish Dr Wilkes' notes himself and was reluctant to release them to someone else.[18] Persuasively, Feilde in a follow up letter dated 23 October 1767, assured Unett that he would give Dr Wilkes all due credit for his work and add to it. He wrote, "My work is intended to be ornamented with views of the principal seats in the County with plates of all kinds of Curiosities that shall be thought worth representing & it is proposed at the same Time to publish a new map of Staffordshire from an actual Survey, in short no pains will be spared to render it a capital Performance".[19] After a long correspondence, it was agreed that Feilde could buy the papers from Unett and publish them. The cost would be £200. Feilde had to pay £100 on receipt of the papers and £50 more when the book was published and, if profitable, then an extra £50, with Dr Wilkes receiving full credit for all the work that he had done.[20] Meanwhile, Feilde was anxious that his book should progress immediately, and even before he received Dr Wilkes' work, was asking if he could borrow, immediately, just two or three letters to show to some friends.[21]

When, in 1767, Reverend Thomas Muchall took over from Feilde as vicar of Brewood church, Feilde used his free time to organise the publication of his book. At the end of November, Feilde contacted Mr Wright of Worcester to find out how much it would cost to print his illustrations. Twenty drawings of views would cost £3 3s each, engravings were more expensive, and at the "size enclosed" would cost £10 10s each making an additional charge of £210. The printing of 20,000 prints at 6 shillings per hundred would cost £60 and 20 reams of paper at £1 5s 0d per ream was £25, making a grand total of £358. Feilde's income from subscriptions was £42 11s 6d, which left a substantial shortfall of cash. The engraving was to be done by Mr Hancock.[22] This was probably Robert Hancock, a master engraver who, at the time of Feilde's correspondence, would have been working at Worcester Porcelain Works.[23]

In December 1767 Feilde advertised in the newspapers that he would welcome subscriptions, at a guinea a time for his forthcoming *General History of Staffordshire* based on Wilkes' manuscripts but with his own additions to them. Feilde planned that his work would be one volume of 120 pages or more, priced at 1 ½ guineas to subscribers, 1 guinea to be paid in advance. Subscribers came from all over Britain and included Trinity College, Cambridge, James Beauclerk, Bishop of Hereford and John Hornyold, the Roman Catholic vicar apostolic of Midland District who lived at Long Birch, Brewood, as well as Feilde's relations: Mrs Feilde of Hoddesdon, Hertfordshire, Paule Feilde and Mrs Harrison who ordered two copies.

At the same time, Feilde told the readers that he would welcome any additional information about the history and antiquities of the county and he could be contacted either at Brewood, or via Mr Ralph Taylor, the bookseller, in Stafford.[24]

The response to providing information for his book was more productive than the subscriptions. George Tollet of Betley Hall in North Staffordshire, was particularly supportive of Feilde, and offered to help him, proffering advice and accommodation at Betley. In a letter dated 15 March 1768, for example, Tollet informed Feilde that Mr Loxdale and Mr Bowen had some manuscript collections of Staffordshire and Tollet himself had a copy of Sampson Erdeswick's *A survey of Staffordshire containing the antiquities of that county* with the continuation by John Hurdman of Stone.[25] He continued with offers of help and advice throughout the writing of the book, sending Feilde some items that had been collected during the digging of the canal and tunnel at Harecastle. He also suggested that Feilde contact the authoritative Mr Joshua Platt of Oxford, about his collection and his observations on fossils in Staffordshire. Unett and Feilde were both invited to join Tollet when he opened up a sepulchral barrow on Maer Heath, near Madeley and Whitmore.[26]

Another offer of help came from John Langley of Golding, near Shrewsbury, who had a manuscript copy of the "*Antiquities*" by Sampson Erdeswick of Sandon which he was happy to lend to Feilde, as he thought it had never been published. He even offered to send it by Bather's Waggon to Ivetsey Bank, near Brewood, or by his friend, Mr Fowler of Pendeford, another Trustee of the school.[27]

Other people wrote asking for mistakes of previous histories of Staffordshire to be corrected. William Cotton of Crakemarsh wrote to Feilde, on 28 December 1768, telling him that he had subscribed to Mr Feilde's book at Major Morgan's bookshop at Market Street, Lichfield.[28] He wanted Feilde to correct the injustice that his family had received from Sir Simon Degge's letter, printed at the end of Sampson Erdeswick's Survey, stating that his family were not of good pedigree. Cotton invited Feilde to visit him at Crakemarsh and see the pedigree of the family and a plan of the house. He would also lend Feilde a copy of the new *Anecdotes of British Topography* by Richard Gough, a leading antiquary of the time but who had published the book anonymously.[29]

Feilde was also making his own contacts. He wrote to Erasmus Darwin who suggested that Feilde include Matthew Boulton's works at Soho, as a wonder of art. Darwin told Feilde that Soho, a hill in Staffordshire about two miles from Birmingham, had been bleak barren heathland with a hut, the home of a warrener but Mr Boulton had changed it all. Darwin continued that "The transformation of this place is a recent monument of the effects of trade on population. A beautiful garden, with wood, lawn and water, now covers one side of this hill…..”[30]

Reverend Feilde also asked advice from people. He contacted Reverend Owen Manning, of Godalming, Surrey, asking how he had compiled his *Ancient History of Surrey*. Manning had used questionnaires but for the purpose of discovering unknown private collections. He sent Feilde some notes from Dr Mills who was writing a natural history, which he thought Feilde might find interesting.[31] Manning introduced Feilde to Sir John Peshall of Oxford, who invited Feilde to be his guest at Oxford and also recommended *Anecdotes to Topography*.[32]

Another writer had botany experience which he was happy to share, as he frequently visited Staffordshire finding it "one of the pleasantest counties in England". He wished to remain anonymous but it was likely to have been Richard Hill Waring of Leeward, Flintshire and Hayes, Oswestry. He was a barrister of law, Recorder of Oswestry, and High Sheriff of Flintshire. Waring was also a keen and eminent botanist, had completed the Grand Tour and, soon after he had written to Feilde, became a fellow of the Royal Society. The author advised Feilde to contact Emanuel Mendes Da Costa who had an immense interest in natural history and who had an extensive collection of fossils, minerals and shells. The writer believed that no one else knew the fossils of these islands as well as he, and he thought that Da Costa would be very pleased to assist Feilde.[33]

As the research progressed, work on the history of Staffordshire was becoming more extensive but Feilde was having trouble raising the final £30 he needed to buy Wilkes' papers, and, as a result, had still not received the core material. On 19 August 1768 he wrote a letter to Reverend Unett with a solution. Feilde would give Unett a bond of £80 and all the proceeds from future subscriptions at Mr Taylor's, the bookseller, plus the proceeds from subscriptions amongst Unett's friends until the money was raised, in exchange for receiving the papers immediately. This way Unett would not be taking any risk and Feilde would be able to get the book to a printer as soon as possible. Feilde went on to tell Unett that his *History of Staffordshire* was progressing well and that he had some drawings going forward by Mr Bond of Birmingham, "a very good hand", with the printer ready to begin the work.[34]

The idea of an £80 bond for the papers must have appeared an agreeable solution to Unett as, by the end of November, Feilde was ready to collect the papers, as soon as possible. He requested that the papers be packed up ready in parcels convenient for the carriage, as the daylight hours were getting shorter.[35]

Mr Bond of Birmingham the engraver that Reverend Feilde had chosen was likely to have been John Daniel Bond of Birmingham, who had been born in Stroud, Gloucestershire, son of William Bond, a bookseller and book binder. Daniel Bond had exhibited his landscapes in London at the Society of Artists of Great Britain and had also gained fame within Birmingham School for his landscape painting.[36]

It should be remembered that Feilde would have had the expense of the Grammar School, which all the headmasters found a problem to fund, and he had a large family to feed and clothe too, so money would have been scarce. Time would also have been at a premium. If Feilde was relaying his knowledge of Staffordshire to the pupils at Brewood Grammar School, which it is very likely that he would have done, it would have been a unique opportunity for them to develop a breadth of knowledge of the county and progression in the understanding of new subjects which were just in their early stages of development. However, the pupils also needed a grounding for university, including a classical education. There is no evidence that the pupils at Brewood Grammar School were neglected, but Feilde must have been extremely busy with teaching, parochial duties and family commitments. He was travelling to Hertfordshire to perform clerical duties at Stanstead Abbots and Eastwick churches, and travelling to different destinations across Staffordshire, and further afield to Oxford and London, to do research for his book.

Feilde did contact Emanuel Mendes da Costa, for his help and expertise. Geology, at this time, was a new science, and Feilde was anxious that his book would reflect the latest authoritative ideas on the subject. Da Costa was one of the leading geologists of his day, with a vast collection of shells, minerals and fossils. He was in correspondence with many people, both at home and abroad, including Sir Hans Sloane, whose own collection of material was used in part to begin the British Museum.[37]

Da Costa, was writing his own book *Natural History of Fossils*. Volume one had been published in 1757 and had been widely acclaimed. With the help of William Stukeley, a clergyman and antiquarian, he was elected clerk of the Royal Society in 1763, and later became the Society's Librarian, Keeper of the Repository, Housekeeper and Collector of Subscriptions.[38] However, Da Costa's passion for geology became too expensive and he misappropriated £1500 of the Society's funds. The Royal Society became aware of this in 1767 and Da Costa, his wife and daughter had to leave their rent-free premises at Crane Court, home of the Royal Society, and all their possessions were sold at auction, including the collection of fossils. In November 1768 Da Costa was in King's Bench Debtors' Prison at Southwark, London. He was expelled from both the Royal Society and the Society of Antiquaries.[39]

On 29 January 1769 Feilde wrote to Da Costa, from Brewood, asking him for some assistance in his book with regard to fossils. Feilde explained that whilst his book would be on a variety of subjects, with regard to natural history he only wanted to classify and to describe specimens, but as accurately as possible.[40] Da Costa willingly gave Feilde his advice, and a correspondence between the two men began.[41] Da Costa strongly advised Feilde to write down the local or particular county names of all the natural bodies, as he believed it was important as a record of the English language: Polecat, for example, was called Fitchet in some counties and the Penguin Bird had at least seven local names.[42]

Da Costa told Feilde that he had never visited Staffordshire, but there are records that confirm that he had visited the coalfields at Wednesbury, Staffordshire.[43] He had also acquired some fossils from Staffordshire such as fossils of vegetables taken from the canal near Harecastle Hill.[44] At this time, it was common for quarrymen to sell any fossils that they found to collectors.

Da Costa recommended several places for Feilde to visit, including the lime pits at Dudley in which there was a large quantity of fossils, of which the best collection was with Lord Dudley, but he also thought it worthwhile to check out the lime works at Sedgley and Walsall. Da Costa also recommended contacting Walter Mansfield, at Fordhouses, close to Brewood, who had made a collection of fossils from his neighbourhood, as well as contacting Dr Darwin of Lichfield, but Feilde had already done that. Da Costa's enthusiasm for his subject abounded and he recommended Ecton Hill for a variety of fossils, but also advised that it would be very worthwhile to look at the copper mines as they had not been worked when Dr Plot visited. Da Costa thought that Darwin might be willing to accompany Feilde on this trip. Da Costa continued that mill stones were to be found at Mow Cop, and grindstones at Bilston as well as Branston near Burton.[45]

In addition to writing to the current experts for his now ever-expanding work about Staffordshire, Reverend Feilde also needed to obtain as much historical material that he could find about the county. This would verify Dr Wilkes' work, provide new material and make his own name as an established historian. In order to do this, he had to pay for documents not available locally to be transcribed.

An example was Feilde's correspondence with William Huddesford, writer and curator of the Ashmolean Museum at Oxford.[46] Feilde planned to visit Oxford in the summer, and wanted to see all the material relating to Staffordshire, and the Giffard family.[47] Huddesford was able to send brief details of the material in the museum, but advised that Feilde looked at the documents himself to avoid the great expense of having material transcribed that might not be relevant to him.[48]

Maybe it was because Reverend Feilde was in correspondence with eminent people, passionate about their authoritative fields of research that fuelled his dedication for a comprehensive book about Staffordshire. Feilde had a particular interest in natural history, which remained with him long after he left Staffordshire.

Reverend Feilde and his family leave Brewood

Reverend Feilde resigned from Brewood school in 1769 and a new headmaster was in place by September. The reasons for his resignation are unclear, but the book may have been a factor.

Reverend Feilde was a polite person, who expected high standards of work. This can be seen from the letters that he wrote to people helping him with both the research for his book, the illustrations and the publication of his work. He paid attention to detail but this cost him dear financially. The continued expense of researching and publishing his history of Staffordshire, including the cost of Wilkes' manuscripts, the costs of transcription of documents, the engravings and illustrations for the book, the cost of travelling, meant that Feilde was soon having money concerns. He had borrowed money from a Mr Hughes in about 1757, which had not been entirely repaid.[49]

On 28 April 1770 Feilde wrote a letter from London to Reverend Unett at Stafford saying that it was with much concern that he had to acquaint Unett that there was little probability that he could continue with his history of Staffordshire, due to the unhappy situation of his own private affairs. He tried to sell Wilkes' papers back to Unett for the same price: writing that "as no doubt you are anxious for the fate of Dr Wilkes' papers, I thought myself obliged to make you the first offer of them". If Unett complied with this wish, then all the subscription money could be returned to the subscribers and the manuscripts would be ready for somebody else to use. This may have been a simplistic view as the subscribers had been waiting some time for the book to be published and would have been unhappy with this solution. Feilde continued that he "really had wanted to do justice to the Subject but that there was no resisting necessity". He also asked Reverend Unett to pass on a message to Mr Turton of Sugnall Hall for him: "If you see Mr Turton pray give my Compliments to him and assure him that I will return the Manuscripts he so obligingly lent me in a very little time".[50]

When George Tollet learned that Feilde's plans for the *History of Staffordshire* had ceased he was devastated. He knew the amount of work that had been put into the book by both himself, Feilde, and others to provide an authoritative account of Staffordshire. It was essential for Dr Wilkes' manuscripts to be purchased quickly so that the important research of Dr Wilkes and other Staffordshire historians would not be lost forever to future generations. Tollet wrote quickly to Unett that Dr Wilkes' manuscripts should be purchased back for the benefit of the county and suggested to Reverend Unett that a substantial sum of money should be paid to Feilde for all his work. Mr. Tollet knew that Feilde had left the manuscripts with a relation, and he would personally write to them, but first he wanted to know the price that Feilde had paid for the manuscripts and the financial details of the subscription charges.[51]

On 2 August 1770 Unett replied to Tollet that he was very sorry that the *History of Staffordshire* would not be completed and he felt Feilde had let him down. The agreement that Unett had with Feilde was that all the manuscripts that Unett possessed from Dr Wilkes would be purchased by Mr Feilde for £100 but there was an additional bond payment of £50, one month after the manuscripts were printed and published and a promise of a further £50 if the book was well received. The latter was to be determined by two people: one person chosen by each party. Reverend Unett stated that he still had an interest in the publication of the book, "but from whence all the Money arose that he advanced to me I know not, or what Subscribers he has taken in".[52]

There must have been concerns from certain subscribers to the book that their money was now lost, and there were rumours circulating that Feilde had left the country and gone to America. This was certainly the view of the Reverend Mr Archdeacon Thomas Smalbroke of Lichfield who wrote to Unett for information about Feilde's *History of Staffordshire*. Reverend Unett did not want to be drawn into the financial turmoil and ill will relating to the book, and promptly replied that he had nothing to do with the publication of the *History of Staffordshire*. He had sold Feilde the manuscripts for a sum of money in hand and that he would receive the extra money when the work was published "which I imagine will be when he has settled his affairs for I believe that they have been a good deal embarrassed of late". Unett thought the rumours that Feilde had gone to America were unfounded as he had two good livings at Eastwick and Stanstead Abbots.[53]

Feilde moves to America

On 2 August 1770, the same day that Unett wrote the letter to Tollet, Feilde obtained permission from Richard Terrick, Bishop of London, to do ministerial work in the American Colonies, for which Terrick had the responsibility.

Fielde sailed to Virginia, without his family and applied for the post of minister of Kingston parish, Gloucester County, Virginia.[54] He was one of four candidates, including the Reverend Thomas Baker, who had been acting as an interim minister for three months. The interviews were held on 19 December 1770 and Feilde was successful, beginning work on 5 January 1771. Feilde lived in one of the most heavily populated parishes and was allocated a house, with a tobacco plantation and farmland of 500 acres where he could raise pigs, sheep and cattle, close to the great Bay of Chesapeake. In 1774 it is recorded that Feilde had seven adult slaves working for him and baptised seven hundred slaves during his time as minister of Kingston.[55]

In August 1771 Elizabeth had joined her husband in Kingston bringing with her some of the children: William, aged 15, Edmund, aged 12, Elizabeth aged 10 and James aged 2. They sailed on the ship *Virginia*, owned by John Norton and his sons, George F. Norton and John Hatley Norton, the tobacconists of Yorktown, Virginia and London. John Hatley Norton was one of Feilde's friends and had suggested that he moved to Virginia. Norton also knew Emanuel Mendes de Costa. George requested that his brother John ensured that Mrs Feilde and the family were well looked after on the journey.[56]

Feilde's passion for science and research continued in America. He wrote to Dr Colin Mackenzie in London, on 16 February 1771, saying that he had an intense interest in gaining a natural knowledge of America, and making visits into the country to look for curiosities. Feilde had already learned about the shell strata of coastal Virginia, the soil composition, and how to plant Indian corn. He had also collected some specimens to send to Mackenzie. Feilde, in return, wanted Dr Mackenzie to send him some potatoes, lucerne seed and some 'turnip cabbage seed' so that he could experiment with different crops. Colin Mackenzie was an eminent midwife whose work and research in obstetrics and gynaecology was ground breaking. He had attended University of Leiden in the Netherlands and Edinburgh University where he had been a pupil of William Smellie. He also worked and lectured at Guy's and St Thomas' Hospitals, Southwick, London.[57]

Feilde continued to write to Da Costa via Mackenzie and through his scientific network in America, Feilde was happy to do anything that would help with the progress of natural history both for Mackenzie and

Da Costa. Reverend Thomas Feilde soon gained respect in the area and was included in the Governors and Visitors of the College of William and Mary in 1773.[58] It was at this college that William Small, a member of the Lunar Society and friend to Erasmus Darwin, had been a professor.

However, whilst Feilde was establishing new friends, Da Costa was feeling a little neglected. He had not received any fossils or letters from Feilde and was very keen to hear about the post of Library and Museum Keeper which was vacant at the College of William and Mary, Williamsburg. For whatever reasons, Reverend Feilde was not rushing to send him the details.[59] Mrs Feilde was also unhappy that in America she did not have sufficient income to be able to offer guests even a glass of wine.

During 1775 the American War of Independence was underway and Thomas Feilde's position as minister of Kingston Parish was under threat. He had refused to take the oath of abjuration of the King and allegiance to Congress, but this did not come to a head until July 1777, when he was relieved of his clerical duties at Kingston. A few months later, on 2 February 1778, his sons William and Edmund, by that time aged 23 and 19, managed to make their escape by canoe into Chesapeake Bay and were picked up by the British ship, the *Richmond*.[60] In 1780, William returned to America to fight the rebels and Edmund joined the East India Company.

Reverend Feilde and the rest of the family were given a pass by Patrick Henry, the first Governor of independent Virginia, and major participant in the American War of Independence. The pass allowed Feilde and his family to travel to the British Army at New York. Here, Feilde became a chaplain under the command of Brigadier General Oliver De Lancey, as well as interim minister of St Andrew's church on Staten Island.[61] In order to reach New York, the Feildes had to sell everything that they could at very low prices. Times were hard and on 25 September 1779 Thomas Feilde, John Agnew, John Hamilton Rowland and William Duncan, who had all been rectors of parishes in Virginia but were now living in New York, wrote to Robert Lowth, Bishop of London, informing him they did not have sufficient income to support themselves and their families.

A few years later, in February 1781, Reverend Feilde died, and the family were destitute. Reverend Samuel Seabury and Reverend Charles Inglis petitioned that Feilde's widow, Elizabeth, should be given a pension. This allowed her to return to England, and in March 1784 she lived at the King's Road, Chelsea, with three of the children. She petitioned for a permanent pension and financial reimbursement for money lost due to her husband's loyalty to King and Country. She died on 31 August 1785 and is buried at St. Mary's church, Lewisham. Elizabeth, her daughter, died on 18 June 1790 aged only 29 years, and was buried alongside her mother.

The *History of Staffordshire* was finally completed by the antiquarian Stebbing Shaw who requested any information on the location of Dr Wilkes' papers in January 1792 in the *Gentleman's Magazine*.[62] Feilde had left the papers with his cousin Paul Feilde who had died in 1783 and who, in turn, had left them with Martha Kemp, Feilde's eldest daughter. Martha Kemp, fortunately saw the advertisement and allowed Shaw to have the material, and her father's work with them, but only if the subscriptions already paid to Feilde were honoured.

On 4 September 1775 during the American War of Independence, an advertisement was placed in *Aris's Birmingham Gazette*, the local newspaper at the time for Brewood, asking for any creditors of Reverend Mr Feilde to meet at the "Flour-de-Luce Inn", Brewood, on Saturday 16 September at 3 o'clock in the afternoon "in order to assent or dissent from the Proposal made by Mr Fielde [sic] for the Payment of his Debts". Anyone wanting to make a claim needed to deliver an account of the debts to Mr Morton, attorney, Wolverhampton.[63] Clearly Feilde and his family wanted to settle all their debts but they were struggling financially, so this gesture appears to be aimed at returning to England without facing bankruptcy.

Notes

1 *Aris's Birmingham Gazette*, 4 January 1762, p. 3.
2 Sarah Brewer (ed.), *The Early Letters of Richard Hurd, 1739 to 1762*, (Church of England Record Society, 1995), Letter 254, 23 December 1761.
3 Dr Darwin lived at nearby Lichfield and would become grandfather of Charles Darwin.

4 Brewer, Letter 256, 1 January 1762.

5 Thomas Feilde the elder had been born at Stanstead Abbots Hertfordshire and had attended Eton School, and St John's College, Cambridge. Reverend Feilde and his young wife Rebeckah Willson, were married by licence on 26 May 1728 at North Wingfield church.

6 Will of Thomas Fielde, clerk, 1739 at SRO/LRO, 31 October 1739.

7 R.F. Scott, *Admissions of the College of St John the Evangelist, Cambridge, part III*, 1903, and queried in later editions of *Venn's Alumni Cantabrigienses.*

8 Desmond King-Hele, *Letters of Erasmus Darwin*, (CUP, 1985), pp. 7, 9 and Desmond King-Hele, *Erasmus Darwin: A life of unequalled Achievement*, (DLM, 1999), pp. 31, 41. Darwin was an established Lichfield doctor.

9 *Clergy of the Church of England database* and WSL, CB Feilde/2.

10 WSL, CB Feilde/1 in reference to a letter at Hertfordshire County Archives.

11 *Aris's Birmingham Gazette*, 11 January 1762, p. 3.

12 WSL, CB Feilde/2 and Neil Ker (ed.) *A Directory of the Parochial Libraries of the Church of England and the Church in Wales*, revised by Michael Perkin, (London Bibliographical Society, 2004), p. 203; Reverend Allen bequeathed a substantial library of over 1,700 books to the church.

13 WSL, CB Feilde.

14 My thanks to Randle Knight for this observation. William Day was curate of Stanstead Abbots in 1766 and vicar of Roydon, Essex from 1752. He did officiate at Stanstead Abbots in 1767.

15 Frances Wrottesley was the widow of Heigham Bendish. She married Richard Wilkes at St Michael and All Angels church at Tettenhall on 9 October 1756.

16 WSL, S.MS 439/11/2/1 15 October 1767.

17 Michael W. Greenslade, *The Staffordshire Historians*, (Staffordshire Record Society, 1982), p. 93 and *Venn database*. Reverend Unett was the grandson of Ann Wilkes and her husband George Unett, a Wolverhampton bookseller.

18 WSL, S.MS 439/11/1/1 Letter from Tollet to Unett, 6 October 1766.

19 WSL, S.MS 439/11/2/2.

20 Otto Lohrenz, *Parson, Naturalist and Loyalist: Thomas Feilde of England and Revolutionary Virginia and New York, Southern Studies,* New Series, Volume 12, Numbers 3 and 4, 2005, pp 105–128.

21 WSL, S.MS 439/11/2/313 Letter from Feilde to Unett, 13 November 1767.

22 WSL, S.MS 342/5/155.

23 ODNB: Robert Hancock.

24 WSL, S.MS 439 and Greenslade p. 94.

25 Stebbing Shaw: *Vol II* p. xvii. The notebooks belonging to George Tollet relating to the *History of Staffordshire* are at the William Salt Library.

The notebooks include the methods of observation on pits, mining, etc and two volumes of *Topography of Staffordshire* from the library of George Tollet.

26 WSL, S.MS 439/12/1/7.

27 WSL, S.MS 342/6/2–6 from Reverend Feilde's bundle *and* Stebbing Shaw, *Volume 2*: Adverts pp. XVI–XXI.

28 The bookshop was the birthplace of Samuel Johnson, and is now the Samuel Johnson Birthplace Museum.

29 WSL, S.MS 342/6/104.

30 Desmond King-Hele, *Collected letters of Erasmus Darwin*, (CUP, 2007).

31 WSL, S.MS 342/6/7 Letter from Reverend Owen Manning of Godalming, 26 June 1768.

32 WSL, S.MS 342/6/8 and ODNB. John Peshall, antiquary, was eldest son of Thomas Pearsall of Eccleshall. He was ordained and had experience as a schoolmaster at Highgate, London.

33 Reverend Nightingale, *Beauties of England and Wales, 1813, Vol XIII, part I and* WSL, S.MS 342/6/3-6 p xviii; *Stebbing Shaw, Volume 2*: 12 September 1768, unsigned letter.

34 WSL, S.MS 439/11/2/5.

35 WSL, S.MS 439/11/2/6.

36 ODNB: Daniel Bond.

37 *Bulletin of the British Museum, 1977, Historical series 6 (1):* P.J.P. Whitehead, *Emanuel Mendes Da Costa, [1717–1791] and the Conchology, or natural history of Shells,* p.7.

38 William Stukeley was the first secretary of the Society of Antiquaries. He helped to establish the modern methods of archaeology, and had a particular interest in Stonehenge.

39 ODNB: Mendes Da Costa.

40 WSL, S.MS 439/12/1/1.

41 WSL, S.MS 439/12/1/3.

42 WSL, S.MS 439/12/1/4.

43 WSL, S.MS 439/12/1/6.

44 WSL, S.MS 439/12/1/4.

45 WSL, S.MS 439/12/1/6.

46 William Huddesford (Keeper 1755-1772), followed his father as Keeper, and was very diligent in his duties. He catalogued the collections as well as making an audit of the objects, some of which were in such a bad state that they had to be eliminated from the collection. However, he acquired new material and his enthusiasm encouraged new collections including the fossils from Joshua Platt. http://britisharchaeology.ashmus.ox.ac.uk/collections/history-18thcentury.html

47 WSL, S.MS 439/12/1/3.

48 WSL, S.MS 342/6/1.

49 WSL, CB Feilde/1 and CB Feilde/2.

50 WSL, S.MS 439/11/3/1 Letter from Feilde in Holborn, London to Reverend Mr Unett at Stafford, 28 April 1770.

51 WSL, S.MS 439/11/3/2.

52 WSL, S.MS 439/11/3/3.

53 WSL, S.MS 439/11/3/5.

54 This part of Gloucester County, was renamed Mathews County in 1791.

55 Barbara DeWolfe, *Discoveries of America,* (CUP, 1997), pp. 164-169.

56 *Guide to the John Norton and Sons Papers* in Library Special Collections, Colonial Williamsburg Foundation, 1990, Letter 28 May 1771 George Norton to John Norton.

57 ODNB: Colin Mackenzie, *Gentleman's Magazine, January – June 1812,* p. 514; Harry Owen, *Simulation in Health Care education: an Extensive history,* p. 33, Springer, 2016; W.I.C. Morris: *Colin Mackenzie MD (St Andrews) an estranged pupil of William Smellie* in *British Journal of Obstetrics and Gynaecology*, volume 82, No. 10, October 1975.

58 WSL, CB Feilde/2.

59 WSL, S.MS 478/4/1/3-5 and *Stebbing Shaw,* Volume 2, advertisement, p. xxi.

60 WSL, CB Feilde/2.

61 Otto Lohrenz, pp. 105–128.

62 *Gentleman's Magazine,* Volume 62, part 2, August 1792, p. 108.

63 *Aris's Birmingham Gazette,* 4 September 1775, p. 3.

Chapter Six

Reverend Timothy Colebatch

Reverend Timothy Colebatch succeeded Thomas Feilde as headmaster at Brewood Free Grammar School in 1769. He was the eldest son of Timothy Colebatch an attorney of Cleobury Mortimer, Shropshire and his wife, Mary, who had been born at Wildmore, Trysull, Staffordshire. Their home, at Cleobury Mortimer was not far from Bitterley where Mary's brother, Thomas Devey, had been elected master of the Grammar School in 1764.

Timothy Colebatch was christened at St. Mary the Virgin's church, Cleobury Mortimer on 10 November 1730. It is not known which school he attended but his university education was at Wadham College, Oxford, where he matriculated on 28 February 1748/9, aged 18. He was awarded his B.A. on 20 November 1752. In the *Alumni Oxonienses*, he is listed as the son of Timothy Colebatch of Weston, Shropshire, but there is no evidence that he had any connection with Weston-under-Lizard, so close to Brewood.[1]

On 22 September 1755 the younger Timothy Colebatch took his oath to conform to the liturgy of the Church of England and was licenced to the chapel of Chilcot in the parish of Clifton Campville with Chilcote, Staffordshire. He may have been appointed to teach in the new schoolroom at Clifton Campville church, which was above the chantry chapel and reached by a spiral staircase.[2]

Reverend Colebatch taught at King Edward's School, Birmingham, before his appointment as headmaster of Brewood Grammar School in 1769.[3] He was also appointed as perpetual curate of Shareshill, resigning his position at Chilcote.[4] Colebatch advertised in the November newspapers that he would be ready to take boarders by Candlemas, if not before. Any gentlemen wishing to entrust their sons to his care would be assured of the utmost care being given to their sons' instruction and morals. Fees were sixteen pounds per annum and two guineas entrance.[5]

A few months later, on 13 January 1770, at St Peter's church, Coreley, Shropshire, Timothy married Margaret Baldwin, the rector's daughter. Margaret's brother, Reverend John Baldwin, married the couple. He was the new rector of the parish, succeeding his father, Reverend Andrew Baldwin, who had died in 1761. John Baldwin, like Timothy Colebatch, had also attended Wadham College.[6]

On 21 July 1771, Margaret and Timothy's son Polydore was christened at Brewood church. He appears to have been their only child.

Little is known about Reverend Colebatch's teaching and presence at Brewood but he subscribed to buy thirty copies of *Thirteen Sermons on various subjects* written by the late J. Brailsford, M.A., Headmaster of the Free School, Birmingham, published in 1776. They were presumably for the use of Brewood Grammar School pupils.

Some sources claim that William Huskisson, statesman and first railway passenger to be killed by a train, notably Stephenson's *Rocket,* may have been a pupil at the school during Colebatch's time as headmaster. Huskisson's father had inherited property at Oxley, near Brewood, and moved there from Birchmorton Court, Worcester in 1776, but *The Sun* newspaper of London, clarifying some incorrect facts after the sudden death of Huskisson, records that William Huskisson was placed in an infant school in Brewood, just after the death of his mother, in 1774.[7] Huskisson would have been initially too young to be taught by the usher at Brewood Grammar School, Thomas Careless, but may have progressed to that school from a local school, perhaps in Dean Street, there being no records to verify or disprove this fact. *The Sun* newspaper then records that Huskisson went to school in Albrighton before moving in 1782 to Appleby Grammar School. where his father had been taught. He only stayed here a short while before moving to France in 1783.[8]

After nine years at the school, Reverend Colebatch died suddenly and unexpectedly.[9] He was buried at St Mary and St Chad's churchyard in Brewood on 10 August 1778. Reverend Colebatch had not made a will and his wife had to register probate, which she did before Reverend William Horton, at Brewood, on 18 November 1778. With her at this time were some friends, Thomas Careless, usher at Brewood Grammar School, Robert Talbot of Brewood, shoemaker, who had been a pupil at the school and also a relative, Frances Colebatch, who stated that she was unmarried.

The post for a new headmaster was advertised immediately, in the same newspaper as the death notice.[10] Colebatch's successor was Reverend John Pickering whose father, Reverend John Pickering was, at the time, vicar and schoolmaster at Mackworth, Derby.

Reverend Timothy Colebatch had owned some property in Brewood which was sold by auction at the Fleur de Lys Inn, Market Place, many years after his death, on Tuesday 24 November 1795. One property was described in the *Staffordshire Advertiser* as a well-built dwelling house with outbuildings, garden and appurtenances, which was situated in the most "centrical" and pleasant part of the town of Brewood, ideal for a genteel family and at the moment occupied by Mrs Lees. In addition, there was a house with barn, stable, outbuildings and land at Eyke's Lane, now known as Shop Lane. There were also two pieces of enclosed land at Cross Field, and also another piece of land at Suteing [Shooting] Butt Lane now in the occupation of William Wallers. Any interest in the sale was to be addressed to Mr Careless, usher of Brewood Grammar School, or John Woodward, attorney at law, Cleobury Mortimer.[11]

Mrs Colebatch remained in Brewood, and it would seem likely that her son, Polydore Colebatch, remained at the school too, but little is known about him. It may be that this is the same Polydore Colebatch who was working on the merchant vessel *Cotton Planter* which carried coffee and cotton. The merchant vessel was captured in 1798 during the Napoleonic Wars and Polydore Colebatch became a prisoner of war. He was taken to Brionne, Normandy, on 2 May 1798 and then to Fontainebleau on 25 July. He was exchanged as a prisoner on 16 January 1799 and arrived back at Dover on the boat *Le Charles* in March 1799.

After Reverend Colebatch's death, his wife was struggling financially. In 1803 she applied for charity from Reverend Thomas Gisborne's relief fund for the widows of "necessitous clergymen" within the archdeaconry of Stafford, and was awarded 14 guineas out of the £300 collected. Messrs Stevenson & Salt of Lombard Street, London, were the bankers dealing with the finances.[12] William Salt, whose collection of material began the William Salt Library in Stafford, was a partner in the Stevenson Salt Bank.

Notes

1 R. B. Gardner, *The Registers of Wadham College, Oxford, Part II, from 1719–1871,* (George Bell and Sons, 1895).
2 www.cliftoncampville.com
3 *Aris's Birmingham Gazette,* 13 November 1769, p. 3.
4 *Clergy of the Church of England database.*
5 *Aris's Birmingham Gazette,* 13 November 1769, p. 3.
6 R.B. Gardner, *Register of Wadham College.*
7 *Sun* (London), 25 October 1830, p. 3.
8 C.R. Fay, *Huskisson and his Age*, (Longmans, Green and Co, 1951), pp. 302-313.
9 *Aris's Birmingham Gazette,* 17 August 1778, p. 3.
10 *Aris's Birmingham Gazette,* 17 August 1778, p. 1.
11 *Staffordshire Advertiser,* 21 November 1795, p. 1.
12 WSL, S.MS 478/2/121/18.

Chapter Seven

Reverend John Pickering

The unexpected death of Reverend Mr Colebatch in August 1778, made it necessary to quickly find his replacement. Mr Careless was a very competent undermaster, and so it can be assumed that he was in charge until a new headmaster was appointed. Careless did not have the necessary Bachelor of Arts degree to take on the position himself. The school had an excellent academic reputation and attracted the attention of local wealthy gentry who wanted to send their sons to university.

An advertisement was placed in the newspapers highlighting that Brewood was a small healthy and pleasant town in the county of Stafford. The Headmaster's House was described as "large and commodious, capable of containing a great number of Boarders together with an Estate which at very low rents produces to the Headmaster not less than £50 per annum". Any further information regarding the position could be obtained by applying to Mr Careless, undermaster, or Mr Perks, estate manager and attorney for the school, who lived at Saredon, near Shareshill. A list of the Trustees could also be obtained from Mr Allen, an attorney at No 14 Furnival's Inn, London.[1]

On 28 September 1778 Moreton Walhouse, one of the Trustees, contacted Mr Perks, informing him that he would like the candidates to be asked if they would be prepared to receive boarders into the house immediately after Christmas. He felt that the students had already waited too long for the replacement headmaster, and that their education was being disrupted.[2] Letters were to be sent to the distant candidates by 7 October 1778, so that they would be prepared for the election of a headmaster on Monday 19 October. There was no interview procedure, candidates just had to provide written testimonials and recommendations.

There were 15 letters of interest for the appointment of headmaster, including Reverend Mr Pickering who was teaching at Penryn, Cornwall,

Reverend Mr Haden who gave his address as Castle Bromwich, Reverend Mr Thomas Middleton of Kedleston and Reverend Mr Benjamin Woolfe, Master at Dilhorne Free Grammar School. Three other people later declined to be considered for the post including Reverend Mr George Croft of Beverley, Ripon.

The Trustees of the Free Grammar School of Brewood duly met on Monday 19 October 1778 at the Fleur de Lys, Market Place, Brewood, at 11 o'clock, with dinner at the nearby Red Lion at 2 p.m., to decide on the successor to Reverend Colebatch.[3] The Trustees included the Honourable Viscount Lord Dudley and Ward of Himley near Wolverhampton; Sir Edward Littleton, Baronet, of Teddesley Park near Rugeley; Mr William Bagot of Blithfield near Wolseley Bridge; Sir Theophilus Biddulph, 4th Baronet of Westcombe, Kent who had inherited Elmshurst, near Lichfield from his cousin Theophilus Biddulph; Charles Baldwyn of Aqualate, near Newport, Shropshire; Thomas Hoo of Barr, near Birmingham; John Lane of Kings Street, Covent Garden, London; Thomas Fowler, of Penford, Wolverhampton; Moreton Walhouse of Hatherton, near Cannock and Reverend Mr Stafford of Penkridge, near Stafford. All the Trustees were requested to attend as the opportunity could be taken to renew the legalities of the Trust.

The Trustees decided to appoint Reverend Mr Pickering M.A. to be the new headmaster. John Pickering was the son of the Reverend John Pickering of Mackworth, Derbyshire and his wife, Mary, daughter of Anthony Blackwall, the headmaster who had educated William Budworth at Derby Grammar School. Reverend John Pickering, the elder, was a tutor and lecturer of some note. He had an interest in scientific discovery and mathematics, which was reflected in a portrait of him painted by Joseph Wright of Derby. This Reverend Pickering had officiated at the marriage of Reverend Feilde and his wife, Elizabeth, daughter of the rector, Reverend Henry Fletcher, of nearby Boylestone. It is inevitable, with these connections, that Reverend Pickering would have received some information about Reverend Feilde at Brewood Grammar School and his work on the history of Staffordshire.

Reverend John Pickering of Mackworth may have taught his own son, John Pickering, as he later taught privately Thomas Gisborne who became a clergyman, poet and advocate of the abolition of slavery.[4] John Pickering the younger was born on 12 February 1737 and christened on 21 March 1737 at All Saints' church, Mackworth. He continued his education at New College, Oxford where he was awarded his B.A. in 1760 and his M.A. in 1763. He became a deacon in 1760 and a priest in 1762.

John Pickering then moved to Redruth, Cornwall, where he was clerk and curate of the church of St Uny. On 23 December 1763 he married Catherine Bowler at Gwennap, Cornwall.[5] It was an area known for its tin and copper mining, and visited, at the time the young couple were living there, by John Wesley.

Reverend John Pickering, the younger, like his father was also interested in science, and both he and his father subscribed to a new book about minerals, mines and mining, published by William Pryce of Redruth, Cornwall. The short title was *Mineralogia Cornubiensis* and was published in 1778. However, in 1774, in order to encourage subscribers to his work in progress, William Pryce published *The plan of a work entituled Mineralogia Cornubiensis et Leges Stannariae or a general treatise upon minerals, mines and mining......* and in it he thanked his deserving friend Reverend Mr Pickering of Redruth for making corrections. The book was published on 9 November 1778, priced £2 16s 0d.[6] Pryce mentioned that he and a group of friends: Reverend John Pickering, Mr R. Phillips and Mr Waltire, a travelling lecturer in philosophy and astronomy and an authority on Stonehenge, climbed the ancient hill settlement of Carn Brea, near Redruth, taking one of Mr Waltire's best barometers.[7] Pryce's book became a classic, being the first book published about Cornish mining, and is mentioned in Winston Graham's *The Angry Tide*, part of the Poldark series.

During the 1760s and early 1770s Reverend John Pickering and his new family continued to live at Redruth. It may be possible to speculate that he had contact with Josiah Wedgwood because of their mutual interest in Cornish geology. In June 1775, Wedgwood and his friend and fellow potter, John Turner of Lane End, Staffordshire, and Brewood Hall, had toured Cornwall in search of the perfect clay. If Pickering, Wedgwood and Turner had met, it was at the very time John Pickering was appointed as headmaster at the newly established Grammar School at Lostwithiel, a clean and healthy town. The school opened on Monday 17 July and the young gentlemen attending the school were instructed in the classics as well as their morals.[8] Almost three years later, the school was doing well and had twenty pupils, some of whom boarded.[9] However, in 1778, Reverend Pickering decided to take a new position as headmaster at Bodmin Grammar School, which was going to open in midsummer. He intended to take boarders, at a house "situated in an open and healthy part of the town for that purpose". His terms for boarding were 14 guineas per annum.[10]

Bodmin Grammar School dated back to the time of Queen Elizabeth I, and was situated by the church of St Petroc's. Reverend Pickering only stayed a few months there before moving to become headmaster at Brewood Grammar School. An advertisement was placed in the newspapers, that a new headmaster was needed at Bodmin as the Reverend Mr Pickering preferred "a valuable living in the North of England".[11] It was in the same year that an Act of Parliament was granted to build three new penal institutions at Bodmin, one as the County Gaol for serious offenders, one as a Debtors Prison and one as a House of Correction. Although it was a prison that was built as a pioneer of prison reform, it would not have been the ideal location for genteel families.[12]

When Reverend Pickering was appointed headmaster of Brewood Grammar School, he was also appointed curate of Shareshill church and he swore his allegiance on 6 February 1779. He also sometimes performed ministerial duties at Brewood church.

Reverend Pickering's experience with mining must have been very valuable knowledge to be imparted to his pupils. However, his appointment was short as he died unexpectedly on Saturday 11 March 1780 of gout in the head. It was a sad time for the school, and his death was "deeply lamented".[13] He was buried on 15 March at Brewood parish church, just a few weeks after the christening of his daughter Ann, on 22 December 1779.

John and Catherine had a large family, but not all the children survived childhood. When Reverend Pickering's father, Reverend John Pickering of Mackworth, wrote his will in 1790[14] he provided for his daughter-in-law and her children. He left Catherine, widow of his son, John, £30 a year for her natural life and gave his grandchildren John, Henry, James and George each £100 and his grand-daughters Alicia and Ann each £50 exclusive of their shares in a British Tontine, which they had already received.[15]

Catherine Pickering moved to Bodmin and died in April 1810 aged 64.[16]

Reverend Pickering's appointment at the school was unexpectedly brief, and the process of appointing a successor began again.

Notes

1 SRO, D1416/4/2/1.

2 SRO, D1416/4/2/1.

3 The Fleur de Lys inn, also known as Flower- de-Luce. It had been a public house and a barber and peruke makers shop since at least 1713. *Aris's Birmingham Gazette*, 21 February 1763, p.2.

4 Thomas Gisborne was born in Bridge Gate, Derby and later moved to Yoxall Lodge, Staffordshire.

5 *Cornwall Online Parish Clerks database.*

6 William Pryce, *The plan of a work entituled Mineralogia Cornubiensis et Leges Stannariae or a general treatise upon minerals, mines and mining……* pp. 11 and 214.

7 *Western Flying Post and Sherbourne and Yeovil Mercury,* 9 November 1778, p. 2.

8 *Western Flying Post and Sherbourne and Yeovil Mercury,* 26 June 1775, p. 1 _also_ 12 June 1775, p. 3 and 19 June 1775, p. 1.

9 *Western Flying Post and Sherbourne and Yeovil Mercury,* 27 January 1778, p. 1 _also_ 16 February 1778, p. 1.

10 *Western Flying Post and Sherbourne and Yeovil Mercury,* 4 May 1778, p. 2.

11 *Western Flying Post and Sherbourne and Yeovil Mercury,* 9 November 1778, p. 3.

12 www.bodmingaol.org.

13 *Aris's Birmingham Gazette,* 20 March 1780, p. 3.

14 Reverend Pickering of Mackworth, born 1705, died 22 December 1790, will proved at Mackworth in 1792. *Will of Reverend John Pickering, clerk, Vicar of Mackworth, Derbyshire 26 April 1792;* National Archives, PROB 11/1217/250.

15 John and Catherine Pickering had 11 children, one of whom, George, christened 22 December 1777 at Lostwithiel, attended Jesus College Cambridge and became curate of Mackworth church in 1800, then vicar of Mackworth from 1802 until his death on 11 June 1858. Alicia was buried at Brewood in 1795.

16 *Gloucester Journal,* 23 April 1810, p. 4.

Chapter Eight

Reverend George Croft

The sudden death of Reverend Pickering was upsetting for both school and community but plans had to be quickly implemented to appoint a new headmaster. An advertisement for the post described Brewood as a small, healthy and pleasant town near Wolverhampton, with a large school house and the capacity to take a great number of boarders, providing a good income.[1]

The candidates were to send their testimonials to Mr Careless, undermaster, who would forward them to the Trustees. The candidates' personal attendance for an interview was not required but the appointment would be made on Tuesday 20 June 1780 when the Trustees met at the Fleur de Lys Inn, Market Place, Brewood, owned by John Simpson, verger and clerk at St. Mary and St Chad's church.[2]

Sir Edward Littleton sent a letter to his friend Samuel Johnson who was living in Fleet Street, London, asking for his opinion about an unnamed candidate. This is very likely to have been George Croft, whom Samuel Johnson had regarded highly at Oxford. In a subsequent letter to Mrs Thrale, Johnson wrote that he understood that there were seventeen applicants for the post of headmaster at Brewood Grammar School.[3]

The Trustees were unanimous that Reverend George Croft of Beverley, York, D.D., Fellow of University College Oxford should be appointed. When Reverend Colebatch died, Croft had applied for the position of headmaster, but then withdrew, no record exists as to why this happened. Sir Edward Littleton and Bishop Hurd may have been expecting that Croft would be a headmaster of the same calibre as Reverend Budworth, as he was certainly a respected teacher and an academic.

Croft had been born at Beamsley, Skipton, in the chapelry of Bolton Abbey and was baptised on 29 March 1747. He was the second son of

Samuel Croft. The biographical accounts of George's childhood state that he was of "humble parentage". There is no known record of the name of his mother, but George did have an elder brother, John, who was christened in 1744 and died, in his youth, of consumption.[4]

Croft had been educated at Bolton Abbey Grammar School by Reverend Thomas Carr, a member of an established family of clergymen and teachers who had been in the locality for many years. Croft was extremely intelligent, hard-working and had a retentive memory. Carr provided Croft with both a free education and provided his books, as his parents were unable to afford the cost. Carr was so proud of his pupil that he allowed visitors to the school to test Croft on his knowledge of the classics and the Bible, and the boy was usually able to give a more detailed answer than was expected to any question.[5] It also gave Carr the opportunity to ask his friends and acquaintances for help in funding Croft's university education.

In 1762 when George Croft was only 15 years of age he was admitted to University College, Oxford, as a servitor. He was also chosen to be a Bible clerk, which provided him with a little more income. Croft excelled at university, winning exhibitions and prizes, including the Oxford University Chancellor's newly established English essay prize for writing in prose, which had to be read at the Sheldonian Theatre during the Commemoration of the Founders and Benefactors.[6]

At University College, Croft became friends with Samuel Johnson and also the Scott brothers from Newcastle upon Tyne: John Scott, later Lord Eldon, and William Scott, later Lord Stowell. The latter had been a tutor in ancient history, a subject which interested George Croft a great deal. William Scott also became a judge of the High Court of the Admiralty and a jurist. John Scott, his brother, also attended University College, Oxford and was later to become Lord High Chancellor of Great Britain after first becoming a barrister and politician.

Croft graduated with a B.A. on 16 February 1768, and deliberated about becoming a fellow of Oriel College, Oxford. His friend Samuel Johnson supported this and on 17 March 1768, wrote to his friend Thomas Apperley, who had attended Oriel College, praising the social and literary merits of Croft for a fellowship, and clearly hinting that Croft needed a benefactor and help in progressing his career.[7] Apperley's son, Charles, was to become the famous sports writer, Nimrod, who lived in Brewood for a while in the early nineteenth century.[8] Instead of pursuing a fellowship at Oriel in December 1768, George Croft accepted the post of master of Beverley Grammar School. The next year, Croft received his M.A. and was also ordained deacon, and in 1771 he became a priest.

Croft was ambitious and learned. He felt that there was a need for a book about teaching. In 1775, whilst master at Beverley School, Croft wrote *General observations concerning education, applied to the author's method in particular*, where he advocated the value of a classical education. Croft wrote about his teaching methods. He felt that his pupils should keep up to date by reading newspapers and journals and, in Croft's opinion, if his students read various compositions of English writers in both verse and prose it would help them eradicate 'the barbarous dialect of the locality'.[9] The dialect issue was a continuing concern of Croft's, and possibly had some resonance with his childhood.

One of Croft's students at Beverley Grammar School was Smithson Tennant who, in 1804, discovered iridium and osmium. Tennant enjoyed natural philosophy and was competent in Greek and Latin, reading for pleasure books in both languages, perhaps reflecting the teaching he had received from Croft.[10] He wanted to study science under Joseph Priestley, but as Priestley travelled so much it never happened.[11] However, it would have been ironic if he had succeeded, as Dr Croft and Joseph Priestley were soon arguing strongly over religion.

In 1773 Croft became domestic chaplain to the young Thomas Bruce, 7th Earl of Elgin and 11th Earl of Kincardine.[12] He was then appointed perpetual curate at St. Mary's church, Watton, Yorkshire, just north of Beverley in 1776. During these years, Croft was also working hard at University College, Oxford, gaining a number of exhibitions. He was elected a fellow of University College on 16 July 1779 and, by December 1779, University College had appointed Croft as vicar of Arncliffe, near Skipton, in Yorkshire. His ambition did not wane and in January 1780 Croft took the respective degrees of Bachelor of Divinity and Doctor of Divinity.

Croft is appointed headmaster at Brewood Grammar School

George Croft had taught at Beverley Grammar School for 11 years but in June 1780 he accepted the post of headmaster at Brewood Grammar School. He was also awarded the perpetual curacy at Shareshill church by Sir Edward Littleton, which provided extra income but was not an automatic right of appointment for headmasters of the school. Croft was now able to visit University College, Oxford, more frequently as it was much closer than when he was living at Beverley but he was also headmaster of an established, highly regarded school, in pleasant surroundings.

On 4 September 1780 George Croft put an announcement in the newspapers saying that Brewood Grammar School would open at Michaelmas with the "proper assistants". The charge would be 20 guineas per annum, with two guineas entrance. He apologised for the delay, due to his "present Engagement" but it would be remedied by "stricter Attendance".[13]

On 12 October 1780 George Croft married Ann Grimston at Ripon Cathedral then, three days later, the couple moved to Brewood. Ann was the daughter of William and Ann Grimston of Ripon. Although George was described as being from a "humble" background his wife's family certainly were not. William Grimston, was several times mayor of Ripon and an alderman, as well as being a long-standing member of Ripon Corporation.[14] Ann Grimston, Croft's new mother-in-law, was the sister of John and Edmund Hutchinson who were both apothecaries. John Hutchinson was also an alderman of Ripon. Edmund Hutchinson moved his apothecary business to Bath where he became active on the town council, from 1782–1791, and a freeman there in 1782.[15]

George and Ann Croft's first child, Ann, was baptised on 1 September 1781 at Ripon Cathedral. Her grandfather, Alderman Grimston, bequeathed her £400. The young couple were to have nine other children, six of whom were christened at Brewood: John Hutchinson Croft, born on 30 December 1782 at Brewood but died 22 May 1785; Hannah christened on 4 October 1784; Maria on 26 July 1786; Edmund on 9 February 1788; Isabella on 4 December 1789; George Grimston was christened on 30 September 1791 but did not survive and was buried the next day.

Eliza and Harriot, twin daughters, were born in Birmingham on 12 December 1794 and christened 10 August 1798 at St Martin's church, Birmingham, and George William born 27 April 1798 but buried 25 April 1799 at St Martin's church, Birmingham.

George Croft maintained his friendship with the Scott brothers and William Scott, on 5 January 1784, sent George Croft two dozen prayer books of the *Whole duty of Man* and one dozen small prayer books for use at Brewood Grammar School. It is not clear if they were a gift or if Scott was just posting them for his friend. They were delivered by the Shrewsbury Wagon Company to the Crown, Watling Street, Brewood.[16] In that same year, after the death of the young Reverend Lawrence Owen in November 1784, Croft became a curate at Brewood church. The vicar of the church, Reverend Thomas Muchall, was also a Trustee of the school. He lived at Longdon, Staffordshire, and welcomed the help of others to preach sermons at Brewood. In 1785, Reverend Gartham, another friend of Croft's, helped with the church duties and taught at the school. He later became headmaster of Skipton Grammar School.

Croft as an Educationalist

In 1784, Croft published *A Plan of Education, delineated and vindicated. To which are added a Letter to a Young Gentleman designed for the University and for Holy Orders. And a short Dissertation upon the stated provision and reasonable expectations of Publick Teachers*. On the title page, the author was given as "George Croft D.D., Vicar of Arncliffe, Master of Brewood School and Chaplain to the Right Hon. The Earl of Elgin".[17] These positions of importance were to be commented on at a future date. The *Plan of Education* was dedicated to a group of people, which, although not actually acknowledged as such, were the Trustees of Brewood Free Grammar School.

The Plan, like Croft's book of *General Observations* written in 1775, describes Croft's methods of teaching at Brewood Free Grammar School. It also gives a good insight into the character of George Croft. The book was aimed as a teaching guide for those new to the profession and included a fairly comprehensive list of books for each subject. Croft wrote that many people who talked about how to teach successfully had never actually taught, nor understood the difficulties and obstacles that confront the teacher. After criticising books about education written by both John Locke and John Milton, he then admonished Sir Richard Steele, co-founder of the *Tatler.* Reverend Croft thought that Steele had no understanding of teaching. Croft believed that parents read Steele's comments and believed that all children were always meek, gentle and good, but never naughty, which Croft believed was not necessarily true. Croft thought that a child should only be disciplined when absolutely necessary, but the "evil propensities of children grow up with their good ones" and that "whoso spareth the rod, hateth his son". Croft acknowledged that learning was not always pleasant, however popular the teacher, and that the way forward would at times, "be sufficiently rugged", and the ascent would "sometimes be slippery and steep".

Croft thought that children were quite capable of embroidering the truth when recounting their school day. He was not surprised that "parents should be blind to their second selves", but believed teachers were more impartial and, in any case, children should not be encouraged to tell tales on others. Croft also wrote, bearing in mind that the book was dedicated to the Trustees, that he believed a public school education was better than a private one with a tutor. He elaborated that some people believed that a public education made a better scholar but a private one a better man. Croft thought that an education with just a child and his tutor would make the child "grow indifferent to the concerns of others" and he would have difficulty in mixing in either company or society; friendships at an early age became lasting ones, and pupils should help each other, working together. Croft defended the numerous holidays at grammar schools, by explaining that pupils needed additional curriculum exercises, but should not be idle.

The Plan then continued with "Reading and Pronunciations Observations" where children, he claimed, learnt at a very early age those "provincial inaccuracies and dialects, that can stay with them for the rest of their lives". Croft believed that many hours of reading newspapers and history books would help to correct poor English and simultaneously educate them with the intelligence of the day, supplemented by the *Annual Register and Monthly Review* for the senior classes. When reading out loud, Croft wanted the articulation to be distinct and the emphasis good, but not vehement. "Loud Vociferation should be left to those troublesome Members of Society known by the Name of Spouters." He added that a self-confident child was a dangerous child and could be offensive to all those around him.

Croft wanted the use of a common grammar book for all schools across the country, as children frequently changed schools, and with it the curriculum, causing the child problems. He believed that nouns and verbs should be learnt first and revised weekly with spelling tests on Saturday mornings. The younger children should be taught from Gay's *Fables*,[18] and as the children progressed in their education Croft believed that they should learn Latin and Greek poetry and translations, reading Phaedrus's *Fables* and progressing to Ovid.

Croft then gave his thoughts about rhetoric, which was needed for university. Just repeating facts alone, he thought, was tedious and unprofitable. Some knowledge behind the facts was far more useful, and for this he recommended the book by Thomas Farnaby entitled *Rhetorical flowers of diction*. Croft believed that children should learn history, supplementing their learning of the subject with interesting one sentence facts, and historical lists, such as knowledge of the Royal Household.

Natural history should be taught and also geography, using maps, and referring to places mentioned in the classics and in history. French, dancing, music, drawing could all be taught to the pupil or omitted at the discretion of the parent or guardian. However, writing and accounts, which were often also discretionary, were subjects that were particularly useful to the child. Croft advised that each afternoon there should be one and a half hours allowed in the school timetable for these subjects, with the morning given to classical instruction. Copying passages from good authors was essential until the pupil could write well.

George Croft advocated the teaching of religion as an indispensable part of the curriculum, with the teaching of the catechisms as essential learning, as well as the psalms. Sermons should be preached on Sunday evenings to the pupils, and the Greek testament should also be taught.

George Croft's booklet, *A Letter to a Young Gentleman designed for the University, and for Holy Orders*, published in 1784, outlined how the student could make best use of his study time. He advised the student to divide the study day into three, in particular putting the morning to good use. Of course, there were no electric lights at the time, and so working only by candlelight would not have been easy, daylight would have been preferable. Croft advised making sure that the study was varied but Sundays should be kept for divinity, and studying sacred writings in the original language, until the theological studies commenced. He advised that lessons should be read in Greek, and occasionally in Hebrew, but that the Book of Common Prayer should only be read in English, otherwise it was not praying, but studying.

Croft also wrote a pamphlet *On the Endowments of Schools and other Emoluments of Publick Instructors* published with the *Plan of Education*. The pamphlet was, again, dedicated to the Trustees of Brewood Grammar School. In the opening paragraph George Croft wrote that "This subject requires no small degree of delicacy". He continued that it was no secret to the writer's friends that, like his two predecessors, he was given false promises. This appears to indicate that he and the two previous headmasters, Colebatch and Pickering, had taken on the position of headmaster with promises from the Trustees, which had not materialised.[19] This happened again with future headmasters. Perhaps the broken promises were connected with plans to improve the school as, at some point during Croft's time as headmaster, he had bought two houses, with their gardens, in Deans End, opposite the school. These houses had been built by John Howle, skinner and glover of Brewood in 1778, and then owned by Thomas Pitt of Pierce Hay, Brewood, who had married John Howle's daughter, Elizabeth.[20] It is likely that Croft saw an opportunity to expand the school and make it one of the most prestigious in the country. However, nothing happened, and it was not until his successor arrived that these properties were eventually bought by the Trustees and converted to the usher's school and residence, now known as Rushall House.

George Croft was of the opinion that some masters taught through necessity, not ability. To be a teacher a person needed not only learning and morality, but also patience and perseverance. If masters taught through necessity, they would find teaching 'a drudgery'. If a child was difficult, a teacher tended to have to deal with both child and parent. If the parent was influential and friendly with other parents, and wished to withdrew the child from the school, other parents followed their lead. The teacher then lost the income of several children through one child's behaviour and the teacher would suffer in both reputation and profit. Croft also believed that some grammar schools were suffering a loss of pupils because the rich wanted their children to be educated in the south of the country. This may have been a reflection on what was happening at Brewood Grammar School, as there began to be a decline in the number of sons and relatives of gentry attending the school.

Croft wrote that pupils should be kept away from "any Communication with the Rabble of the Place". He continued that if the school was situated in a large market town, and here Croft may have been referring in part to Brewood as it was considered to be a town at that time, "the Inhabitants have it within their power to lessen, if they cannot entirely remove the Inconvenience". Brewood residents were always keen to let their feelings be known about anything happening at Brewood Free Grammar School, particularly during the nineteenth century.

Croft wanted a good headmaster to get a higher salary because an improved school attracted better teachers and more students. Croft was a good headmaster. He felt that there was a minimum income necessary for a master to appear respectable to the students, especially if he was teaching the children of gentry. If a teacher appeared impoverished and dependent on the pupils it would make him "contemptible" in their eyes and they should be holding their teachers in high regard. The teacher might also be tempted to relax discipline. This would encourage pupils to think that they had the upper hand, as the teacher was dependent on their fees to provide his income. The result would soon be disobedient and insolent pupils.

Croft, Priestley and Dissenters

In 1780 Reverend Bampton, Canon of Salisbury, had bequeathed some money so that each year one person with a Master of Arts degree from either the University of Oxford or Cambridge would be chosen to preach eight divinity lecture sermons at St. Mary's church in Oxford.

The sermons had to promote the Christian faith, and they would be published in a book. It was a prestigious award, and in 1786, Reverend George Croft was honoured to receive the prize. In his lectures he publicly gave his support for the Church of England against the dissenting sects.

In the same year, Joseph Priestley, the well-educated, renowned scientist and deeply religious Dissenting Minister, wrote a paper entitled *History of Early opinions concerning Jesus Christ* which questioned the Virgin birth, the Trinity and the Atonement. Priestley, like Croft, had been born in the West Riding of Yorkshire but had lived and worked in various parts of the country including, in 1758, Nantwich, Cheshire, where he had opened a school and taught languages and science. He also sometimes preached at the Unitarian Church at Newcastle-under-Lyme, Staffordshire. Priestley was an inspiring teacher and, like Croft, had written books which could be used as teaching aids. In 1765 he wrote *Essay on a Course of Liberal Education* which argued that there was a need for a revised curriculum for children who were intending to enter commercial professions. These children needed less emphasis on languages other than English and more education in science and history.

Priestley was respected academically for his scientific research. He had been on the Grand Tour with William Petty, second Earl of Shelbourne, and was also a member of the Lunar Society which had, amongst its members Matthew Boulton, Erasmus Darwin, James Watt and Josiah Wedgwood.

In 1780 Priestley moved to Sparkbrook, Birmingham where he established his laboratory. This was the same year that George Croft moved to Brewood. Priestley continued his religious teaching as minister of the New Meeting House, Moor Street, which had one of the largest and more powerful dissenting congregations in England. Here he established a school for children and young adults.[21] He was also active in improving Birmingham's library service, which had been formed in 1779.

In 1782 Priestley wrote a paper entitled *History of Corruptions of Christianity* which included the rejection of the doctrine of the Trinity, angering and upsetting the clergy of the Church of England.[22] It particularly upset Dr Croft, as did the attempts by the Dissenters to repeal the Test and Corporation Acts which, since the seventeenth century had banned Roman Catholics and Nonconformists from holding public office unless they took the Church of England's Holy Communion.

In 1788 Croft published a paper against Dr Priestley's religious views entitled *Cursory Observations in Respect to Dr Priestley,* claiming that the Dissenters supported republicanism, and disagreeing with Dr Priestley's views about the Trinity. In May 1789 an attempt by Henry Beaufoy in the House of Commons to repeal the Test Acts was only narrowly defeated. On 5 November 1789 Joseph Priestley published another sermon entitled *The conduct to be observed by Dissenters in order to procure the repeal of the Corporation and Test Acts.*

As Priestly lived and worked in Birmingham, the Anglican clergy in the area responded strongly to Priestley's public sermons about the repeal of the Test Act, and his views on the Trinity. Reverend Dr George Croft, Reverend Spencer Madan who was rector at St Philip's church, Reverend Charles Curtis rector of St Martin's church, Birmingham and St Alphege church, Solihull and Reverend Edward Burn, lecturer of St Mary's church, Birmingham all spoke out against Priestley and the Dissenters.

Croft defended the Test Laws in a powerful sermon at St Philip's church, Birmingham on 3 January 1790. It was a large church capable of seating 2,000 people, and is now the cathedral of Birmingham. The sermon that Dr Croft preached was published as *The Test Laws defended, with a preface containing Remarks on Dr Price's Revolution Sermon and other Publications*. He started the preface by telling the readers to pardon the many imperfections within in it, but to be kind as much of his time is taken with being a public instructor of youth and a parish minister.[23] In his sermon Reverend Croft advised his audience to read certain religious books, which he named, including the Bampton Lectures of 1786, which he had written. His sermon again attacked Joseph Priestley and the Dissenters. Reverend Croft quoted an example at Beverley, Yorkshire, where, he claimed, a minister "sinking under age and infirmity" had been treated cruelly by the Dissenters. The Dissenters at Hull, Croft claimed, were united by a common hostility against the words of truth and soberness delivered by the regular clergy. At West Bromwich, Croft said, there was a more ecumenical approach by one teacher who took his pupils alternately to the church and the meeting house for their religion and at his death he had a funeral sermon at both. Reverend Croft did not see this in a positive light.[24]

Soon after the publication of Croft's sermons against the Test Laws, there was a reply by the Reverend John Hobson of Kingswood Unitarian chapel who, whilst he thought that the Dissenters had nothing to fear from George Croft's sermons, he did think that some people were in awe of titles. The sermons had been written by "George Croft, D.D., Late fellow of University College, Vicar of Arncliffe, Master of the Grammar School, Brewood and chaplain to the Earl of Elgin". Hobson thought that a sermon delivered by titled and academic George Croft held more weight for some people than one delivered by plain George Croft.[25]

Reverend Spencer Madan, rector of St Philip's church, Birmingham, continued the argument about repealing the Test and Corporation Acts by publishing a sermon on 14 February 1790 entitled *The Principal Claims of the Dissenters considered*. In this he claimed that the Dissenters could not be loyal to either Church or State if they were trying to get the Test and Corporation Acts repealed.[26] This opinion was shared by George Croft, who thought that those who did not believe in the Trinity, which was fundamental to the Church of England, did not understand Christianity and were thus diminishing both Church and State.

In the meanwhile, there was a fear that following the American and French Revolutions, the British people might also revolt and overturn both church and monarchy. George III was not always in good enough health to rule the country, and his son George, later Prince Regent, was considered extravagant, and insensitive to the poverty in the country. Priestley, a very educated man, was considered to be a supporter of both revolutions and a dangerous man to the British establishment. Anger against the Dissenters was growing, and getting nastier with Priestley receiving anonymous letters to be wary, because as an enemy of Church and State his presence would not be tolerated in Birmingham. Croft's sermon at St Philip's Church in January had been powerful and eloquent, although he was not the only clergyman who spoke out against the Dissenters.

The French Revolution had touched Brewood, bringing the fear of a revolution nearer to home. This may have, in a small way, influenced

Croft's lecture. John Turner, the eminent potter of Lane End, Stoke-on-Trent, and friend of Wedgwood, lived at Brewood Hall. In 1784, he had been appointed potter to the Prince of Wales but when Turner died in December 1787, his sons, John and William carried on the business, supplying a fine dinner service to Thomas and Charlotte Giffard on their wedding day in 1788. The Turner's also supplied their chinaware to Holland and France. However, with the unrest abroad the Turner brothers were having trouble obtaining money owed to them. William went across to France to try and retrieve some of the debts. Some sources claim that whilst he was there, he was caught up in the storming of the Bastille and then arrested in Paris as a Dutch spy as the Turners had a decorating factory in Delft. Other sources, such as Simenon Shaw's account, describe William Turner as being in France at the wrong time. All sources agree that William Turner was imprisoned and was expecting be sentenced to death, but at the last moment freed with the help of the ambassador in Paris, Sir George Granville Leveson-Gower, Earl Gower of Trentham, later Duke of Sutherland, who was about to board a ship and return to Britain.[27]

The Birmingham riots

On 14 July 1791 there was a plan to have a grand dinner at the prestigious Dadley's *Hotel* in Temple Street, to celebrate Bastille Day. Whilst many of the guests were Dissenters, some were members of the Church of England, including the chairman, James Keir, who was also a member of the Lunar Society to which Priestley belonged. A few days before the dinner was due to take place some handbills were circulated around Birmingham highlighting the extravagance of the royal family when taxes for the people were so high. The handbills also encouraged a public celebration of the anniversary of Bastille Day.

The handbills were anonymous but the Dissenters were blamed for their publication. Priestley denied all knowledge and claimed that that they were printed by Church and State supporters to create mischief, and stop the dinner from taking place.[28] Discussions took place as to the best solution to the problem and given that all the food had been bought by the hotel manager, it was decided to have the dinner as planned, but to start the meal at 3.00 p.m. and finish at 5.00 p.m. Joseph Priestley was not one of the 90 people who attended as he thought his presence would make matters worse.

The magistrates of Birmingham, including Dr Benjamin Spencer who was the vicar of Aston and Joseph Carles of Handsworth, arranged to have dinner at the nearby Swan Inn, Bull Street, Birmingham, in order to keep an eye on events. Spencer and Carles were responsible for maintaining law and order, and were respected by the Dissenters. As late as March 1791 Joseph Priestley and William Russell, an ironmaster and also a Dissenter, had both supported a petition which was presented to William Pitt, prime minister, praising the excellent work that Carles was doing for the town of Birmingham.

During the dinner at Dadley's *Hotel*, the size of the mob outside grew, and became more restless. The *Hotel* windows began to be broken and it was alleged that the magistrates told the crowd not to damage the *Hotel* but "if you wish to be revenged go down to the meetings" which the crowd took to mean go down to the New and Old Meeting Houses.[29] With that the rioting in Birmingham began. The Old and New Meeting Houses were burnt down, the mob then continued to Priestley's house at Fair Hill, Sparkbrook where they set fire to his home, laboratory, manuscripts and library, all his work was destroyed. The mob then marched to target specific properties over a large area within the town, also destroying them by fire, all the homes of Dissenters. No homes of Church of England members were touched, not even the home of James Keir who had chaired the meeting. However, even though the destruction of houses was specific, neighbouring properties were also catching fire. Finally, after four days of intense destruction, the Light Horse Infantry arrived from Nottingham, and the crowd dispersed. Twenty-seven houses had been attacked of which twenty of them were destroyed. Many of the owners of these properties employed large numbers of people in the city, which now put jobs at risk.

Many argued, including William Hutton the bookseller and historian of the town, that the magistrates were behind the riots, inciting the mob and encouraging them to alcohol. The magistrates certainly did not rush to call in the army, some of whom were nearby, or read the Riot Act, and it has been argued that when the Army did arrive to help, they had been sent for privately, possibly by Lord Aylesford of Packington Hall, Warwickshire. Out of an estimated 2,000 rioters, only 20 were apprehended, only five were found guilty and out of the five, only three were executed.

When the New Meeting House, where Joseph Priestley had been pastor, had been burnt to the ground in the riots, the register of Dissenters required by the Toleration Act, had also been destroyed. This was needed before any financial compensation could be given for the destruction. Sir Robert Lawley, of Canwell Hall, near Tamworth, one of the Trustees of Brewood Free Grammar School, presented a petition to Parliament for compensation for the Dissenters. Lawley believed the riots to be of a political nature not a religious one.

Samuel Whitbread, of Whitbread brewery and an M.P., also wanted an investigation into the riots and his petition was presented to parliament on the same day, 21 May 1792. Whitbread believed that the riots were caused by arguments about religion, based on the fact that only the houses of Dissenters had been targeted and only a very few people of the thousands of rioters had been brought to justice. Dr Priestley and Mr Keir also believed that the riots were caused by 'religious bigotry' and not because of the commemoration of the French Revolution, proven by the targeting only of Dissenters houses in the riots.[30]

Whitbread also felt that the magistrates had done little to quell the riots, and were negligent in their duty. He argued that the magistrates were fuelling the riots with their cries of "Church and King" at every opportunity to the mob. A recruiting party for the army that happened to be in Birmingham offered to help disperse the mob, but the magistrates refused their help. They did warn those targeted that they could not use armed weapons to disperse the crowd, or they would be held to account by the law. Thirty-six affidavits were signed charging the magistrates with gross neglect of duty.

Whitbread argued that the law existed for the protection of all whether they were members of the established church or not. He continued that whilst Priestley's wish to repeal the Corporation and Test Acts had started the argument, the sermons of Mr Madan, Dr Croft and other clergymen in

Birmingham had fuelled the fire for the riots. He quoted from Dr Croft's sermon on 3 January 1790 that "the charge of republican principles against them [the Dissenters], harsh as it may be thought is well founded". William Smith, M.P. and a Dissenter, also quoted Dr Croft as saying "It is the firm belief of our clergy that while their meeting houses are open, they are weakening and almost demolishing the whole fabric of Christianity" and then continued with another quote from Dr Croft: "The fabric of our constitution was built on a solid foundation, the dissenters wish to destroy it". Smith also quoted Madan as saying that "Their (Dissenters) possession of offices has proved incompatible with the welfare of the established church and the safety of the civil government".

The public enquiry of May 1792 debated if the riots were caused by politics or religion. Parts of the sermons delivered by Dr Croft and Reverend Madan were read out, but Croft was never mentioned as having been in Birmingham at the time of the riots. Brewood Grammar School was closed from 18 June until 25 July 1791, but remained open for two hours a day for writing and accounts, taught by a different teacher.[31] The implication is that Croft was neither in Brewood, nor Birmingham as various members of the clergy in Birmingham at the time claimed that they had rushed to remonstrate with the mob, and help the Dissenters who were the victims of the riot. Croft's name was not mentioned then or later, by Priestley, who claimed that the clergy had not tried to help the Dissenters, and dispel the mob.

Many of the leaders of the Church who tried to help the victims were known to George Croft. Some like Dr William Gilby M.D., famous at the time for his research into paralysis and diabetes, were mentioned in Dr Croft's will as executors. Dr Gilby, had seen a handbill circulating around Birmingham, which he thought might instigate trouble so had tried to get Carles to request military help from William Pitt, the Prime Minister.

Samuel Whitbread lost his petition to parliament for an enquiry into the riots. One hundred and eighty-nine members of parliament voted against the motion, with only forty-six members of parliament supporting him.

Joseph Priestley moved to Hackney, London, and taught at Hackney College, a college for Dissenters, before he moved to America in 1794.

A few years later, in 1800, John Simpson, owner of the Fleur de Lys Inn, Brewood, established a Congregationalist church for Dissenters at Brewood. Mr Simpson had disagreed with the vicar and Trustee of Brewood Free Grammar School, Reverend Thomas Muchall, about something undisclosed, and left the Church of England. John Simpson and his brother-in-law, James Neale of St Paul's Churchyard London, built the Congregational Chapel in Sandy Lane, which opened on 3 May 1803. In 1806 Brewood welcomed students from Hackney Dissenters College who came in the summer and conducted open air services in the area.[32]

Resignation of Croft from Brewood Grammar School

In August 1791, Sir Edward Littleton was worried that Dr Croft would resign from Brewood Grammar School for a lectureship at Birmingham but Richard Hurd, Bishop of Worcester doubted that Dr Croft, after further consideration, would want to leave such an establishment as Brewood.[33] Nothing was said of Dr Croft's involvement, intentional or otherwise, with the riots, and the effect that the public enquiry would have on the school. Croft had firm principles and strongly believed in the sovereign and the constitution, but perhaps he had not expected the riots at all, or realised the impact of his words.

Dr Croft, however, did accept the lectureship at Birmingham at St Martin's church and later also accepted the chaplaincy of St Bartholomew's chapel, a chapel of ease, for the parish of St Martin's. He remained headmaster at Brewood School until the summer, but lived in Birmingham from December 1791. On 5 December 1791 Croft put a notice in *Aris's Birmingham Gazette* to the Trustees, and also friends of the school and the inhabitants of the "Town of Birmingham", which should have read "Town of Brewood", that he was anticipating to be "relieved from the labour of instruction". He was going though, to suspend his resignation for a few months and had appointed a respectable graduate from the University of Oxford, who had been his associate for seven years to take his place. This unnamed person was Reverend Thomas Gartham.

Croft and his family, lived at the St Martin's parsonage, Smallbrook Street, Birmingham. It was old and "a curious, low, straggling building" surrounded by a moat and situated between Smallbrook Street and Bromsgrove Street, close to Ladywell Baths. A large tithe barn went with the parsonage, which by 1825 was being used as warehouses and shopping. The buildings were demolished by 1837 and the moat filled in to provide a housing development.[34] Croft liked living at St Martin's vicarage and actively participated in the development of the town of Birmingham, helping those in need with advice and support.

The process began again to appoint a new headmaster at Brewood. In late April, Hurd was discussing with Littleton, the necessary qualifications for the ideal candidate, and a way of streamlining the selection process, whilst the school was without a headmaster, Croft being in Birmingham.[35]

On 1 June 1792 Thomas Birks, of Horsebrook, received payment of £3 6s 0d from Thomas Careless for carriage of a load of goods to Birmingham for Reverend Dr Croft.[36]

The Trustees placed an advertisement in the newspapers on 23 June 1792 for Croft's replacement. Just over a week later, on 1 July 1792, John Byng, 5th Viscount Torrington, visited Brewood on his tour around Britain on horseback. He had visited Tong, then Boscobel House, White Ladies, then Black Ladies, before hurrying to Brewood, "whose tall spire was in sight for dinner". He was not happy with his experience of the town of Brewood, but then he was not happy with many places. The inn at Ivetsey Bank he described as "a horror of a place", Penkridge as an "ill-paved little market town" and although at Chillington, he liked the ride through "one of the finest avenues" he thought that the house, which was under repair, "an ugly staring thing". He described Brewood as a "mean market town where the Red Lion alehouse receiv'd me; and being put into a white-washed room, got a miserable neither-hot-nor-cold dinner…". [37]

Croft and his wish to return to teaching

In 1797 Croft wanted to return to teaching and applied to become headmaster of King Edward VI Grammar School, New Street, Birmingham. He was shortlisted with the current second master of the school, the Reverend John Cooke, but the latter was appointed. Reverend Madan, one of the governors of the school, and a friend of Reverend

Dr Croft, was furious about the unconstitutional way that the appointment had been handled. Madan argued that some of the governors who had voted for the appointment of Reverend Cooke were not empowered to do so as they were no longer resident in the town, parish, manor or lordship of Birmingham, as required by the school constitution. A booklet was published entitled *An Abstract of the Charter of King Edward the sixth for Founding the Free School in Birmingham to which are added remarks on the clause requiring residence* by George Croft, D.D. and an appendix containing letters from the Reverend Spencer Madan stating the *Reasons why he resigned the Office of Governour [sic] and his previous Proposal of Reference*. Reverend Dr Croft stated that at every election of future governors or masters of the school the *Act of 31 Elizabeth, Chapter 6, Section 4* should be read out as this authorises and directs the proceedings. If this had been done then the governors would have realised that they did not have a legal quota of governors. Reverend Madan thought that the candidate had not been chosen on merit but rather through family connections. He claimed that he was angry because of the principle, not the person.

On the same day that Reverend Cooke received his promotion, the governors of the school wanted to appoint a second master to replace him. After the row, the genteel and courteous, Reverend Jeremiah Smith from Brewood was appointed second master at King Edward VI Grammar School later to become headmaster, or High Master as the position was known, of Manchester Grammar School. He had been a pupil of Dr Croft at Brewood Free Grammar School, and one of his future sons was James Hicks Smith, barrister and historian of Brewood, who later lived at Dawscroft.

Arncliffe

With regard to Arncliffe, Dr Croft although vicar there since 1779, hardly ever visited the parish causing some of his congregation to complain. It was a long distance from Brewood Grammar School, being approximately 133 miles away. He was not unique in being an absentee vicar of a church, but Croft told his parishioners that when he took up the living at Arncliffe, the Archbishop of York, William Markham, had condoned his absence as he had care of a school, but the parishioners did not agree that this was sufficient reason.

The church at Arncliffe did not provide him with a good income, and Croft said that had it done so, he would have been "free from the troublesome office of teaching", an indication that he had not enjoyed his position as headmaster at Brewood Grammar School.[38] In 1804 following a complaint from Croft about the poor income of the parish of Arncliffe, Hugh Moises, bursar of University College, wrote to the Archbishop.[39] Moises tried to ascertain if Croft was able to have two livings so far apart, probably with a view to his relinquishing Arncliffe, although that did not happen.[40]

Dr Croft received complaints from the churchwardens, one of whom wanted an exemption from tithes and the lead roof of the church replaced with slate. Reverend Croft replied from Brewood, on 10 August 1790, in the negative. Croft agreed that "the blasts of winter were disagreeable", but he had given permission for every repair needed.

On another occasion Dr Croft replied to a complaint about a Mr Bolland. Writing from Brewood, on 1 September 1790, Croft stated that he would not expect churches to be crowded on weekdays but a poor living was no excuse for poor preaching. Croft replied to another letter on 24 November 1790: "if people on weekdays in Lent be so inattentive as not to go to Church, I think, whatever the former custom might be, a Clergyman cannot be expected to read to the bare walls". Again, the churchwardens raised the matter of the roof being better in slate than lead as the valley was subject to violent hurricanes.[41]

In 1802 John Scott, Lord Eldon awarded George Croft the rectory of Thwing in the East Riding, which he was allowed to hold by a dispensation, with the vicarage of Arncliffe. This gave Dr Croft more income and was of benefit to Mrs Ann Croft who, after the death of her husband, received benefits from the rectory for many years.[42] In 1805, the same Lord Eldon in his capacity as Lord High Chancellor, ruled in the Leeds Grammar School case that the intentions of the founders of the endowed grammar schools had to be carried out. The endowments were for the grammatic teaching of the learned languages and so the subjects of Latin and Greek had to be taught to pupils and at no charge. This ruling had a huge impact on endowed grammar schools for many years.

The death of Reverend George Croft

George Croft died on 11 May 1809, at his home in Birmingham, aged 62 years. He was buried in the north aisle of St Martin's church, where a memorial to him was erected by his parishioners in gratitude for his valuable services as a lecturer at St Martin's church. They acknowledged "their respect for his learning as a scholar and his zeal as a supporter of the Establishment in Church and State; of their esteem for his integrity as a man, his hospitality as a neighbour, his active and unwearied benevolence as a counsellor of the poor, and his virtues in private life as a husband and father".[43]

Croft's reputation was such that he had an obituary in both the *Athenaeum Magazine* and the *Gentleman's Magazine*. Croft was described as having a strong mind and opinion, highly improved by classical erudition. He was well versed in Hebrew, Syrian and most modern languages and had extensive knowledge of ecclesiastical law. His character had been firm and decisive, with a strong belief in the constitution of church and monarchy. He was averse to any dissent from principles which he considered to be those of the British constitution. Although he had been hostile to modern times, he was highly esteemed for his hospitality, steady in friendship, he did his duty, was a counsellor to the poor and had an amiable disposition as a husband and father.[44] *Showell's Dictionary of Birmingham* described Croft as "one of the good old sort of Church and King parsons" but not popular with the majority of his parishioners.[45]

After the riots, Croft had donated a substantial amount of money annually to the fund for the relief of the suffering clergy of France. He was keen to help all those in need, giving free advice and assistance to the poor, who came to his house. He helped widows and orphans of soldiers and sailors as well, aiding them to claim their monetary entitlements from the government, and he took an active role in Birmingham life. During his lifetime, he had also supported his parents and an uncle.[46]

In his will, written on 29 January 1806, Croft wanted his esteemed friends William Gilby of Birmingham, doctor of physic and John Cope of Birmingham, druggist, as well as his only son Edmund Hutchinson Croft to be trustees of his estate. John Cope had married Ann Bromley, daughter of the former headmaster Reverend Bromley. In 1798 Dr Croft and his friends William Gilby and John Cope had all contributed to a tontine deed for new premises for the Library of Birmingham.

George Croft wanted his wife to have full use of the household furniture for her life, and to use his financial assets for the education and support of his children. Upon the death of his wife, all the money should be divided equally between his six daughters: Ann, Hannah, Maria, Isabella and the twins, Eliza and Harriet. They were to have equal shares, but as Ann had received £400 as a bequest from her late grandfather, Alderman Grimston of Ripon, then this should be taken into consideration in the final distribution of the property amongst the six children. Reverend Croft wanted Ann "together with and including her Legacy of four hundred pounds" to have £200 more than the other five daughters. Croft expected his only living son, Edmund Hutchinson Croft, to inherit a moiety of £1,800, which had been lent to the Commissioners for the improvement of Bath. Edmund could expect to inherit this money after the decease Mrs Hannah Hutchinson, a relative living at Bath. He was also expecting Edmund Hutchinson Croft to be a benefactor of her leasehold house, No. 2, Paragon Buildings next to the house where Jane Austin had stayed with her aunt and uncle Leigh-Perrot.[47] In his will, Croft wanted the trustees to lend his son money to complete his education, but proper security had to be given to the trustees upon the moiety of £1800 and upon the leasehold house at Paragon Buildings. His son was also to have the option of buying the books from his personal library at half the price than would be obtained by their sale. His daughters could choose some of the popular books in English or French, and the exact price need not be given, only an appropriate amount of money.

Reverend Croft had lent money to Reverend Thomas Gartham, who had been a teacher at Brewood Grammar School before becoming headmaster of Skipton Grammar School in 1796. Gartham had been in financial trouble from 1802, but the boys of the parish received a free education, and this did cause financial problems for many of the masters of endowed schools. Croft wrote in his will that the interest of Gartham's debt was to be discharged before any transfer of the writings which were in Reverend Croft's possession.[48]

In 1811 the sermons that Croft had preached at Oxford were published as *Sermons including a series of discourse of the minor prophets, preached before University of Oxford.* They were published in two volumes and dedicated to Lord Eldon. Ann Croft, George's wife, wrote an eloquent letter to Lord Eldon published in Volume 1, and Rann Kennedy, master of King Edward VI Grammar School, Birmingham, wrote the short biography of Croft. Almost 600 copies of the book were subscribed to from many people across the country before its publication, including the following Brewood residents: Reverend Harrison, Thomas Grundy, Moses Anslow, Mrs Pitt and Reverend Dr Jeremiah Smith.

Mrs Croft died on 11 February 1838, at Ward End, Aston, Birmingham, aged 85. The family: Ann, Maria, Harriet and Edmund continued to live in the parish of Aston until their deaths, although Edmund attended University College, Oxford, matriculating in 1808. Isabella did not live with them but may be the same Miss Isabella Croft, of Water Eaton who was buried at St Mary and St Chad church, Brewood, in 1814, although only listed as aged 22 years.

Dr Croft, whilst his name was linked with the Birmingham riots, was a good and steady headmaster at the school, strong in his religious beliefs, rather than a trouble maker intent on causing the riots. He was well respected for his integrity, and his steady friendships.[49] The new headmaster, Reverend Harrison, was to rule the school in a different way.

Notes

1 SRO, D1416/4/2/1 n.d,? March-June 1780.
2 SRO, D1416/4/2/1; also written as Fleur de Lis.
3 R.W. Chapman (ed.), *The Letters of Samuel Johnson, with Mrs Thrale's genuine letters to him*, Volume II, 1755–1782, Letter 672, Samuel Johnson at Bath to Mrs Thrale, Thursday 25 May 1780.
4 *ODNB*: George Croft; Rann Kennedy, Introduction in *Sermons including a series of Discourses of the minor prophets preached before the University of Oxford* by George Croft, Volume 1, pp xxv-xxxiv; *Gentleman's magazine*, Volume 79, Part I, 1809, p. 485.
5 Kennedy, Volume 1, p. xxvi.
6 ODNB and Oxford University Calendar 1813.

7 R.W. Chapman (ed.), *The Letters of Samuel Johnson, with Mrs Thrale's genuine Letters to him,* Volume 1, 1719–1774, Letter 198, Samuel Johnson to Thomas Apperley, 17 March 1768.

8 Thomas Apperley was also a friend and guardian of Sir Watkin Williams Wynn, another student at Oriel College. Apperley had accompanied Wynn on a Grand Tour of Europe from June 1768 until February 1769. It was whilst on these travels that Wynn met Sir William Hamilton at Naples. He had a large collection of historic Greek and Italian vases and had produced an expensive illustrated catalogue of his collection, published by Baron d'Hancarville. Wynn bought a copy and lent it to Josiah Wedgwood to use at his new Etruria factory in Barlaston for his Etruria ware _see_ Wrexham government –*The Holiday of a Lifetime: The Grand Tour of Sir Watkin Williams Wynn 1768–1769,* Exhibition 2013 at Wrexham County Borough Museum, Paul Hernon, guest curator, 2012.

9 Ian Michael, *The Teaching of English from 16th century to 1870* (Cambridge University Press, 1987), pp. 206 and 432.

10 David Lewis, *The early life of Smithson Tennant, FRS (1761–1815).* Platinum Metals Review, 2011 **55** (3) pp. 196–200.

11 John Whishaw, *Some account of the late Smithson Tennant, Esq. F.R.S. Professor of Chemistry in the University of Cambridge,* 1815.

12 Lord Elgin became a soldier, politician, ambassador, and patron of fine arts.

13 *Aris's Birmingham Gazette,* 4 September 1780, p.1.

14 Yorkshire Indexes, *Tourist guide to York, and History of Ripon,* 2nd edition, 1806; *Gentleman's Magazine,* volume 76, part 1, 1806, which gives the obituary.

15 Trevor Fawcett, compiler: *Bath Council Members 1700–1835.*

16 WSL, S.MS 479/19/21.

17 WSL, pbox/Brewood-22 George Croft, *A Plan of Education, delineated and vindicated. To which are added a Letter to a Young Gentleman designed for the University and for Holy Orders. And a short Dissertation upon the stated provision and reasonable expectations of Publick Teachers.*

18 John Gay [1685–1732], English poet and dramatist.

19 WSL, pbox/BREWOOD/22.

20 David Horovitz, *Brewood. Some notes on the history of Brewood in Staffordshire, with an account of the escape of Charles II after the Battle of Worcester on 3rd September 1651* (David Horovitz, 1992), p. 228.

21 *Joseph Priestley and the Birmingham riots,* 16 January 2023, Archives and Collections@the Library of Birmingham, theironroom.wordpress.com.

22 Jenny Uglow, *The Lunar Men, The Friends who made the Future,* (Faber and Faber, 2002), p. 407 and Jonathan Atherton: *Rioting, Dissent and the Church in late eighteenth century Britain: The Priestley riots of 1791,* p. 93.

23 WSL, George Croft, *The Test Laws Defended: A Sermon preached at St Philip's Church in Birmingham on Sunday January the 3rd, 1790. With a preface containing Remarks on Dr Price's Revolution Sermon and other Publications,* (Birmingham, 1790).

24 WSL, George Croft, *The Test Laws Defended: A Sermon preached at St Philip's Church,* p. v.

25 WSL, John Hobson, *A Series of Remarks upon a Sermon Preached at St Philip's Church, in Birmingham on Sunday, January 3 1790 entitled The Test Laws Defended by George Croft,* pp. 5–6.

26 Atherton, p. 102.

27 Bevis Hillier, *Master Potters of the Industrial Revolution, The Turners of Lane End,* (Cory, Adams and Mackay, 1965), pp. 48-49.

28 George L. Craik and Charles MacFarlane, *The Pictorial Story of England during the reign of George III being a history of the people as well as a history of the Kingdom,* Volume II, 1842 p. 58.

29 William Corbett, *The Parliamentary history of England from the Earliest period to the Year 1803,* Vol XXIX 22 March 1791- 13 December 1792, published by T.C. Hansard, 1817: Debate on Mr Whitbread's motion respecting the Riots at Birmingham May 21 32 George III [1792] pp. 1431–1464 [p. 1438].

30 Corbett, p. 1434.

31 *Aris's Birmingham Gazette* 13 June 1791, p. 1.

32 Horovitz, p. 331.

33 SRO, D1413/1, Letter from Richard Hurd, Bishop of Worcester, to Sir Edward Littleton, 16 August 1792.

34 *The Picture of Birmingham,* 1825 and 3rd edition, 1837.

35 SRO, D1413/1 Letter from Bishop Hurd, Hartlebury Castle, to Sir Edward Littleton, 29 April 1792.

36 SRO, D1416/4/2/1.

37 John Byng, Viscount Torrington, *Rides Round Britain: Tour to the North 1792,* (Folio Society 1996), p. 371.

38 William Arthur Shuffrey, *Some Craven Worthies,* (F.E Robinson and Co., 1903), p.160.

39 Hugh Moises was the son of Hugh Moises, headmaster of Newcastle-upon-Tyne Free School, who had taught both John Scott, later Earl of Eldon and William Scott, later Lord Stowell, the friends of George Croft

40 https://www.univ.ox.ac.uk/sites/www4.univ.ox.ac.uk/files/uce4.pdf: The rectory of Arncliffe, University College, Oxford.

41 Shuffrey, p. 159.

42 David John Bowes, *The Church of England in East Yorkshire from 1743 to c 1840 with particular reference to economic matters.* Summary of Theses for Ph.D. degree, March 2006, pp. 321-2.

43 Shuffrey, p. 179.

44 *Athenaeum magazine*, January – June 1809, p. 561; *Gentleman's Magazine obituary*, Volume 1 [79], 1809, p. 485.

45 Walter Showell and Thomas T. Harman, *Showell's Dictionary of Birmingham: A history and guide*, 1885, p. 206.

46 Kennedy; Shuffrey, pp. 158 and 178.

47 Mrs Hannah Hutchinson was the third wife of Edmund Hutchinson, apothecary of Bath. Edmund Hutchinson had died in 1791 and in his will, he bequeathed No 2 Paragon buildings to his third wife as long as she lived, but on her decease then it would go to George Croft, John Bell and Robert Bell, sons of Ralph Bell of Thirsk for the rest of the term of the lease.

48 Thomas Gartham was the son of James Gartham of Pocklington, York, born 1760, died 1825. He gained his M.A. from Queen's College, Oxford in 1787, and later became a fellow of Lincoln College, Oxford. He was appointed headmaster of Skipton Grammar School from 1796 until 1822, when he was removed from his post by the vicar and churchwardens for 'malversation in his office'.

49 *Gentleman's Magazine*, 1809, p. 485.

Chapter Nine

Reverend Hamlet Harrison

Dr Croft moved to Birmingham at the end of December 1791 and Brewood Grammar School was without an elected headmaster for several months. Croft had arranged for a colleague at the school, Reverend Gartham, to deputise for him. He then publicly resigned in April 1792 by writing a notice in the newspapers that he wished to devote the remaining part of his life to "Literary Pursuits". He proposed to give the "Keys of the House" to his successor at midsummer.[1]

The process for Croft's replacement lacked urgency and the advertisement was not placed in the newspapers until July. However, Dr Hurd and Sir Edward Littleton had been corresponding on the subject and, in late April, Hurd had written to Littleton that he expected the Trustees to agree that the new appointment would be a clergyman of the Church of England in full holy orders with at least a Master of Arts degree from either Oxford or Cambridge.[2] Hurd also had the innovative idea that instead of printing a list of Trustees for the candidates to contact with their testimonials, they should send them post-paid to one person only such as Mr Careless, the usher. The testimonials could then be presented to the Trustees at one meeting for them to inspect and then, at a later date, elect Croft's successor. This would save both candidates and Trustees a great deal of trouble. The selection of the new headmaster was to be based solely on testimonials, not by interview, and the unsuccessful applicants would be advised by John Perks of Saredon, secretary to the Trustees.

The advertisement that appeared in the newspapers did not mention that the candidates needed to be in holy orders, but candidates were required to have a Master of Arts degree from either Oxford or Cambridge. The new headmaster could expect a salary of £100 per annum from the school estates with additional income from boarders. The curacy of St Mary and St Luke's church at Shareshill, whose patron was Sir Edward Littleton, was also available and provided an additional income of £50 per year with duties only on Sundays and holidays.[3]

There were only sixteen applicants for the post but although Croft had left Brewood in December 1791 the Trustees did not meet to select his replacement until 20 September 1792, and then not at Brewood but at Wolseley Bridge, Colwich. Reverend Hamlet Harrison was the successful candidate, but others that had anticipated a career move to flourishing rural Brewood included the "pious, sober and honest" Daniel Mathias, who had attended Brasenose College, Oxford, but was not yet in holy orders, and Reverend Edward Baldwyn, Fellow of St John's College, Oxford who, at the time of the advertisement, was teaching at Bradford Grammar School. Reverend Baldwyn had established a thriving school of seventy boys in Bradford, with two ushers and a new School House. He wanted to move to Brewood to enjoy more church duties, and to also be closer to his churches at Clee St Margaret, and Abdon in Shropshire, near Ludlow. He was an author, sometimes writing under the pseudonym "Trim".

Hamlet Harrison was born in 1764, at Penketh, near Warrington, Lancashire. He and his siblings were the children of farmer Peter Harrison and his wife Elizabeth Hamblet. It is not known where Harrison went to school, but he possibly attended the Free Grammar School, Farnworth as he had been baptised at Farnworth church. There is no evidence, as is sometimes claimed, that Hamlet Harrison had attended Manchester Grammar School, although Reverend Harrison's nephew, Peter, had been a pupil there.[4] Hamlet Harrison obtained his B.A. and M.A. degrees from Brasenose College, Oxford, and also became a Founders' Fellow at Brasenose in 1788. He was ordained a deacon and a priest in 1780 at Oxford. Littleton appointed Harrison to the curacy of Shareshill on 29 September 1792, Croft continuing his duties at the church until that date, but Harrison was the last headmaster of Brewood Grammar School to receive that privilege.[5]

Harrison was an enthusiastic headmaster with big plans for the school. As soon as he took up his appointment, he wanted to substantially raise the school fees for boarders, from 20 guineas to 30 guineas per annum. He could not do this without the approval of the Trustees and wrote to

Littleton for permission who, in turn, discussed the matter with Hurd. These Trustees had both been pupils at the school and were passionately interested in its continued success. Baldwyn, the applicant from Bradford, had proposed charging 20 guineas at Brewood even though he was charging 30 guineas per boarder at his own school. He argued that 20 guineas would be a preferable rate at Brewood due to the competition with Wolverhampton Grammar School.

Hurd agreed that an increase in the school fees could be justified as there had been a rise in the cost of living but as Littleton preferred to retain the lower fees Hurd was happy to agree. He expected Harrison to be an excellent headmaster, but confided in Littleton that Harrison should find himself "a prudent and good wife as his credit and success at Brewood would depend on it".[6] This never happened. There is no documentary evidence to indicate where Harrison had taught before coming to Brewood, or why Hurd and Littleton anticipated that Harrison should be a worthy headmaster.

The headmaster had authority over the usher and the Lower School, as well as responsibility for the maintenance of the school building, which comprised a School House, garden, fold yard, brewhouse, coal house, fowl house, pigsty and stables.[7] He received rental from school lands and had the opportunity to farm, ideal for Harrison, the son of a farmer. At Brewood Free Grammar School, the headmaster's School House and garden had always been rent free but the headmaster was expected to pay for any building repairs. Mr Budworth, headmaster from 1731-1745, had purchased some land to build a brewhouse and made some additions to the house and garden which had incurred a debt.[8] The Trustees felt that the subsequent headmasters had enjoyed the benefit of the improvement, so they were expected to take on the debt and pay the interest out of their own salary.[9] In 1794 Dr Hurd gave £100 and Sir Edward Littleton gave £60 to pay off the outstanding money owed, thus relieving the school and future headmasters of the burden, a substantial amount of money for the time.

The Grammar School pupils were expected to attend the parish church at Brewood regularly and, like all the congregation, had certain pews allocated to them, which were usually purchased. Mr Feilde, headmaster from 1762-1769, had bought four pews in the south gallery for the Grammar School pupils but a subsequent headmaster to Feilde had sold them to Mr Careless, the usher, who had then rented them out to other people. Harrison had been promised two pews by Careless and, after a long delay, he sold them to Harrison on 28 September 1797 for eight guineas.[10] However, complications arose after the death of Careless as he had not altered his will, which still stated that the pews in the lower part of the church, being used by Mr Harrison, were bequeathed to the Trustees for ever.[11]

The new school

Mr Harrison was headmaster when the nineteenth century was about to dawn. With hope and positivity, Harrison wanted a state-of-the-art school with a curriculum to suit the needs of his pupils. The building that he had inherited, he complained, was old and dilapidated, occupied a large area of ground and was expensive to maintain. It had been substantially rebuilt between 1731 and 1733, under the headship of Budworth, and had also been renovated from time to time. In 1796 Harrison complained of already having spent £80 of his own money in repairs of this old building, with the year not yet complete. Croft, the previous headmaster, may have had the same problem as he had complained about broken promises by the Trustees in a publication entitled *On the Endowments of Schools and other Emoluments of Publick Instructors*. It is likely that Croft also wanted to make improvements, as he had bought two cottages in Deans End, adjacent to the school and opposite the School House, which were rented out to tenants. Samuel Webb occupied the cottage next to the school and Benjamin Wootton, breeches maker, occupied the adjoining one.

Harrison had been in correspondence with John Perks, secretary to the Trustees, about the cottages from at least 6 October 1796, as well as corresponding with Sir Edward Littleton. In May 1797, with the Trustees approval, Harrison bought the cottages from Dr Croft for £190 plus legal fees.[12] Edward Monckton was consulted about a possible issue regarding heriot tax but the issue had not been resolved by March 1799, with Monckton and Littleton both too busy to meet.

Harrison who did not think a heriot needed to be paid anyway, began the building work on both school and cottages. This worried Hurd who preferred a more cautious approach, but the heriot issue was finally settled at Christmas and the cottages were exempted from the tax.

Hurd was pleased with Harrison's plans to make the school "the most commodious of any that he knew", and he believed that Harrison was a modest, well-qualified master.[13] There was to be a new frontage to the school, with gardens and a new school room for the usher with a dancing room above it. Previously, the pupils had walked across Brewood to the Red Lion and used a room there for dance lessons. The new room was to be rented out to Mr Hales, the dance master, and the rental included candles, heating and a cleaner.[14] Hurd wanted the work to be fully costed before any building work commenced, but Harrison believed that the work could be financed by excavating a seam of coal on school land at Willenhall. Hurd was not keen on this idea, as his elder brother had found to his cost "that miners were 'dangerous' people".[15]

Hurd's concerns continued because as the work on the school began, so the costs increased. Hurd was not prepared to advance any more money to Harrison, and knew that only he and Littleton would provide financial support for the development of the school, not the other Trustees. Eventually, in 1799, Hurd wanted the houses either sold or rented out and the financial support of £200 promised by Hurd and Littleton to be used for some other purpose which would benefit the school.[16]

In spite of Hurd's unease, the new school continued to be built. One of the bought houses would be used by the usher, and the other would be rented out for a contingency fund to keep the school buildings in good repair. Carpentry work on the new building was carried out by John Lewis and James Morris of Brewood, including the provision of new windows in the passage and doorway, one of which was circular. New doors were made which locked, Brewood being a lock-making town. The carpenters also constructed two seats in the "necessary", or toilet and built 100 yards of palisading for the garden fence. In addition, two brick and tiled pigsties were built with a floor paved in stone, one of which was for Benjamin Wootton's house.

Mr Anslow worked on the masonry and John Southern also worked on the building. The new school and dancing room were built using 39,000 bricks. The walls in the school were plastered, and new fire grates were provided. Five waggon loads of lime were used and another 2,000 bricks for the school floor. Work had also been done on the stone stair case, and the paving yard. However, 5,500 old tiles were recycled in the new school. Iron railings were also made for the steps by Mr Meacham. In spite of the different spelling of the name, this is likely to have been Francis Machin, the blacksmith, who lived near to the school and provided the iron railings for the Sunday School steps in January 1800.

In October 1799 the bill for the work to the school totalled nearly £400. Included in this sum was a moderate amount of ale for the workmen, which cost £8.[17] Hurd and Littleton each paid £100 towards the cost but there was a remaining £183 18s 10d to be financed, plus legal fees, so Littleton raised a mortgage of £200, but paid the legal fees himself. Bishop Hurd, who was almost 80 years old, wanted Mr Careless, the usher, an "old, deserving man" to receive the rent of one house, even if he did not live in it himself, but this would only apply to Careless.[18] Mr Careless died a few weeks later, on 1 February 1800, aged 65, and was buried in the churchyard a few days later. He was an esteemed member of both school and community.

Harrison, frustrated by the delays to his new modern school, had drawn up a school plan, printed the school fees onto cards and circulated them publicly, without authorisation and too late for the Trustees to do anything about it. To publicise the new school at its best, Harrison had commissioned some drawings, for which he was taking subscriptions. He had the agreement again of Hurd and Littleton, both of whom subscribed to some prints, but Hurd specifically wanted the dedication at the bottom of the drawings to be to the Trustees at large without any special mention of either of them.[19]

Richard Paddy was the chosen artist. He was a painter and engraver who lived in Wolverhampton. He had worked with famous artists, including the eminent engraver, Francis Jukes. Paddy was a drawing master at both Wolverhampton Free Grammar School and at the Catholic Seminary at Sedgley Park. Amongst his works of art were the south-east view of the church of St Peter, Wolverhampton, the view of Dudley Castle and views of the abbeys of Lilleshall and Buildwas in Shropshire.[20]

The drawing of Brewood Grammar School was published on 30 January 1799, and dated as such. It shows the school on the right-hand side of the painting with the Usher's House, now Rushall Hall, on the left-hand side, enclosed in the school grounds. There are problems tallying the date of the drawing with the original documents held at Staffordshire Archives relating to the building work. The new road, which was diverted from the school yard to the back of the Usher's House, now known as School Road, was not diverted until 1800.[21] This allowed the school and school croft to be formed into an enclosure, with a wall built across the old road to enclose the school space. The wall and gate are shown on the January 1799 drawing of the new school, but it is likely to have been the intended view, an advertisement, for the new school as it was perceived when completed.

To the Trustees of Brewood Free Grammar School from their most obliged and obedient servant, R. Paddy. Dated 30th January 1799. WSL, SV-II.137

Reproduced courtesy of the Trustees of the William Salt Library.

111

Coloured pen drawing of Brewood Grammar School,
anonymous but attributed to R. Paddy, 1799.
WSL, SV-II.135

Reproduced courtesy of the Trustees of the William Salt Library.

After the death of Thomas Careless, a new usher needed to be appointed and Littleton asked Harrison to employ some temporary teachers for the school until the vacancy was filled. Mr Harrison was to receive all the property rent income to the school, including that belonging to the usher during the vacancy, but in return he had to pay a salary to the teachers and pay for the repairs of the property rentals.[22] James Morris, the carpenter, was again employed, this time to make a new writing table, some forms for the pupils, and some repairs on the palings to the Usher's House.[23] The temporary teachers included Reverend Kemsey, who was eventually appointed usher, Richard Talbot who taught accounts,[24] and Waldron Ladbury of Dean Street, Brewood, who taught the boys drawing, writing and also accounts.[25]

In May 1800, several residents of Brewood and parents of pupils, met at the Fleur-de-Lis and agreed that the new usher should be required to teach the pupils English grammar and other useful subjects for the "middle class of life", rather than just the rudiments of Latin.[26]

The residents were not the only ones seeking change. Harrison also wanted to make modifications in the teaching methods at the school, and to modernise the curriculum but he had to have the approval of the Trustees. Hurd advised Harrison to check the rules of the foundation and the school charity, because new ideas could not just be implemented. Hurd was of the opinion that two masters could be employed at the school: the headmaster to teach Latin and Greek; and the usher to teach English, the rudiments of Latin, writing and accounts. The usher was subordinate to the headmaster and had to teach from books approved by both headmaster and Trustees. Harrison wanted the usher to teach writing and accounts to the whole school, not just the Lower School, to which Hurd could see no problem. Harrison also wanted only day pupils in the Lower School to have their lessons taught for free, in line with the foundation, but he wanted Upper School pupils to be charged for lessons, at a sum agreed by the Trustees. The usher could also receive boarders if the house allocated to him was large enough, and then boarders in the Lower School could attend the Upper School when the headmaster felt they were of sufficient ability.[27]

Harrison had to present his new ideas to the Trustees, and in Staffordshire Archives there is a lengthy document detailing his background research.[28] It also gives interesting detail of both curriculum and pupils. Harrison asked old pupils about their recollections of school. The responses were that the usher had always taught the scholars the rudiments of Latin, beginning with the Accidence and then progressing so that they could translate easy passages from English into Latin. John Clarke's *Introduction to the making of Latin* was used as the examining book for entry into the Upper School by previous headmasters at the school, from at least the time of Mr Budworth. The boys were also taught from books such as *Lily's Grammar of Latin* and *Corderius Latin dialogues* by the usher, and when they had passed the Upper School examination they were taught by the headmaster to a higher level of classical education.

Richard Talbot, cordwainer and a man of good character had been a day scholar when Mr Blake was usher and during the headmasterships of both Budworth and Bromley. His school friends included the late Thomas Careless, usher, and William Weate, son of Reverend William Weate, vicar of Lapley church from 1736.[29] Richard Talbot particularly remembered when out of the six boys tested, only the above three mentioned boys passed and went into the Upper School. The three boys that had failed the test had to stay in the Lower School, until they reached the required standard for entry. This was the system used by Mr Budworth and continued by Mr Bromley and Mr Feilde.

Thomas Pendrell Rock, aged about 72, had also been instructed by Mr Blake, as had Mr Rock's eldest brother, William, who was in the same class as Edward Littleton.[30] The Rock brothers were the sons of William Rock, the apothecary who lived and worked at the house now known as Speedwell Castle. Thomas Pendrell Rock remembered that Eusebius Holmes, the grandson of Stephen Onions, an ironmaster who had lived at Brewood, and Joseph Webb, were both instructed by Mr Blake and then admitted into the Upper School with Mr Budworth. They were in Budworth's class along with Fisher Littleton, brother of Sir Edward Littleton, Moreton Walhouse of Hatherton, and William Simpson. Other pupils that were at school with Thomas Rock were Nathanial Bradshaw from Gunston, John Toncks from Codsall, William Bedford from near Codsall, John Lane from Bentley, William and John Thomas from Edgford, Thomas Watson of Longdon, and the Barrett brothers of Oaken, near Codsall.

Joseph Pursall, aged 73, was a day scholar under Mr Blake. His father was a shoemaker and made Mr Blake's shoes in payment for his son's school bills. Thomas Baker, was taught by both Blake and Bromley, and Joseph Lloyd, now aged about 74, had been a day scholar whose grandfather, Richard Lloyd, paid Mr Blake for teaching him writing and accounts.

Mr Harrison believed that there was originally only one master at the school who received payment from the foundation. In 1726, a second master, known as the usher, was appointed to help the headmaster in his duties. The salary of the usher was £23 9s 9d per annum, which even in

1749 was considered to be a very low salary. In order to supplement his income, the usher was allowed to instruct the boys in writing and accounts, for which there was a charge. As these were not in the definition of his essential duties they were not mentioned in the original legal documentation for the Grammar School. Harrison argued that if the usher taught writing and accounts, then they should also be taught in the Upper School. He also argued that the terms of "Headmaster" and "Usher" were not defined in the original documentation for the school but were understood to both be teachers in a "School of Learning or Grammar School". Harrison believed that the usher had the duties of "ushering in" or introducing young scholars to learning. As the scholars became older and progressed in their abilities the headmaster would then instruct them to a higher level of education.

During Mr Harrison's headship, there were between 30 to 40 boys in the Lower School, but sometimes as many as 50, all of whom were taught English free of charge. Harrison thought that if the boys were charged a small amount of money for English, then it would be beneficial to the school, and increase the usher's salary. As the new usher would also be expected to teach the boys Latin, it made sense to appoint a person who was both a competent classical scholar and writing master so that the boys in the Lower School would benefit from classical instruction and then take this level of education further. Mr Harrison was also well aware that there was a loophole in the free education for local Brewood Grammar School boys. There were some people in Brewood who were boarding boys at their houses for lower rents than the school charged. As the boys were technically living in Brewood they were entitled to free education at Brewood Free Grammar School so that the school was providing free education not just for the boys in the parish of Brewood, but "to all the world at large". Harrison argued that if subjects were taught free of expense, it devalued them and encouraged the pupils to miss school when they felt like it and so stunt their progress in education. This may have related to seasonal times, when children were needed by their parents to help on the farm, especially at harvest time.

Harrison was keen to state that he had the good of the school at heart and wanted to enhance its reputation. He had personally worked very hard and spent a substantial part of his income on improvements for the school.

He felt that the Trustees believed that he wanted to shrink from his duties but he stated that he owed his character and honour to the Trustees and the foundation which gave him shelter and support. He added, "I am ready, so help me God! to fulfil the views & intention of the Founder, whatever they be, & if I have mistaken the strict line of duty in adhering to the path which my Predecessors have all trodden in before me, I would sooner resign the situation".[31] He later may have regretted writing this statement.

At the Trustees meeting on 17 October 1801 Littleton and Hurd confirmed that they had provided a substantial amount of money towards the rebuilding of the school and that Littleton had also taken out a mortgage of £200 to pay the debt on the new school room for the usher with the dancing room above it. After the meeting Hurd told Littleton that he was against the idea of a mortgage and thought that it would be better to settle the debt immediately, in case either he or Littleton "dropped down dead". With that in mind, Hurd and Littleton each paid £300, for the new school, again kindly releasing the trust, and the masters, of any debt. It was officially written in the minutes of the meeting that the usher was to receive one of the houses free of charge, as long as he lived in the house, otherwise, if he sub-let the house, he had to pay a rent. The rent of the other house was to be used as a contingency fund for the school.

At the same meeting, the Trustees ruled that a recently introduced charge of £2 2s 0d per annum to day pupils in the Upper School should be dropped but Mr Harrison, instead, would be appointed to the position of receiver of the rents and be paid £1 per year. The Trustees made it clear that the headmaster should teach Latin and Greek but the new usher must teach the Lower School pupils English, writing and accounts as well as the rudiments of Latin in preparation for the pupils to progress to the Upper School, in line with the rules of the foundation. The usher was to be paid, as usual, for teaching writing and accounts in the Lower School.[32] This had been introduced in the Lower School as a benevolent fund to an earlier usher, Mr Blake, when he became blind during his old age. Later, in 1810, the Trustees decided to drop the charge but only when the present usher, Mr Kemsey, had ceased teaching at the school, which did not happen until 1840.

At the meeting the new usher was appointed. The candidates had to provide testimonials and were interviewed at the School House.[33] The successful candidate was Reverend Matthew Kemsey who had been employed as assistant master at Brewood Grammar School since at least 1798 when he is listed as donating some money for the defence of the nation appeal at the school. Kemsey officially began his appointment as usher at Brewood Grammar School in September 1801, at Michaelmas. He had been second master at Wolverhampton Grammar School from December 1799, where he was allowed to receive 12 boarders.[34] He officially left Wolverhampton Grammar School at Christmas 1801. Kemsey was the son of Matthew Kemsey of Lapley, and had graduated from St Edmund Hall, Oxford in 1797. He remained teaching at Brewood until his retirement in 1840. Kemsey was also a curate at St. Nicholas' church, Codsall, from 1801 until his death in 1846.

Kemsey was not the only person from Brewood Grammar School making a donation to the defence of the nation against France. Reverend Hamlet Harrison donated five guineas at Brasenose College, Oxford, one guinea at Shareshill and two guineas at Brewood. Reverend Kemsey donated one guinea, Mr Harrison's boarders each donated five shillings: S. Mountfort, T. Hurd, J. Metcalfe, J. Kyffin, J. Smith, W. Marshall, C. Molineux, T. Aspinall, W. Worsey, R. B. Marsh, William Bradney Pershouse, J. Horton, G. Brookes, T. Marsh, Philip Monckton, Willis Beebee, Claud Monckton, William Aspinall, along with Mrs E. Highfield the housekeeper and Thomas Careless the usher. Other parishioners also contributed such as the Monckton, Bill and Vaughton families, Smith Muchall, William Shenstone, Mrs Bromley, James Morris the builder and an old man of the age of 80, unnamed, who gave his earnings of two days labour at eight pence a day.[35]

Whilst Reverend Harrison wanted a new state-of-the-art school in Brewood, the poorer members of the parish were facing hardship. On 26 December 1799 it had been decided at the church vestry meeting, of which both Reverends Harrison and Kemsey were on the committee, to buy a substantial amount of wheat at market price and ration it out to families. At other times of poverty, soup kitchens were provided.

Dismissal of Mr Harrison

Despite Harrison's claim to have the best interests of the school in mind, support for the headmaster from the Trustees was waning, and by 1809 the Trustees were determined to have him dismissed. Douglas Thompson, a history teacher at Brewood Grammar School and an author of *A History of Brewood Grammar School 1553-1953* claims that Harrison "... either seriously abused his position, or else local jealousy was too much for him".[36] The Trustees cited Harrison's preference to farm rather than teach as their reason, and there is no doubt that Harrison enjoyed farming. There may have been other issues, such as his discipline of the pupils.

On 12 May 1809, George Chetwynd, a Trustee, enlisted the legal help of Mr Serjeant Joseph Williams, for Harrison's dismissal. Williams was of the opinion that the Trustees were answerable to the Charity Commissioners but, as the Trustees appointed both headmasters and ushers this gave the Trustees responsibility for the masters' conduct and for the way the pupils were instructed. In other words, the Trustees had the power to expel any master who neglected his duties. Secondly, if Mr Harrison was farming rather than performing his duties as headmaster, he could have his farm taken from him and be prevented from taking another, on "Pain of being displaced". On a third matter raised by George Chetwynd, Williams suggested that "Papism" or an act of violence, were good reasons to dismiss a headmaster. One accusation against Harrison appears to have been that he used unduly harsh punishments on boys that boarded with him. Williams argued though, that as Harrison was under no obligation to take boarders this accusation might not stand up in court.

Williams also advised the Trustees on two other matters about which they had doubts. One concerned the collection of rents from school land leaseholders and another arose from Harrison's request to be able to appoint a deputy during absences from school. Harrison had been appointed receiver of the rents of the school estates, at a salary of 20 shillings per annum, but the Trustees had the power to have this rescinded. Williams advised the Trustees to appoint a solvent person so that there was no risk to the funds.[37] This advice was taken and Harrison's appointment as receiver of the rents was rescinded. John Perks was appointed in his place, but he had to give a security to the Trustees.

He was also appointed solicitor for the Trustees in place of his father, who had died.

In the matter of having a deputy, Mr Harrison had asked the Trustees if he could appoint a master to take his place if he needed to reside in Oxford, the answer was firmly in the negative. In 1808 Harrison had obtained his Bachelor of Divinity and a year later became rector of Stratford-le-Bow in London as well as rector of the first portion of Pontesbury church, Shropshire. If Harrison ceased to do his duty as headmaster at the school, and resided elsewhere, then the Trustees were entitled to dismiss him. This had not happened with Croft though, when he moved to Birmingham in December 1791, and had publicly stated in the newspapers that he would not resign yet, but appoint a deputy in his place.[38]

It is possible that Dr Croft's opinion was sought on aspects of Harrison's administration to judge by a letter he wrote on 29 February 1809, a few weeks before his death. The Trustees wanted to know detail about certain procedures such as, boys transferring from the Lower to the Upper School and the fees paid by local boys. Croft explained that when Mr Budworth was headmaster, the "Boys of the Town were not admitted into the Upper School until they could write short sentences in Clarke's introduction to the making of Latin". Croft personally had expected the local children when they transferred to the Upper School to pay some money for the first two years, but only what the parents could afford. Dr Croft had continued the practice of the previous headmaster, Reverend Pickering, and had taken into account the opinions of the local people, who did not like too much encroachment from the school.[39]

Croft further reported that when Reverend Budworth had been headmaster of Brewood School he did not farm and only had enough land for two saddle horses and a summer and winter cow. The boys in the Upper School never associated with the boys in the Lower School. The Upper School boys had the privilege of playing in the school croft, which was adjacent to the school garden. As soon as the school day finished, the Lower School boys were expected to go to their friends' houses, but over time this lapsed.

With the legal issue of Mr Harrison's dismissal clarified, a notice was put in the newspaper stating that there would be a meeting of all Trustees on the 6 July in the school room at 11.00 a.m. for "the purpose of taking into account the state of the charity and for other purposes".[40] It must have been a topic of conversation in Brewood. There is no documentation written by Harrison about the meeting but documentation relating to the meeting, written for the Trustees, survives at Staffordshire Record Office.[41]

The first meeting to dismiss Mr Harrison held on 6 July 1809 in the school room

Sir Edward Littleton chaired the meeting with nineteen Trustees of the Free Grammar School of Brewood in attendance: the Honourable Edward Monckton; Sir John Wrottesley, Baronet; Sir George Pigot, Baronet; John Woodhouse, the Reverend Dean of Lichfield; Edward Monckton, junior; George Chetwynd; John Lane; Francis Eld; Francis Eld, Junior; John Sparrow; Henry Crockett; Phineas Hussey; Moreton Walhouse; Thomas L. Fowler; Reverend George Talbot; Reverend Baptist John Proby; Reverend Egerton Bagot and Reverend Richard Slaney.

Nine charges were brought against Mr Harrison at this meeting including the very serious charge of Harrison's gross neglect of his duties as headmaster. Harrison was in attendance.[42]

The Trustees at this meeting agreed clear rules to which the master and usher should abide. Firstly, the Upper and Lower Schools which Reverend Harrison had converted for other purposes be reinstated. Harrison had received permission from several Trustees but was found guilty. The headmaster should be constantly at his desk in the Upper School during school hours, unless prevented from doing this due to illness. The headmaster was required to open the doors that separated the two schools and read prayers to the pupils of both schools every morning at 9 o'clock which was the custom of all former headmasters. It was also agreed that the headmaster's chair which Mr Harrison had removed from the Upper School to enable him to teach the boys in his study, should be returned to the Upper School.

The Trustees also ruled that the usher was expected to "preside and sit constantly" during school hours in the Lower School, and both masters could only be absent from school in the school holidays, unless five Trustees had signed an order. If this was not adhered to then the headmaster could be expelled.

With regard to Mr Harrison farming rather than teaching, the Trustees agreed that both the headmaster and the usher had to leave their lands by next Lady Day, and in future could only have land that was necessary for themselves and their family, as by the decree relating to the school of 1725/1726. As Mr Harrison did not have a wife and family this limited the land he could rent from the school. In fact, Mr Harrison had a large farm of about 90 acres, almost half of which was school land. The Trustees ruled that Reverend Harrison was guilty of obtaining some of the school lands without their consent or that of their agent.

Lastly, a sub-committee of Trustees was formed to meet annually, the first meeting being in October, to ensure that the resolutions agreed at the meeting were being complied with, and that the tenants of the school estate were not paying their rents to the headmaster, rather than John Perks.

The meeting was then adjourned until 2 August.

The second meeting relating to the charges against Reverend Harrison

The Trustees again came out in force. At the start of the meeting, it was agreed that there should be a survey of the school and grounds and all expenses incurred in carrying out the investigation into the conduct of Reverend Harrison would be paid for out of the Littleton fund.

The charges were then heard against Reverend Harrison for misconduct in his office. He was accused of not spending enough time either teaching or on school business but instead using his time to work on the farm or do other personal business.

Mr Harrison was able to defend himself and was allowed to present evidence from other people, who confirmed that he was teaching at the school during school hours rather than farming in the fields. Mrs Highfield, the housekeeper, Mr Ladbury of Dean Street, the writing master, and a Thomas Hatchett,[43] all gave evidence that Mr Harrison had taught his classes from 7 o'clock in the morning until breakfast at 9 o'clock. At 10 o'clock, when school recommenced, Mr Harrison would teach again, then after dinner, he taught from half past 3 until 5 o'clock, Mr Harrison used his study to teach his pupils so that he could refer to the reference books when necessary. As soon as Mr Harrison had finished teaching the first class, a boy was sent to get the second class.

Mr Kemsey, the usher, was questioned about the length of time it took Mr Harrison to hear his exam classes. Mr Kemsey said that the time varied according to the lessons. Mr Kemsey did not believe that Harrison neglected his teaching to the school boys, but sometimes Mr Harrison taught in school, and sometimes out of school and he would sometimes teach the boys before school, and sometimes afterwards. Kemsey confirmed that Harrison gave sufficient time to each lesson, and instructed the boys well and carefully.

Mr Harrison had support from many people who either said that they had not seen Mr Harrison working on the farm, or only infrequently. These included William Bagnall, James Daw, Thomas Willets, Thomas Mullard and John Willets who lived opposite Mr Harrison's farm. William Griffith, who had been employed by Mr Harrison for more than 15 years working in the school garden, also testified that Mr Harrison taught in the school, rather than spending his time at the farm. He could confirm that because Mr Harrison was angry with him at least four times a week.

Mr Purchase, Benjamin Wootton, and Thomas Careless, eldest son of the late Mr Thomas Careless, usher of the school, had all seen Harrison farming, but could not give the exact times. Thomas Careless confirmed that he had seen Harrison go past his window when going to his rickyard, and he had also seen Harrison tend to his lambs in the churchyard. Benjamin Wootton had seen Harrison swearing violently against Mr Till, one of his farm employees, who had been working in the fields but could not be specific about the time.

Mr Purchase who lived in Brewood and rented land from the Trustees, claimed to have seen Mr Harrison frequently at his farm. As recently as

23 March he was with his young lambs in the churchyard, and he had also seen Mr Harrison with his mare and colt at the school croft.[44] Purchase would not commit to the amount of time that Harrison spent on his farm, but did remember that he had seen him when he was repairing "The Way" at Deans End, which, as it had taken three months to repair, included both holiday and term times. Harrison was found guilty of the charge of insufficient time teaching and spending, instead, time on the farm or working on other personal business. Harrison claimed that John Perks, solicitor for the Trustees, had threatened the tenants with eviction unless they spoke against Harrison.

Reverend Harrison was then charged with using the School Croft, a field adjoining the School House, for his own purposes so that the pupils did not have the school playground, provided from time immemorial and considered necessary for the children's health, exercise and amusement. This charged was proved.

The next charge against Reverend Harrison stated that he neglected to read prayers in the school according to established usage, and to instruct the scholars in their moral and religious duties. When he had accepted the post of headmaster, Reverend Harrison had to swear that he would teach according to the rules of the established church. However, whilst Harrison did not read prayers to the scholars on Sunday mornings or any other mornings, he did read prayers in the evenings and the curate, Reverend Hutton, read them in the mornings. However, in spite of this evidence the charge was proved against Harrison on 2 August.

The sixth charge against Mr Harrison accused him of conducting himself towards the scholars with intemperance and passion, using improper modes of correction, and been unreasonably severe in his punishments. In other words, in modern terms, he was accused of having a quick temper and was severe in his punishment of the children. Mr Chetwynd, junior, recalled that Harrison had poured beer over his brother James Read Chetwynd when he complained that the beer the school provided was bad. James Read Chetwynd suffered from rheumatism and also had, at the time, a school fever. Mr Chetwynd stated that even on his death bed, in 1808, his brother complained about Harrison. Harrison is reported to have severely punished the boys and once dragged a boy from his sick bed saying, "See, I can work miracles; I can make the lame to walk".[45] Thomas Hatchett did not think that Mr Harrison ill-treated the pupils, but Mr Eld agreed that his son had been badly treated too. The charges were proved on 2 August.

The seventh charge against Harrison related to his lack of accounting for certain rents and profits. The charge appeared to specifically relate to the rent that Mr Harrison received from Mr Hales for the use of the new dancing room above the school room: an annual rent of two guineas. Mr Harrison claimed that this was not rent for the room, but covered the costs for lighting the fires and sweeping the room for the convenience of the dancing master. The Trustees found Mr Harrison guilty.

Reverend Harrison was also charged by the Trustees of having received all the school rents of the usher whilst there had been a vacancy for the position following the death of Mr Careless on 1 February 1800. The position was not filled until Michaelmas 1801. Mr Harrison's total gain from this income of £126 12s 2 ½ d was only £1 2s 0 ¾ d. Mr Harrison pointed out that he had also had to pay £25 for the advertisement for the vacancy of headmaster when he succeeded Dr Croft, and £5 3s 2d for the title of the two houses in Deans End. The Trustees would not re-imburse him and the case was proven.

Mr Harrison was found guilty by the Trustees of the eighth charge of cutting down a considerable amount of timber belonging to the school estate, some of which he had used and some he had sold, all allegedly without the knowledge and consent of the Trustees. Mr Harrison admitted that he had cut down some firs and elms from the headmaster's garden soon after his appointment as headmaster in 1792, and he had used the wood for a stable. However, he claimed that he had been given permission for this to happen and that the timber he had used in the School House and buildings were necessary, as the buildings were no better than a ruin when he came to the school. The dilapidated state of the school seems to be a common theme with each new headmaster. Mr Harrison claimed that he had a promise of assistance from the Trustees when he began the improvements and he had only spent between £700 to £800 on the school.[46] Harrison was found guilty.

All the charges against Reverend Harrison except the one of gross neglect of his duty as headmaster were proved at the meeting with the Trustees on the 2 August 1809. The ninth, last and most serious charge was postponed until 15 September at 11 o'clock, at the Littleton Arms in Penkridge on account of Reverend Harrison disputing the visitational power of the Trustees. He was not going to leave the school easily and wanted to fight for his reputation and his position as headmaster at the school.

The charge against Reverend Harrison of gross neglect of duty as headmaster

The day of the meeting at the Littleton Arms, Penkridge arrived. The charge of gross neglect of duty of Harrison as headmaster was considered. Harrison was asked if he allowed the Trustees their visitational power or not. His reply was "I neither allow it, or deny it". In view of his answer, the Trustees formally told him that he was discharged from his position as headmaster of Brewood Free Grammar School and he would be expected to vacate the school on 20 December 1809, with John Perks, the Trustees solicitor being present. The Trustees would then meet as soon as possible after that date to appoint a new headmaster. It was also resolved that a sub-committee would be chaired by the Honourable Edward Monckton, to look at the accounts of Reverend Harrison, and collect all outstanding money due to the charity.

On the 28 September 1809 the Trustees of the school met at Wolseley Bridge to examine the accounts and other matters relating to the school. The only concerns, in the end, related to the rent of one of the cottages at Deans End, the money he had received for timber belonging to the school since he started, 17 years ago, and the 14 years of rent for the dance room.

Reverend Harrison refused to leave the school on the 20 December. A Trustees meeting was held at Wolseley Bridge, two days later, with Monckton chairing the meeting. It was agreed that advice to evict Harrison should be sought from Sir Vicary Gibbs and Sir Samuel Romilly, the latter having petitioned an Act in relation to Charitable Trusts. In the meanwhile, a new headmaster would be appointed. An advertisement was placed in the Birmingham, Stafford, Oxford and Cambridge newspapers and also in the *Courier* for the purpose of receiving testimonials and proposals from prospective candidates.

On the front page of the *Staffordshire Advertiser* for 6 January 1810, Harrison stated that he wanted to respectfully inform the public that he had no intention of leaving the school. He was open for boarders and all pupils, and was expecting his character to be vindicated either through the press or a court of law. Immediately underneath this notice was the advertisement for a new headmaster at the school. Candidates were requested to have their testimonials and proposals submitted by 27 January and the new headmaster would be elected on 15 February. It was also noted on the advertisement that the curacy of Shareshill was usually given to the headmaster of the school and was worth about £70, but this, in fact, did not happen. Testimonials were to be sent to Mr Perks, at Wolverhampton, not to the school.

Sir Edward Littleton presided at the Trustees meeting at the Littleton Arms, Penkridge on 15 February. The rules and regulations of the school were again re-affirmed but it was also stated that the headmaster and all future headmasters should be expected to give a bond of £1,000. In future, if the majority of Trustees believed, and proved, that the headmaster was guilty of immorality, neglect of duty, or any other sufficient cause of complaint, then the headmaster would have to resign.

At the same meeting it was agreed that the field known as the School Croft, which adjoined the School House, would be used as the playground for the boys of the Upper School. It was also thought that a rule was needed to state that the entrance to the Usher's House should be the entrance opposite the School House.

Tenants renting school land

A committee of Trustees met again on Thursday the 15 March 1810 at Wolseley Bridge to look at the re-submission by tenants for their land and premises. All tenants could re-apply, except Reverend Harrison. The tenants were made aware that they had to retain their pasture land, and could not break it up. Any meadow or mowing ground needed a quantity of manure put on in proportion to the quantity of hay produced. No more than three crops could be grown each year, and when the last crop had been collected at least 10 lbs of red clover and 3lbs of Dutch or white clover and one bushel of good grass seeds should be sown. Finally, not more than one third of the plough land should at any one time be in tillage. The Trustees required that the fields were farmed in a good husband-like manner with appropriate seeds sown. Fences were to be kept in good repair and the ditches and drains properly cleansed and opened. Rents were to be paid half yearly free from all payments, except property tax, and the tenant had a half year's notice to quit, if required. They could not let any of the land without the agreement of the Trustees in writing and under no circumstances were trees to be cropped or copped on the land. [47]

The headmaster and usher were to be given a specific allocation of land. The headmaster was allowed, exclusive of the School House, garden and croft: Mason's Field, Pinfold Croft, and Round Bush, otherwise known as Robin's Croft. This piece of land was described as close to the footpath connecting the two roads leading from Brewood to Giffard's Cross and a road leading past Deans Hall Farm over the canal in the direction of Chillington called Hadens Lane, now known as Hyde Mill Lane.[48] The usher was allocated The Great Peas Croft, Echill, Chandlers Croft and Stoker's Croft.

Reverend Kemsey was to be given both his salary and the money due to him from the rents of the estate from last Michaelmas. However, proceedings would begin to evict Mr Harrison from both the school and the school lands.

The Trustees also began to get tougher on the tenants of the properties as well as the masters of the school but it was acknowledged that some "trifling" repairs were necessary at several small dwelling houses belonging to the charity. If tenants neglected to keep their houses in good repair, they would now be evicted.

Will Harrison stay or leave the school?

Mr Harrison may have been evicted by the Trustees, but he would not leave the school. On 15 June 1810, George Bennet of Penkridge, acting solicitor for the Trustees after the death of John Perks of Saredon, attempted to serve an affidavit on Reverend Harrison. Mary Brant, who worked at the school, told the solicitor that Harrison had left Brewood on the 11 June and was not expected to return before next Tuesday or Wednesday. This was confirmed by other people, who believed that Harrison had gone to London to avoid being served with the ejectment notice.

The Trustees had advertised for a new headmaster and the appointment was made on 10 July 1810 at the Littleton Arms, Penkridge. There were seven candidates shortlisted out of many, one of which was Reverend Alfred Hadfield who had been employed as assistant classical master to Hamlet Harrison for six years and was well respected. The choice for headmaster soon became a clear contest between him and Reverend Kempson, who had recently been appointed headmaster at the Collegiate School, Southwell, Nottingham. Hadfield received a lot of support from the Trustees, including that of Sir Edward Littleton, but Kempson was appointed.[49] Hadfield may have lost the vote not because of his ability, but because of the fear of some Trustees that it would be even more difficult to evict Hamlet Harrison from the position of headmaster if his successor was already at the school. Hadfield did not stay at Brewood Grammar School but moved first to Breightmet, near Bolton and then to Everton where he ran a private school.

The Trustees again had to seek legal advice about how to evict Harrison. This time Thomas Lowton, a distinguished, solicitor, a member of Inner Temple and founder of the Lowtonian Society gave his opinion. He suggested giving George Bennet the power to serve notices to quit, as well as being receiver of the rents. All rents should be collected before the notice to quit was served, to ensure that the money was received before the eviction of Mr Harrison on Lady Day or Michaelmas 1811. This advice was taken, and George Bennet prepared the papers.

On 1 September 1810, some sources give the date as 31 August, Mr Bennet arrived at the school driven in a chaise. As the chaise approached the gate, the front door was opened and two men were in the hall. Reverend Hutton was one, and when Bennet asked him if Mr Harrison was home, he replied in the negative and did not know when he would return.[50] Mrs Highfield, the housekeeper, then came to the door and directed Bennet to the cornfields, but whilst Mr Bennet was exchanging remarks with Mr Hutton about the weather, Harrison appeared. George Bennet asked him for the names of the late tenants and the amount of their rents, to which Harrison responded that they were in Perks papers and, if that was the sole purpose of the journey he objected to being charged for the chaise. Bennet reasoned that he needed the chaise for his gout and that he had shared a lift for part of the way, which would defer some of the cost. Hutton wanted to leave but Harrison asked him to stay, as a witness.

On the death of Mr Perks, no accounts in his capacity as receiver of the rents for the school could be found amongst his papers. Mr Bennet only had the accounts of Mr Careless, which ended in 1798. Bennet might have received some help from Harrison under different circumstances, but he either would not or could not help Bennet. Harrison wanted to know the current valuation of the land, and the amount of rent that he was owed and pointed out to Bennet that as Perks had been appointed receiver of the rents in place of Harrison, the matter was nothing to do with him. Harrison did advise that he received two thirds of the rent of the school lands and had paid his rent to Mr Perks, so keeping it simple.

However, Harrison had his own problems with the now deceased Perks. The receiver, had not given Harrison a receipt for the rents he had paid for the last half year. Reverend Harrison had paid his rent via Mr Parke of Stafford Street, his hairdresser, but when Parke had paid the rent and was being given a receipt, Perks had torn it into pieces, and would not give another.

Bennet also wanted Harrison to supply him with the name of the tenants whilst he was receiver but Mr Harrison countered that he did not know the names now, as the Trustees had turned old men off the land and put in new tenants. He added that Benjamin Taylor did not have his tenancy renewed because he would not speak against Mr Harrison, and had been threatened by Perks. When Benjamin Taylor had lost a horse, Mr Harrison had given him five guineas. The conversation ended with Bennet delivering the resolution of the Trustees to Harrison, which was to be followed, at a later date, by an ejectment notice. As Bennet left, he claimed that Harrison violently slammed the door shut.

On 12 November 1810 there was another Trustees' meeting about the conduct of Mr Harrison as a headmaster. The Trustees discussed whether or not Harrison should be given notice of the meeting as it was felt that his temper would lead him to lock up the entrance to the school and prevent their admission.[51] The decision was to send a letter to Harrison telling him that, at the meeting of 15 September 1809, it had been agreed by the Trustees that Harrison should be discharged from his duties as headmaster and was to vacate the school on 20 December 1809. He had not complied and had been served again with a copy of the original resolution, on 31 August 1810. The Trustees now required Reverend Harrison to leave the school on 20 December 1810.

On 10 December 1810 Mr Harrison was still trying to obtain his share of the arrears of the rents and profits of the estates to which he was entitled. The Trustees replied that when the accounts between the Trustees and Mr Harrison had been properly examined, he would receive the approved balance, if any was due to him. The amount of money that Mr Harrison should have received until Michaelmas 1811 when he actually left the school was a substantial amount of money for the time: £504 16s 3d.

Mr Harrison again refused to leave the school at Christmas and a meeting was held by the Trustees on 27 December 1810 at Wolseley Bridge. Mr Bennet was instructed to apply for information into a *quo warranto* for Mr Harrison to show by what right he continued to hold the office of headmaster at the school.

Reverend Kempson had already been appointed in July 1810 to replace him, but had not yet taken up the post.

On 31 December 1810 another letter was sent to Thomas Lowton from the Trustees querying three points on the expulsion of office of Harrison.[52] The first question was about the notice to quit, served by Mr Perks. As the Trustees had no copy or proof of the delivery, Thomas Lowton was happy to send another draft of the ejectment. The second point was whether Mr Harrison could be made to produce the served notice. Thomas Lowton thought that whilst this could legally happen, a Judge could not compel Mr Harrison to produce the notice. Finally, the Trustees hoped to move for a *quo warranto* against Mr Harrison so that he would have to explain why he was still master of the school but

Lowton dismissed this as the Court of King's Bench had no jurisdiction over the school.

On 16 January 1811 an action of ejectment was drawn up for the Trustees by Justice Le Blanc, Lord Ellenborough, to take possession from Mr Harrison of four houses, four orchards, four gardens, 70 acres of land, 70 acres of pasture and 70 acres of meadows with appurtenances in the parish of Brewood. At this time Brewood town had a population of 919 people with 210 houses.[53]

On 1 May 1811 Harrison again wrote to Bennet trying to obtain the rent money that he was owed. He required a written answer enclosing the new rental of the school estate and for it to be paid to a Mr Truss. The Trustees were doubtful if Harrison should be entitled to any money as he had been dismissed as headmaster effective from 20 December 1809.

Resignation of Hamlet Harrison

On 24 June 1811 Reverend Harrison sent a letter of resignation to the Trustees via Mr Bennet.[54] He had succeeded to a church preferment which would be "incompatible" with his residence at Brewood so he would be leaving at Michaelmas. He gave the Trustees early notice, so that they could take the necessary measures to appoint his successor. Harrison signed himself "Your obedient Servant, Hamlet Harrison, B.D.". As Mr Kempson was already appointed, the election of a new headmaster was easy.

Joseph Harrison of Park Stile, Walton-on-the-Hill, West Derby, Lancashire, Hamlet Harrison's brother, had bought the first portion of the advowson of Pontesbury with part of the garden fold and buildings on 20 October 1809, transferring the portion in trust for Reverend Harrison of Brewood on 15 March 1810.[55] Harrison only had to preach at Pontesbury for half the year which left him time for his duties as rector of St Mary parish church, Stratford-le-Bow, Middlesex of which Brasenose College was the patron, and he still had time to farm.[56]

On 30 September 1811 when the new term had started, Harrison would be happy to return the keys of the school, but only as long as he received his share of the arrears of the rents which he was owed. This was not going to happen as Bennet would not give Harrison any rent money until he had received and examined Harrison's accounts, but Harrison did return the keys. The correspondence continued with Harrison wanting to meet Bennet at Newport, Shropshire with his own solicitor, Mr Morris, so that they could all discuss the arrears in rent due to Harrison from Michaelmas 1809 to Michaelmas 1811. Harrison also wanted to know the value per acre of the School Field as more than half an acre had been taken from it to make the field square and had been added to Pinfold Croft and so he wanted the rent to be altered accordingly. Bennet had no intention of meeting Harrison, only his representative. He did, however, in November 1811 present Harrison with a bill for the necessary repairs needed at the school, which amounted to £27 18s 0d.

George Chetwynd and Reverend Richard Slaney, Trustees, investigated the accounts of Mr Harrison whilst he was headmaster. It was believed that Harrison owed ten years rent on the house which was used as income for incidental expenses at the school. Mr Harrison agreed that he had divided the rent of the house annually between himself and the usher in the same proportion as other rents instead of setting it apart, as he should have done, as an incidental fund. It was decided not to ask for the rent for that, given the time lapse, but Mr Harrison did agree that he lived in the other part of the house, and was charged the annual rent of £2 12s 6d.

Reverend Hamlet Harrison takes his case to the Charity Commissioners

Harrison was not happy that his reputation as a headmaster was in tatters as a result of the Trustees, and took the matter of his dismissal as headmaster to the Charity Commissioners.

The Commissioners did not present their report until 1820, several years after Harrison's dismissal, and concentrated on the financial affairs. They raised concerns that Mr Harrison had needed to pay for the advertisement for headmaster, the position to which he was elected and had also had to pay Mr Perks' bill for taking Counsel's opinion relating to the two houses in Deans End. They did request more clarification from Harrison about the rent received for the house used as a contingency fund for the school.

They studied 14 years of accounts relating to the new dancing room and did not agree with the Trustees that Harrison was guilty of any misdemeanour relating to the charges or accounts.

The Commissioners also examined the charge about the cutting down of a large amount of timber from the school estate, which the Trustees claimed had been felled without their knowledge. The Commissioners examined the accounts, and spoke to the tenants, but could only find that Mr Harrison had sold one portion of pollards at Willenhall in 1796 for seven guineas. This money had been divided between the two masters in the usual proportions but some compensation had been made to the tenant for a new barn, for which the pollards were not suitable. The Commissioners, felt that the charge of the timber was insignificant and that in any case Harrison had also spent considerable sums of his own money in improving the School House and other premises. Harrison had claimed that the timber he had used in the School House and buildings were necessary for the improvement of the school.

Mr Harrison felt that he was due money from school rentals whilst headmaster at the school. After Harrison had left the school, he continually came to Brewood, and also visited George Bennet at his home in Penkridge, wanting the arrears of rent and land tax owed to him, in his opinion, by the Trustees. In this matter, the Commissioners felt that as the Trustees had the right to dismiss a headmaster if they felt that it was necessary, and as Harrison had refused to leave the school by 20 December 1809, as demanded by the Trustees, he had put himself in the position of trespasser from that date, and so had no legal claim to the rents. However, as Harrison had felt that he had a right to remain as headmaster and he had kept the school in "a flourishing state", the Commissioners advised the Trustees to decide on an appropriate amount of compensation.

Reverend Harrison at Pontesbury, Shropshire, Stratford-Le-Bow, London and Brewood

When Reverend Harrison became rector of the first portion of St George's church at Pontesbury, the church was unstable, and in 1820 the church tower collapsed. In 1825 the nave and aisles had to be pulled down for safety reasons. The parishioners wanted three new churches as they had three portions but Harrison and the rector of the third portion both opposed the idea so one new church was built. The architect was John Turner of Whitchurch, the choice of Reverend Harrison.[57]

When the church re-opened in 1829 Reverend Hamlet Harrison gave a sermon about the problems that had been encountered, not least financial. He said "A public subscription of distinguished magnitude and value gave vigour to our first efforts and every order among us, with the exception of an individual or two of wealth and property, but poor in spirit and generosity...." [58] Reverend Harrison lived in the deanery at Pontesbury but he still had a presence in Brewood through some land that he had retained and continued to be named on Brewood's electoral roll. In the *Wolverhampton Chronicle and Staffordshire Advertiser* for 1 April 1835, Reverend H. Harrison of Pontesbury, Salop, advertised the rental of an excellent family house, with rich and fertile land, not exceeding 15 acre at Brewood. It was recently the residence of the vicar but claimed that it could easily be a boarding house for pupils at Brewood Grammar School, as the day scholars were "admitted free of every charge, except writing and accompts". Alternatively, the premises could be used for selling beer as it was near the "wharfs of the Birmingham and Liverpool Junction Canal".[59]

In January 1842 there was a petition against Reverend Harrison by the parishioners of Stratford-Le-Bow, relating to a bequest to the church for charitable purposes by Mrs Margaretta Brown which had been invested in the names of three executors, including Harrison, the rector. After the death of one of the executors, another one was appointed at a church vestry meeting, a Mr Hunter. Harrison was not happy with the appointment, believing Hunter to be too advanced in years, and so another person was elected in his place. However, this was not legal, Hunter objected and took the case to court. Mr Hunter won his case and Harrison had to pay all costs.[60]

In March 1842 there was another court case against Reverend Harrison relating to "brawling" in the vestry of the church at Pontesbury. *The Hereford Times* reported that there had, for a long time, been unresolved differences between Reverend Harrison and his parishioners and this court case had been pending for two years. The parishioners were not happy that Harrison was allowing his horses and cattle to roam freely in the churchyard as they were damaging the walks, graves and gravestones. The parishioners believed the churchyard should be sacred and undefiled. William Bowen of Pool Place, Pontesford, Pontesbury, claimed that on 5 December 1839 Reverend Harrison had, with disregard to the sacredness of the church vestry, spoken to him in a loud, brawling and quarrelsome manner. Reverend Harrison responded that Mr Bowen had continuously interrupted him whenever he tried to speak, as had Edward Dicken and William Eddowes, a surgeon of Pontesbury. All charges were dropped by both parties. The court ruled that it would have been no credit to Reverend Harrison, or the church, if they had continued.[61]

Reverend Harrison was a successful farmer at Pontesbury, and was famous for breeding Durham bulls. In 1819, the *New Monthly Magazine and Universal Register*, recorded that a Durham bull bred by Reverend Harrison had a carcass weighing 1892 lb.[62]

On 2 October 1843, Reverend Hamlet Harrison died at Pontesbury, aged 80. He was buried in a classical iron tomb near the eastern gateway to the church at Pontesbury. During his lifetime Harrison had been a magistrate for Shropshire, farmer, rector, curate, headmaster and a valued member of Brasenose College. *The Gentleman's Magazine* of 1843 wrote that Harrison had carried out his duties as headmaster of Brewood Grammar School with "credit and satisfaction". However, Lord Hatherton, in his diary, described Hamlet Harrison as having a "very defective system of education. His love of more gainful pursuits, the little attention he paid to the school and his violent temper completely disqualified him from the situation".[63] Lord Hatherton did not send his children to Brewood Grammar School.

Brasenose College, Oxford had, on 20 December 1805, presented Reverend Harrison with a large silver salver valued at fifty guineas, as an acknowledgement of his skill and attention to the landed property of the Society of Brasenose College. Harrison bequeathed this to his great-nephew William Harrison who became rector of Pontesbury in 1847. Hamlet Harrison wanted it to become a family heirloom.

Reverend Harrison also bequeathed to his great-nephew, if he became a priest, the advowson and first portion of the parish church of Pontesbury with a small parcel of land, part of the garden yard and buildings belonging to the parsonage house.[64] William Harrison and other members of his family were incumbents at Pontesbury for most of the 19th century.

On Thursday 30 November and Friday 1 December 1843, at the rectory in Pontesbury, there was a sale of Reverend Harrison's furniture, china, glass, fine and rare prints and prime wines. Also for sale were his livestock and the grain, hay, turnips, potatoes, wool, timber and trees such as oak, poplar and ash. Added to this were the farming implements that Harrison had owned such as portable threshing and winnowing machines and a blacksmith bellows and anvil.[65] In September 1844 the leases of coal mines and lime works at Pontesbury which had not yet expired and belonged to Reverend Harrison were put up for sale.[66]

Later still, in November 1853, there was a notice in the local newspapers that there would be a sale by auction, either in late December or early January, of some property held by Reverend Hamlet Harrison, in accordance with the terms of his will. The auction was to be held at the Lion Hotel, Shrewsbury and it related to property in Brewood and also at Pontesbury, Church Stretton, Worthen and Westbury in Shropshire. The property in Brewood was a beerhouse called Vauxhall, later known as Brook House, which had stables, a coach-house, a cowhouse, barn and outbuildings, with a productive garden, orchard, rich arable meadows and pasture land totalling about 17 acres. Brook House is situated opposite Hyde Mill Lane. It was occupied by Joseph Fox, who afterwards moved to The Angel Inn. The property came up for auction at the Lion Inn, Brewood on Monday 30 January 1854.

Another house, workshop and garden near Brewood was also offered for sale and this was in the occupation of Joseph Lloyd, locksmith. On the 1851 census, Mr Lloyd was living on the Wolverhampton Road. The printed particulars, for both properties, could be obtained from Mr Thomas Harrison of Norris Green, West Derby, and the other trustees of the estate, all of whom were relatives of Reverend Hamlet Harrison.[67]

Reverend Kempson's headmastership, was to bring stability to the school, after the turbulent court case for Reverend Harrison.

Notes

1 *Aris's Birmingham Gazette,* 9 April 1792, p. 3.
2 SRO, D1413/1 Letter from Bishop Hurd, Hartlebury Castle, to Sir Edward Littleton, 29 April 1792.
3 *Jackson's Oxford Journal,* 23 June 1792, p. 1.
4 Peter was the son of Hamlet's elder brother, Thomas. *The Manchester School's Admissions Register* has made no claim to Hamlet Harrison being educated there. The *Register* was edited by Reverend Jeremiah Finch Smith, the eldest son of Reverend Dr Jeremiah Smith, headmaster of Manchester School and past teacher and pupil at Brewood Grammar School who still had a home and property in the village. The Smith's would both have been aware if Harrison had attended Manchester School.
5 Reverend John Hayes Petit of Queen's College, Cambridge succeeded Reverend Harrison at Shareshill church on 16 February 1811. His son was the Reverend John Louis Petit, the renowned watercolour artist.
6 SRO, D260/M/P/5/133, Hurd to Littleton.
7 SRO, D1416/1/1/2.
8 This debt was possibly incurred as Budworth would have expected a substantial amount of money to be awarded him from the court case, regarding his wife's inheritance. He would then have been able to repay the debt himself, if required.
9 SRO, D1416/1/4/1, Letter from Harrison to Littleton, 8 June 1794.
10 SRO, D1416/1/4/1.
11 Mr Careless wrote his will on 1 February 1796 and died on 1 February 1800.
12 SRO, D1416/1/4/1-2.
13 SRO, D260/M/F/5/133, Letter from Hurd to Littleton, 11 January 1797.
14 SRO, D1416/4/2/6.
15 SRO, D260/M/P/5/133. Hurd's elder brother, John Hurd, of Hatton, Shifnal, died in 1792.
16 SRO, D260/M/P/5, 18 April 1799.
17 SRO, D1416/1/4/1.
18 SRO, D260/M/P/5/133, 2 November 1799.
19 SRO, D260/M/P/5/133, 14 July 1798.
20 *The Investigator or Quarterly Magazine,* Volumes 5–6, 1822-23, p. 467. Richard Paddy was buried at St Peter's church, Wolverhampton, 5 December 1821, aged 71.

21 James Hicks Smith, *Brewood: A résumé historical and topographical* (William Parke, 2nd edition, 1874), p. 27.

22 SRO, CEG/2/1, p. 557.

23 A James Morris is listed as joiner and builder of Sandy Lane in 1818 trade directory for Brewood.

24 SRO, D1416/4/2/6. Richard Talbot may have been related to Richard Talbot, the cordwainer, who spoke at a Trustees meeting about Hamlet Harrison's teaching.

25 Waldron Ladbury was employed at the school from 1799 but on 5 December 1807, he put a notice in the *Staffordshire Advertiser* for his new school in Deans End which could accommodate twelve young gentlemen. After Waldron Ladbury's death on 2 February 1837 there was a sale of his furniture. Items included a fine-tuned pianoforte by Christopher Ganer, Kidderminster carpets, an eight-day mahogany clock, oil paintings and a variety of other goods. *Wolverhampton and Staffordshire Advertiser,* 21 June 1837, p. 2.

26 *Staffordshire Advertiser*, 24 May 1800, p. 1.

27 SRO, D260/M/P/5/133.

28 SRO, D1416/5/1, Teaching at Brewood School, 1801, p. v.

29 Lapley parish registers.

30 Thomas Pendrell Rock was christened in 1727 and died in 1815, at Brewood.

31 SRO, D1416/5/1, Teaching at Brewood School 1801, p. v.

32 SRO, D260/M/E/128.

33 *Staffordshire Advertiser,* 10 October 1801, p. 1.

34 *Aris's Birmingham Gazette,* 30 December 1799, p. 1.

35 SRO, D1/A/PZ/35.

36 Douglas Thompson, *A History of Brewood Grammar School, 1553–1953,* (Brewood Grammar School, June 1953), p. 23.

37 SRO, D1416/4/2/3.

38 *Aris's Birmingham Gazette,* 5 December 1791, p. 3.

39 SRO, D1416/4/2/3.

40 *Staffordshire Advertiser*, 24 June 1809, p. 4.

41 SRO, D1416/4/2/3.

42 SRO, D1416/4/2/3.

43 Thomas Hatchett was possibly Thomas Bulkeley Hatchett who matriculated to Brasenose College, Oxford in 1808, aged 17 years, and transferred to Trinity Hall, Cambridge in 1809. He was the son of Bulkeley Hatchett of St Chad's, Shrewsbury and Ellesmere, Shropshire. He changed his name to Thomas Bulkeley Owen and lived at Tedsmore Hall, West Felton, Shropshire.

44 SRO, D1416/4/2/3.

45 C.R. Fay, *Huskisson and his age,* (Longmans Green and Co, 1951), p. 312.

46 SRO, CEG/2/1 p.557 and D1416/4/2/6.

47 SRO, D1416/1/4/4.

48 SRO, D1416/1/4/1, Letter from Corser and Fowler Solicitors to R. Walker, 18 February 1879.

49 SRO, D1416/4/2/7.

50 Reverend John Hutton was buried at Brewood on 21 November 1818, aged 41.

51 SRO, D1416/4/2/4.

52 SRO, D1416/5/2/5, Letter from Thomas Lowton, Stockbridge to the Trustees, 5 January 1811.

53 VCH Brewood, *quoting from* William Pitt, *A Topographical History of Staffordshire,* 1817.

54 SRO, D1416/4/2/3, Letter from Reverend Hamlet Harrison to the Trustees, 24 June 1811.

55 Durham University, UND/F3/C3/B3/7-8.

56 John Whiteside, *The Churches and Chapels of Pontesbury Parish*, (Robert Pither and Local Heritage Initiative, n.d.).

57 Whiteside.

58 Handwritten document at Shropshire Archives, Shrewsbury *quoted in* Appendix 14, p. 168 of Whiteside.

59 *Wolverhampton Chronicle and Staffordshire Advertiser*, 1 April 1835, p. 2.

60 *Globe,* 14 January 1842, p. 4.

61 *Hereford Times,* 12 March 1842, p. 3.

62 *New Monthly Magazine and Universal Register*, Volume 11, p. 475.

63 Extract from the end of the Volume 5 of the diaries printed in the Mark Southall: *Diaries of the first Lord Hatherton [Edward Walhouse Littleton] 1791–1863: Diaries 1817–1862 extracts.*

64 Reverend Harrison's will, written on 14 September 1843 was proved on 7 November 1843 and the portion at Pontesbury was presented to the Reverend Richard Tetlow clerk on condition he would resign if Hamlet Harrison's great-nephew, William Harrison became a priest, which he did in 1847. William Harrison was the son of Hamlet Harrison's nephew, also named William and grandson of brother Joseph who had purchased the portion of Pontesbury. William Harrison, the great-nephew was also bequeathed all Hamlet Harrison's books and manuscripts.

65 *Eddowes Journal and General Advertiser for Shropshire and the Principality of Wales,* 29 November 1843, p. 3.

66 *Chester Chronicle*, 13 September 1844, p. 1.

67 *Manchester Courier and Lancashire General Advertiser*, 28 January 1854, p. 12, *Staffordshire Advertiser*, 19 November 1853, p. 8.

A view of Brewood Grammar School drawn in 1842.
It is attributed to John Buckler.
WSL, SV-II. 133a

Reproduced courtesy of the Trustees of the William Salt Library.

Chapter Ten

Reverend Henry Kempson

On 15 February 1810 the Trustees met at the Littleton Arms Inn, Penkridge, in order to select a new headmaster but there was a problem as Mr Harrison had no intention of leaving. Reverend Alfred Hadfield, classical master at Brewood Grammar School for six years and curate at St Mary and St Chad's church at Brewood, was a candidate. He received the vote of Sir Edward Littleton, and seven other Trustees. Other candidates included Reverend Henry Kempson and Reverend Michael Ward of Tamworth. Ward had submitted testimonials from Charles Repington of Amington Hall, Staffordshire, and Lord Townshend of Raynham Hall, Norfolk. Ward ran a small private school at Amington and amongst his pupils had been the children of Sir Robert Peel and Mr Swinfen of Swinfen Hall.[1] Reverend Dr Mogg Bowen, headmaster of St Albans Grammar School; Reverend George John Davies, who later became headmaster of Kingston upon Hull School; Reverend S. W. Millar and Reverend Knight were also shortlisted. It was a narrow victory for Kempson over Hadfield, the former having received the support of Edward Monckton, junior.[2]

Henry Kempson, son of Simon and Lucy Kempson of Birmingham was christened on 17 July 1778 at St Philip's church, Birmingham. Kempson graduated at Christ Church College, Oxford in 1803 and obtained his M.A. in 1806.[3] He became curate at Brinkworth, Salisbury in 1803, chaplain at Christ Church, Oxford, from 1804 until 1811, vicar of St. Mary's church, Long Preston, near Skipton, Yorkshire, in 1809 and stipendiary curate at Weston-under-Lizard, close to Brewood, in 1824.[4] Kempson did not marry until 10 October 1832, when he was 54 years old and his young wife, Mary Ingram, was 32 years old. Mary was the daughter of Reverend Rowland Ingram, B.D., of Settle, headmaster of Giggleswick Grammar School, and his wife, Mary.

In 1809, Reverend Kempson had been appointed headmaster of the Collegiate School at Southwell, Nottingham, receiving an excellent testimonial from the Deans and Canons of Christ Church, Oxford. They described him as being of good character and well qualified for the position, distinguishing himself with the sermons that he had preached at the university. At this school, Kempson had to prepare the students for "Commercial Life" and teach his pupils classics and mathematics to a level to prepare them for university. He was allowed twelve boarders and all of his pupils had "respectable connections". Kempson charged £60 per annum for board, education, writing and arithmetic.[5]

In early 1810 immediately after his appointment at Brewood Grammar School, Kempson wrote to Sir Edward Littleton, whose preferred candidate had been Hadfield, assuring him that he would be faithful in his discharge of duties and promote the interests of the school. Kempson also asked if Sir Edward had any objection to him trying to persuade Harrison to leave the school by next Christmas. He added that he would be very happy to accept the curacy of Shareshill, if it was offered. In the advertisement for headmaster, it had stated that the curacy was "usually given" to the successful candidate, and that had been so since the 1740s, but the curacy this time was given to Reverend John Hayes Petit, father of John Louis Petit, architectural historian and watercolour artist.

Reverend Henry Kempson had to give a bond of £1000 to the Trustees which he provided on 24 December 1811. He also had to sign a legal document promising that at the end of his headmastership of the school he would leave peacefully and that he would neither be guilty of immorality nor neglect of duty. The students at the school were to be instructed in Latin and Greek to the required level for entering university, and none of the pupils were to be charged for this instruction. Mr Kempson was required to be at his desk in the school during school hours and read prayers to the boys every morning at nine o'clock in the school room. The headmaster was not allowed to be absent from his school duties at any time, except for the usual holidays, unless he had permission in writing signed by at least three of the neighbouring Trustee visitors for that purpose. The bond was witnessed by the usher, Matthew Kemsey, who was also a friend of Kempson's father, Simon.[6] This document ensured that the headmaster could be evicted from his post more quickly than had happened with Reverend Harrison.

Reverend Kemsey had also received a university education, was a competent teacher and was qualified to be headmaster at the school, but did not apply. The Trustees did agree that the new headmaster would have charge of only the Upper School, and not the Lower School, which would be entirely the responsibility of Reverend Kemsey. When Mr Harrison had been headmaster, he had been in overall control over both the Upper and Lower Schools, as was the subsequent headmaster, but Reverend Kempson was happy with the arrangement and still received two thirds of the income from the school estates whilst the usher received one third.

Reverend Kempson, headmaster of Brewood Grammar School

When Reverend Kempson moved to Brewood in April 1812, an inventory was taken of the fixtures and fittings in the school, which was normal procedure. The survey was taken by the eminent John Kempson, land surveyor and auctioneer of Birmingham who had published a map, entitled *Town of Birmingham,* in 1808. The inventory gives a guide to what the school would have looked like at the time, for example, it lists the school room and the school dining room, as well as ten bedrooms heated by fire grates. There was a breakfast parlour containing four double bookcases and shelves, a dining parlour and a drawing room. The kitchen contained a knife room as well as the pantry and scullery. A large canvas meat safe, hen pen, brewhouse, ale and wine cellar and an ordinary cellar, helped with the supply of fresh food. The bells, of which there were five as well as the gate bell, were an important fixture, and so were the locks and keys for the school. Outside were a stable and yard.[7]

Reverend Kempson was soon ready to accommodate boarders. The fees were lower in Brewood than he had been charging at Southwell: 45 guineas per year from the time of admission to the school until the age of 14, when the cost increased to 55 guineas. The boys would receive a free classical education suitable for entry to university but there would be an additional charge of two guineas per year for writing and arithmetic. If the boys required tea, this would be charged for separately, similarly with the washing. There was also a two guineas entrance fee.

Kempson had a problem with local residents providing cheaper accommodation for the school's pupils, as had the previous headmasters. A loop-hole in the system meant that any boy living in Brewood or the surrounding parishes was allowed free schooling, even if they were not an "official" resident. Mr Pearson of Brewood was one such competitor. Pearson had a "commodious and convenient house" situated to combine the advantages of both town and country. He advertised that the boarders would have the advantage of instruction from the masters of Brewood Grammar School, free of "every expense" so that each young gentleman would receive at his house, all the advantages of a "perfect" classical education for the "small cost of twenty guineas a year for board". There was an additional charge for washing but each student was required to bring three napkins, a knife, fork and spoon.[8] Pearson failed to mention the charges for mathematics, English, drawing and dancing lessons at Brewood Grammar School.

In 1816 Kempson wanted to increase the school fees that local day pupils were paying, but it was against the rules of the original endowment. The Trustees did provide a new floor to the Lower School, and a cast iron pump as requested by the usher, Reverend Kemsey.

In early 1817 Mr Pearson moved closer to the school into the "spacious and capital mansion" of Brewood Hall.[9] Mrs Bridgen and Miss Fowke, sisters, were also providing competition at their school in Dean Street which they started in 1811. Although they provided education and board for young ladies, they also accepted young gentlemen under the age of 8 years. In 1816 the cost was 18 guineas for pupils over 12 years old, and 16 guineas for younger children.[10] After the death of Mrs Bridgen in early 1835, Miss Fowke continued the school until January 1836 when it was taken over by Miss Isabella Walker, who no longer accepted boys at the school.[11]

The strongest competition for the Grammar School came from Waldon Ladbury who had taught writing, drawing and accounts at Brewood Grammar School for eight years. In January 1808 he established his own school for 12 young gentlemen at his home also in Dean Street. Charging more than the Fowke sisters, the costs were £20 per annum for pupils over the age of ten and 18 guineas for younger children, plus a guinea entrance fee, 10/6d for writing and arithmetic and 15/- for drawing. Ladbury's school prospered and, in November 1810, he extended his house to provide a larger school room, and advertised that his pupils would receive an education in preparation for university at Oxford or Cambridge. The basic fees continued to be the same but other charges increased.[12] Waldron Ladbury was a cousin of Reverend Kempson and, in 1824, Ladbury returned to teaching at Brewood Grammar School.

Kempson tries to raise the status of the school

Brewood Grammar School had received bad publicity when the Trustees tried to terminate Reverend Harrison's appointment. In order to reinstate the school as thriving and elite, Reverend Kempson needed to have new ideas. Most local parents wanted their children to be pupils at the prestigious Brewood Grammar School, but wanted the subjects taught to be more relevant to a commercial career. A few parents, usually those who were richer, wanted their child to attend university and for this a classical education was essential.

Reverend Kempson had the idea to endorse a boarding house which, by providing extra tuition for pupils, would also raise the status of Brewood Grammar School. The new boarding house would be aimed at those wishing to learn the classics and attend university. There was a limit set by the Charity Commissioners on how many boarders the headmaster of the Grammar School could accommodate. Kempson had vacancies for boarders so his plan was solely to raise the status of the school, and make it thrive again, as he stated in an advertisement he placed in the newspapers.

Kempson advertised for a respectable person qualified to assist in a classical school and who could establish and manage a boarding house for the pupils. The person needed to be able to teach Latin, writing, arithmetic and geography. If the proposed plan was successful and the numbers of pupils attending the school increased, and if the assistant was sufficiently competent in the teaching of classics, he might be employed solely in that department. The headmaster wanted this intelligent and active person to assist him in reviving the reputation of the school. He had in mind a good house pleasantly situated in Market Place.[13]

The proposal had the backing of the Trustees. Robert Kenyon, the successful candidate, was the son-in-law of Richard Rhead, schoolmaster at the Orme School, Newcastle-under-Lyme. It is not known precisely where the property was in Market Place, possibly the house to the west of the Swan and adjacent to it. This had been the home of Dr Jeremiah Smith and his parents' family home. Smith had been both a pupil and teacher at the school, and vouched for Kenyon in a court case a few years later. Another possibility for the school's location, and more likely, is Broadgate House which was opposite Smith's home and certainly used as a school in the 1850s.

Photograph of Market Place, Brewood. 1900–1910. The building
with the cyclist outside is a possible site of Kenyon's school.
Reproduced courtesy of Brewood Civic Society.

Photograph of Broadgate House, adjacent in this image to Powell's tea rooms, 1900–1910. This is the more likely site for Robert Kenyon's school.

Reproduced courtesy of Brewood Civic Society.

Broadgate House, Speedwell Castle and Market Place, taken from the corner of Stafford Street and Bargate Street.

As soon as Robert Kenyon had been accepted for the position, he began advertising in the local newspapers. He was able to provide a pleasant and spacious boarding house in the town of Brewood for the "youth" to be educated at Brewood Free Grammar School under the headship of Reverend H. Kempson. The boarders could expect a "complete classical education, according to the practice of the most respectable public schools". To provide this level of education a third classical assistant and writing master had already been appointed.[14] This was Samuel Kenyon, Robert's father.[15] The school would be open to boarders from the 28 July 1817. The fee for each pupil was £25 per annum, which was slightly higher than Pearson's 20 guineas for accommodation at Brewood Hall, and additional tutoring could also be had in subjects such as French and drawing, at an extra charge. Each boy had to bring with him a pair of sheets, and four towels, with a charge for washing them of two guineas per annum.

Kenyon's school had only been open a few weeks before Pearson was complaining that preferential treatment was being given to Reverend Kempson's boarders, rather than the day pupils. His concern was for his own boarders at Brewood Hall who were attending the school as free day pupils. Pearson's concerns were raised with Mr Kempson, and the Trustees were satisfied with his answer. When Pearson advertised his boarding house in the *Staffordshire Advertiser* again, on 17 January 1818, he said that the young gentlemen entrusted to his care, could depend on the strictest attention to their morals, health, and comfort, and the boys would receive the same instruction during the school hours, as those who boarded in the School House.

In January 1818 Robert Kenyon continued to advertise his boarding house at Market Place emphasising that an assistant from the Upper School regularly superintended the private improvement of the young gentlemen entrusted to Mr Kenyon's care. Terms were no longer given but could be requested by letter.[16] The school was clearly not economically viable as, in July 1818, Robert Kenyon was advertising that the accommodation was very comfortable and well adapted to the lowest possible terms. He also added that his boarding house could provide a commercial and mathematical education as well as a classical one.[17] Unfortunately, the new boarding school did not work out for the Kenyons.

In 1821, Robert Kenyon's second son was born in Wheaton Aston, possibly at the farm of his brother-in-law, Richard Rhead.[18]

Robert Kenyon, became a successful agent and traveller for Messrs. Bass Brewery of Burton, He was held in high esteem until he was sent to gaol at the Michaelmas Sessions of Staffordshire Assizes held on 16 October 1838. Kenyon was alleged to have embezzled certain monies, the property of Bass Brewery, on 24 October 1833, 12 September 1836, 15 February 1837, 10 April 1837 and 1 June 1837. He was found not guilty of most of the charges but he pleaded guilty to one charge of the embezzlement of £3. The Reverend Jeremiah Smith D.D., High Master of Manchester Grammar School and resident of Brewood, along with "several other respectable people" vouched for the previous integrity of the prisoner, whom they had known for years, but Robert Kenyon was still imprisoned for twelve months in the county gaol.[19]

School property

Whilst Kempson was battling to raise the prestige of the school, he and Kemsey, worked with the Trustees to purchase prime property for the school. In 1823 William Careless, who lived close to the school at Deans End, was declared bankrupt and his house was bought for the school for £300. In 1827 Kempson and Kemsey also negotiated to buy two houses which adjoined the Usher's House and belonged to Mr Wilday, for a cost of £380.[20] This purchase would prevent any "nuisances which might happen" if anybody else purchased the same properties.[21] This sale did not run smoothly for the masters though. Whilst the idea was an excellent one and the Trustees had approved the purchase, at a subsequent meeting of the Trustees on 20 November 1828, there was an objection raised which forced them to reverse their decision. They were put to the expense of reconveying the premises to Messrs. Kempson and Kemsey and then the properties had to be re-sold as the masters' private property, which was thought to be to the future detriment of the school.

The new canal through the school land

Reverend Kempson was headmaster at the school at a time of great change for Brewood. The new Birmingham and Liverpool Junction

Canal, constructed by Thomas Telford, was to be carved through the school playing fields. Some of the Trustees, such as Honourable Edward Monckton, Edward Littleton, Phineas Hussey, Reverend Proby and Reverend Slaney, felt that it would be injurious both to the school and the masters and they wanted their objections brought to the notice of both Houses of Parliament. The Trustees asked Earl Talbot to present to the House of Lords and Edward John Littleton, later Lord Hatherton, to present to the House of Commons.[22] However, an Act of Parliament was passed for the Birmingham and Liverpool Junction Canal to be built. It was to be a direct route to Liverpool from Wolverhampton, and 21 miles shorter, with less lockage than any other route.[23] This had the support of the other Trustees.

Mr Fleetwood, the solicitor for the Trustees, arranged for the sale of the land owned by the school and required for the building of the canal.[24] In 1830, he obtained £200 per acre with all damage to the school land to be made good. The canal company agreed to build a six-foot high wall to replace a fence and build a bridge for the pupils to cross into the remaining part of their school field, so that their games of cricket could be continued. In July 1833 the Brewood part of the canal was completed, but the whole canal was not open until March 1835 as Shelmore embankment, near Gnosall, proved to be a problem.

A planned use of sharing supplies of water with other canal companies linking with the Birmingham and Liverpool Junction canal did not materialise so Belvide reservoir was built in 1832. It was completed in 1833 but the engineers soon realised, even before the canal was opened, that the reservoir was too small for the anticipated canal traffic and it had to be enlarged in 1836. Thomas Telford never saw the canal operating as he died in 1834.[25]

The top soil had prudently been removed before work started on the canal but the excavation left a huge pile of sand, about 12,100 square yards by seven yards high above the level of the canal. The estimated weight was 84,700 tons. When John Hay became school estate manager in the 1840s he wanted to sell the sand and had been offered 2d per ton which amounted to 3/4d per boat load of 20 tons each. However, he thought that he could obtain 8/- per boat and expected a yield of at least £1500; then, when all the sand had been removed, the land could be sold for building. This did not materialise as Hay had anticipated, and in the 1870s the safety of the sand bank was a major concern for headmaster, James Heber Taylor.

As the new canal opened work was progressing on a new transport link between Birmingham and Liverpool which passed through nearby Penkridge: the Great Junction Railway. Thomas Brassey, one of the greatest railway engineers of all time, had the contract for Penkridge viaduct, and this was completed in 1836, although the railway did not open until 4 July 1837.

The cost of education at Brewood Free Grammar School

Kempson and Kemsey were both popular and active members of the community but, in spite of this, the numbers attending the school began to decline, particularly in the Lower School. In 1820 there were 35 pupils in the Upper School and 25 in the Lower School, but of the 60 pupils, more than half were boarders whose families did not live in Brewood. Of the 35 students in the Upper School, 25 boarded in the Headmaster's House, five boarded in Brewood, leaving only five as day pupils.[26] In 1817 there were 36 pupils attending the Lower School which was a substantial decline in number of pupils and income for the masters. There were a number of reasons for the decline in such a short time: bad harvests which left parents with a diminished income; the establishment of the National School in Brewood, which provided education for 140 children; and the lack of a boarding house for the younger pupils, which was needed for children coming from a distance.

An idea of the cost of attending the school, and the curriculum of the pupils, can be gleaned from a bill for half a year's tuition for pupil C. Greene sent by Kempson to Mr Greene, the surgeon, for his son's education in Christmas 1824.[27]

Writing and arithmetic at	£1 11s 6d
Slate, and two copy for writing at 1/- each	£0 3s 0d
Heating	£0 10s 0d
Pens and ink	£0 7s 6d
Total	£2 12s 0d
Mr Greene was also charged for the use of books:	
Valpy's *A Greek Delectus*	£0 4s 0d
Two Nowell's catechisms	£0 0s 4 ½ d
Total	4s 0d
Final total	£2 16s 9d

A note was also added the school would re-open on 24 January 1825. The Bank of England inflation calculator estimates that the bill, in 2023, would be approximately £257.

Other books used at the school were a book of fables, an English grammar; a Latin grammar, Carpenter's spelling, Hornsey's spelling, Crossman's *History of England*, Nomenclatura for Latin, a Latin dictionary, *Guy's School Geography*, by Joseph Guy, and Reverend J. Goldsmith's *A Grammar of General Geography*. Goldsmith's book included astronomy as well as maps and engravings. There were also additional charges for the use of the terrestrial globe, maps and a tutor.

Kemsey required all of his school bills to be paid before the child returned to the school. He told the parents and guardians that it was very expensive for him to employ an able assistant to help him, but the cost was worth it as the pupils gained from this extra, more individual tuition. One exception though was William Radford, of Bishop's Wood, not a favourite pupil of Mr Kemsey. He was the son of blacksmith, William Radford and his wife Mary. When Kemsey presented their bill, he told them that he had not charged the family the usual 7/6d entrance fee, "The Boy himself must know that everything has been done for him that any Man or Men can do for him to forward his education".[28]

Unrest in Brewood in relation to Brewood Free Grammar School

In 1831 there was again unrest in Brewood about the charges being made at the Grammar School for arithmetic and English which the residents of Brewood always felt should be provided for free. A meeting took place at the church vestry on 7 February, chaired by Charles Wade, a farmer at Hawkshutts Farm, Brewood and whose sons attended the school. There was an impressive list of other attendees including William Shenstone, a miller at Standiford, William Icke of Woolley Farm, John Plant of Bath Farm, Joseph Brewster of Somerford and Joseph Brewster of Brewood. In 1817 William Pitt of Pendeford, Wolverhampton in his book *A topographical history of Staffordshire* had noted Joseph Brewster as one of the principal manufactures at Brewood, making fixed and portable thrashing machines, kibbling mills, and straw engines. These people believed that the founders of the school wanted a curriculum that would meet the needs of the current times and so additional charges for English and arithmetic at the Free Grammar School were both illegal and contrary to the intentions of the founders of the charity. As the charges were hardest for "that class of our population least able to bear it" they should be discontinued, and if they were not, legal action would be taken. The people attending the meeting respected both the headmaster and the usher, but they wanted the school to move with the times.

A few weeks later, on 25 March 1831, the church vestry committee decided that their approach to gaining free education for their children had produced no positive results. The headmaster thought that he had the right to make charges for education, and the Trustees were making "intimations of an unfriendly nature", so the committee decided to seek legal advice, petition the Lord Chancellor and print all their resolutions in the newspapers.

Reverends Kempson and Kemsey were not pleased with this public display and, having been made aware of what was going on printed their own reply in the same newspaper of 2 April 1831. They felt that the school was "properly" denominated a Free "Grammar" School and that the meeting was raising false allegations which were inapplicable to a

"Grammar" School or School of "Learning". The masters claimed that those at the meeting had kept omitting the word Grammar between Free and School. If the petition was sent to the Charity Commissioners their reply would be that the law had defined the founders intentions by stating that the Grammar School was a school for instructing youth in the learned languages. The practice of the school had been, and still was, to instruct children for free from outside the parish as well as children of the parish in grammar learning. Other subjects such as writing, arithmetic and geography were not taught free of charge but the boys attending the school could "acquire these inferior branches of learning elsewhere at other hours". Kempson and Kemsey were basing their views on a court ruling by Lord Eldon in 1805. Leeds Grammar School had wanted to teach modern subjects for free, such as English and arithmetic but Lord Eldon believed that he could not overrule the intentions of the founders of the charity schools. He interpretated that the founders had bequeathed money for a classical education for the scholars, and so modern subjects had to be fee-paying.

In May 1831 the Brewood parishioners continued their battle publicly in the newspapers. They argued that it would "increase the usefulness of the school" to teach writing and arithmetic for free as the future welfare of the country was dependent on the sound education of the middle ranks. This argument, showing the views of the times, continued into November when William Shenstone of Standeford Mill took up the suggestion of the headmaster to write to the Trustees through the Honourable Edward Monckton. Shenstone added that there should also be no heating and entrance fees. As the Trustees had agreed in 1810 not to charge for writing and arithmetic in the Lower School until after Reverend Kemsey had left the school, why should it not be implemented sooner? An article in the *Staffordshire Advertiser* noted that the Court of Chancery had recently ordered grammar schools that could afford to do so, to employ a master for the teaching of writing and arithmetic at the expense of the school. The case had been raised in Monmouth for the Haberdashers Company and the Free Grammar School in the town.[29]

By September the issue still had not been resolved and some of the inhabitants of Brewood were going to institute proceedings in Chancery

154

against the Trustees. They employed Messrs. Wilks and Millithorpe of Finsbury Place, London, as solicitors, and the case would be presented to the Chancellor, Lord Brougham, an advocate of education. The amount of the subscriptions raised to pay the legal costs was £342.[30] The Trustees replied that they were at all times anxious to render the school as useful as possible. The charges for writing lessons continued.

Fear of cholera in Brewood

The problems at the school were overshadowed in 1832 by an epidemic of Asiatic Spasmodic Cholera across Staffordshire and other counties. On 27 August 1832 the inhabitants of Brewood held a special meeting to decide what should be done. Bilston and other towns nearby, were particularly hard-hit by the epidemic and, as the causes of cholera were then not known, there was a real fear that it could quickly spread to Brewood. Thomas Giffard's offer of the Malthouse in Dean Street for a cholera hospital was accepted, as was William Bratt's offer of bedding. Fortunately, there is no evidence that anyone was taken ill in Brewood, and the town was declared free of cholera in September 1832.[31]

Mr Wade and others continued in their quest to obtain a "Free School of Learning" for the inhabitants of Brewood parish, and made their mission public through meetings and the newspapers.[32]

The impact of the 1840 Grammar Schools Act

In 1840 the Grammar Schools Act was passed by parliament and allowed grammar schools to spend endowment funds on modern and commercial subjects, but this was only to be done after the retirement of the master on a pension fund, or after his death. This over-ruled Lord Eldon's decision of 1805 that money from Endowed Schools could only be used for classical subjects.

However, the Act also required grammar school headmasters and ushers to make public the details of their income and the number of pupils. Kempson and Kemsey submitted their returns, which were published in the newspapers. John Hay, Honorary Secretary of the Friends of Brewood Grammar School, commented on the information, publishing his opinion in the newspaper.[33] The headmaster was entitled to two thirds of the income of the rentals of the school and the usher one third, but the published figures, Hay claimed, did not tally. The headmaster and usher were claiming different incomes and some clarification was needed. Hay also noticed that both headmaster and usher had omitted the value of the properties that they lived in, rent free.

The income for both headmaster and usher averaged £420 per annum from 1835 until 1839, after expenses, repairs and collection of rents, exclusive of all losses by bad debts or otherwise. The tenements were old, so the upkeep of the buildings was high, and when rents were not paid either through bad debt or being vacant, the masters lost revenue.

When Kempson took over as headmaster, the Trustees had made him responsible for the Upper School only, but it also became optional for the boys to learn Latin in the Lower School, rather than compulsory. If the pupils wanted to attend the Upper School, then it was essential that they learnt Latin in the Lower School but by 1840 no pupil was learning Latin in the Lower School so, technically, no pupil from the Lower School could progress to the Upper School.

The pupil numbers at the Upper School seemed to rise when Kenyon started his new boarding house in conjunction with the headmaster, but when it failed, the numbers at the school began to decline. In 1834, in spite of an increase of population to 4,000 people in Brewood and district, the numbers of pupils had declined so much that there were only four boarders and one day pupil and the numbers dropped further in 1835. The salary for the masters was dependent on the rental income from the school property, rather than the number of pupils, and so the system did not encourage the masters to increase the number of pupils attending the school.

Between 1813 and 1834, the usher, Reverend Matthew Kemsey received an annual income from the properties which averaged around £134 per annum, fluctuating between £126 and £143. Income was deducted for repairs to the rental properties on the estate and any bad debts. Kemsey stated that he lost income from three insolvent attorneys to the school, who had been appointed by the Trustees. Mr Perks, for example, agent to the Trustees and receiver of the rents had died insolvent in 1810 and Kemsey lost part of his income. The next attorney appointed had died insolvent in 1827 and again owed money to the school estate. The following attorney was dismissed for "unauthorised and extravagant charges" in 1835, and again Kemsey lost income. Reverend Kempson would have also suffered financial loss, for the same reasons.

1813	8 boarders	**1827**	11 boarders and 3 day pupils
1814	10 boarders	**1828**	7 boarders and 5 day pupils
1815	10 boarders	**1829**	6 boarders and 5 day pupils
1816	13 boarders	**1830**	9 boarders and 2 day pupils
1817	17 boarders and 5 day scholars	**1831**	9 boarders and 1 day pupils
1818	17 boarders and 7 day scholars	**1832**	6 boarders and 2 day pupils
1819	20 boarders and 7 day scholars	**1833**	7 boarders and 1 day pupils
1820	24 boarders and 13 day scholars	**1834**	4 boarders and 1 day pupils
1821	24 boarders and 7 day scholars	**1835**	3 boarders and 1 day pupil
1822	23 boarders and 8 day scholars	**1836**	0 boarders and up to six day pupils
1823	19 boarders and 7 day scholars	**1837**	0 boarders and up to six day pupils
1824	18 boarders and 6 day scholars	**1838**	0 boarders and up to six day pupils
1825	13 boarders 9 day scholars	**1839**	0 boarders and up to six day pupils
1826	12 boarders 4 day scholars		

Brewood Upper School, Reverend Kempson, headmaster.

Source: *Wolverhampton Chronicle and Staffordshire Advertiser,* 20 May 1840, p. 3.

With regard to the number of scholars in Lower School, no documents were available for the years 1802-1804, but from 1805 until 1809 Matthew Kemsey had between 23 and 25 pupils per year. Then in 1810 it increased to 30. In 1817 it peaked to 56 students, but usually averaged about 30 students. Note that the 1817 figure of 56 pupils at the Lower School differed from the figure of 36 pupils submitted to the Trustees meeting.

1805	25 pupils	**1823**	17 pupils
1806	25 pupils	**1824**	19 pupils
1807	22 pupils	**1825**	24 pupils
1808	23 pupils	**1826**	31 pupils
1809	23 pupils	**1827**	26 pupils
1810	30 pupils	**1828**	24 pupils
1811	26 pupils	**1829**	20 pupils
1812	33 pupils	**1830**	31 pupils
1813	38 pupils	**1831**	38 pupils
1814	40 pupils	**1832**	49 pupils
1815	53 pupils	**1828**	34 pupils
1816	43 pupils	**1834**	26 pupils
1817	56 pupils	**1835**	32 pupils
1818	40 pupils	**1836**	42 pupils
1819	36 pupils	**1837**	38 pupils
1820	32 pupils	**1838**	43 pupils
1821	21 pupils	**1839**	28 pupils
1822	21 pupils		

Brewood Lower School, Reverend Kemsey, usher.

Source: *Wolverhampton Chronicle and Staffordshire Advertiser,* 20 May 1840, p. 3.

The argument about fees for writing and arithmetic at the Grammar School continued with a public meeting at the Lion Inn at four o'clock in the afternoon of 23 July 1840. Charles Wade chaired the meeting, supported by John Hay, Honorary Secretary of the Friends of Brewood Grammar School and Reverend Fernie, the Congregationalist minister. Those who attended confirmed that they were prepared to take the matter to Chancery but it was decided that first a delegation would speak to the

Trustees at their meeting on Friday 7 August 1840. The Friends also wanted to raise other points of concern, such as their belief that the whole school needed to be under the control of the headmaster, the need for annual examinations and the Friends wanted all pupils of the school to be allowed to use the playground. In addition, there should be no charge for heating.

At the meeting people gave their opinions as to why there should not be a charge for reading, writing and arithmetic. Mr Lister stated that at Birmingham Free Grammar School the Trustees did not charge foundation boys for other branches of learning. Mr Austin and Mr Plant noted that 40 years ago there were also complaints about charges for education at Brewood Free Grammar School and a petition against fees for writing and arithmetic had been signed by 79 people from the parish in November 1800. The present petition was signed by 200 people.

At their meeting of 7 August 1840, the Trustees again looked at the constitution of the Grammar School. They ruled that every boy in the school should be taught Latin, and it was to be enforced. The headmaster was to have the superintendence of the whole school and its management. There were to be regular school examinations presided over by someone outside of the school and the Trustees had to give their permission for each new child to be admitted to the school. It was finally agreed that heating in the School Room would be paid from the funds of the school and that from the 1 January the playground would be open to all the boys of the school without distinction. Mr Robinson, solicitor for the Trustees was appointed as the new receiver of the rents, and had the authority to give tenants notice to quit. The Trustees wanted it known that the resolutions were passed without any reflection on the headmaster or usher.[34]

At their meeting at the Long Room in the Lion Inn, Hay, as Honorary Secretary, addressed a large gathering of people. He felt that the meeting with the Trustees had been very successful and "never had he seen more strikingly displayed the high characters of English noblemen and gentlemen". Hay reported that the Trustees had agreed to six of their seven requests which received loud cheers, especially with regard to no longer having to pay for the heating. The demand of the Friends that fees for writing and arithmetic be dropped was deferred and would be looked at again at the October meeting of the Trustees. The Friends again reiterated that the resolutions did not reflect on either the headmaster or usher, or their management of the school. They had both carried out their duties according to the rules of the Trustees.[35] It would be hard to see why Kempson and Kemsey would not find this a reflection on their teaching.

On 19 August 1840 a notice by a correspondent for the *Wolverhampton Chronicle and Staffordshire Advertiser* claimed that the Trustees' new regulations would soon restore the school to its former glory. Some of the Trustees who were said to have promised this were Earl Talbot, the Earl of Dartmouth, Lord Ingestre, the Dean of Lichfield, T.W. Giffard and E. Monckton. The Trustees had agreed to return to the foundation rules and every boy entering the school would learn Latin. The entire school was to be the responsibility of the headmaster, rather than the Lower School being solely the responsibility of the usher. The Trustees wanted it known that the masters were acting under the existing regulations of the Trustees and that the school could not be under better superintendence than that of Reverend Kempson.[36]

The resignations of Kempson and Kemsey

In spite of the compliment, Mr Kempson was not happy with the outcome of the meeting and felt that he did not want to take on more responsibility for the school. He wrote to Earl Talbot, Chairman of the Trustees, saying that the resolutions of the Trustees meeting were not in accordance with his appointment as headmaster. He was aware that the regulation of the Lower School could be changed even though he had been headmaster of the school for 28 years but it was not fair at this point in his life, to take on more duties than had originally been agreed. He claimed to be too old to take on responsibility for the whole school and the whole management of it. He was happy to continue under the present arrangement but the meaning of the word "responsibility" he felt, was not understood. "Responsibility is a word of import – something materially different from superintending, or inspecting or advising". He was happy to inspect the progress of the boys in Latin and promote their admission to his own School, but the Upper and Lower School had to be fundamentally distinct as to their management.

The usher was appointed by the Trustees, and therefore he had to be accountable to the Trustees in the discharge of his duties.

As for the issue of the playground, when Reverend Kempson was appointed as headmaster, the Trustees had agreed that a field adjoining the Upper School and the premises of the headmaster would be used as a playground solely for the boys of the Upper School, as a privilege to them.

Mr Kempson reminded the Trustees that Section 10 of the new Grammar Schools Act of 1840 allowed for previous agreements to remain, unless the headmaster or usher gave their consent to the changes, which Kempson did not. He had worked with Kemsey for many years, was his friend, and would not have wanted to suddenly undermine his authority. It would not be good for him or Brewood Grammar School. The fact that the Friends of the School had made a public meeting of their success also undermined the authority of the masters, and the Trustees were increasing their powers of authority too. In the end both masters resigned.

At the Trustees meeting of 2 October 1840, Kemsey submitted his resignation from Christmas but wanted the Trustees to agree that he could stay in his house and receive an annuity of £50 for life, out of the funds of the school estates. He also wanted to be exempt from paying the annual five guineas for repairs, as was agreed since 1801. The Trustees agreed and wanted it recorded they appreciated his long service to the school.

A notice for the vacancy of second master was placed in the newspapers by the Trustees. The person appointed would be required to ground the boys in the Latin to qualify them for admission into the Upper School, and to instruct them in the English language, geography, history, writing and arithmetic.

On Thursday 12 November 1840 at 4 pm, the Friends of Brewood Free Grammar School met to discuss this notice which further said that the appointed person would now be allowed to take boarders and could have a church preferment. The Friends did not want the latter points allowed.[37] The Trustees did not listen. On 8 December 1840 they elected Mr Arthur Baynham of Pembroke College, Oxford, to the post. He was allowed to take eight boarders and, if he was in holy orders, to take Sunday duty but not the cure of souls. Mr Baynham also had to execute a bond of £500, and could be relieved of his post if he neglected his duties. Arthur Baynham was not initially ordained but obtained his curacy later at Daventry. He did not stay at the school for long, resigning due to ill health. The post was advertised again, in December 1841, before the official Trustees meeting in January where the Trustees thanked him and expressed their regret that the state of his health had deprived them of his valuable services to the school. Arthur Baynham lived until he was 73, dying at his home on 6 January 1892 at the vicarage, Bishops Lavington, Devizes.

On the 1841 census, Baynham was living in Stafford Street, Brewood, as Kemsey was still residing in the Usher's House. Edmund Clay, an 18-year-old teacher at the school was lodging with Kemsey. They had a servant to look after them, Mary Ann Leadbetter. Kempson was living at the School House, as would be expected. Kempson's faithful deaf and dumb servant Thomas Oldfield was with him, as were his other servants Esther Wilcox and Eliza Reynolds, both aged 20 and both born in Staffordshire.[38] Mary Kempson, the headmaster's wife, was not recorded at Brewood but may possibly have been the Mary Kempson visiting Peter Kempson, miller, and his family at Edgbaston.

Mr Kempson resigned a few months after Reverend Kemsey, but with effect from 29 September 1841, and received a payment of £200. Mr Kempson also gave health issues as his reason for resigning. The Trustees wanted it recorded again that they held Mr Kempson in high esteem and appreciated his long service to the school.

On 4 and 5 October 1841 Reverend Kempson auctioned off his household effects. There were catalogues available at the Grammar School, the offices of John Kempson and Son, auctioneers, at 32 New Street, Birmingham, and the offices of the *Chronicle Newspaper*, Wolverhampton. Amongst the items were four post and tent bedsteads with carved mahogany foot posts clothed in moreen, chintz and other draperies, mahogany chests of drawers, gentlemen's wardrobes, a Grecian couch, Brussels carpets, two large libraries with glazed fronts and cupboards below, ornamental book stands and several clocks.[39]

Kempson leaves Brewood

Reverend Kempson moved to Long Preston, near Skipton in Yorkshire. He had been vicar there from 1809, but absent for a lot of the time. Long Preston was very close to his wife's family, the Ingrams of Giggleswick.

Reverend Kempson remained living at the vicarage at Long Preston until his death on 17 October 1857, aged 78 years. He was buried on 23 October at Long Preston, in spite of his wish to be buried at the family tomb in Handsworth, or the churchyard in Birmingham. However, when his wife died at Giggleswick in May 1870, she was buried, with her husband, at Long Preston.

In his will, Reverend Henry Kempson wanted a mural monument of marble with a brief inscription to be placed where his remains were interred and another similar one in the church of Long Preston, cost not above £50. His name was to be written on the mural tablet already at Handsworth church. The church where his body was interred was to receive £200 stock of new three per cent bank annuities free of legacy duty but the money was to be used to maintain the mural monuments and to form or support a clothing club for the poor of the parish.

Reverend Kempson described his loving wife, Mary, as conscientious and intelligent. He bequeathed her all the books in the house which had belonged to her father, the late Reverend Rowland Ingram, as well as the books she had bought herself for her "own particular use and instruction". Henry Kempson also gave her Scott's *Commentary on the Bible*, Johnson's Dictionary, Chalmers *British Essayists*, James Ingram's *Memorials of Oxford*, and the *Parliamentary Gazetteer*, obviously a learned lady. The rest of his library he wanted shared equally between named family members, but for certain particular tomes he specified his bequests. The manuscript books kept in an iron chest were to remain with Mary Kempson but on her decease were to be given to Reverend Edwin Alfred Kempson. Reverend Henry Kempson had also kept a lengthy diary, but it was not to be published.

Mary Kempson was also bequeathed a substantial amount of money, some relating to investment in the freehold buildings in the Bull Ring,

Birmingham, belonging to Charles Henry Cope of the Sparklings, Spark Hill, and other investments in the towns of Birmingham and Walsall. She was also bequeathed the portrait of the Reverend Rowland Ingram, her father, and other portraits, paintings, plates and historical pictures.

There were many financial bequests to individuals. In Brewood, it was not only his faithful servant, Thomas Oldfield, that received some money, but Waldron Ladbury, Fanny Louisa Ladbury and Selina Ladbury, son and daughters of Reverend Kempson's cousin, Waldron Ladbury of Brewood. The Ladbury sisters ran a school in Brewood and in 1848 moved to larger premises at Speedwell House, as it was then known, not Castle, so that they could take boarders. This was the first time that the building appears to be officially recorded as Speedwell.[40]

Reverend Kempson left a substantial amount of money to the schools in Brewood: Brewood Free Grammar School, the National Schools and for an Infant School at Brewood established or to be established. There was also money provided for Exhibitions for scholars but half-yearly meetings had to be held for the supervision of these Exhibitions, and at one or both of these meetings, there were to be public examinations and recitations by the scholars. A considerable proportion of the Trustees must attend. He wanted the presentation of these Exhibitions to be valued, and for this to happen he knew the Trustees had to support the school by showing their presence.

Reverend Kempson gave money to provide a suitable library for the Free Grammar School but a room had to be provided for the proper care for the books. If the Trustees did not wish to do this then the money would be bequeathed to Christ Church, Oxford, instead.

In his will, Reverend Kempson wanted the Bishop of Lichfield to approve a plan for effective religious instruction at the school, and more religious instruction to be given to the National School children on a similar basis to his own church school at Long Preston.

Reverend Kempson also bequeathed some money for the cost of a tablet or memorial within Brewood Parish church recording the several charitable bequests that he had made. This would not have been done for his memory, but would mean that the charities would continue to receive their due bequests, rather than be forgotten. Kempson also made money available for the vicar to distribute clothing and fuel to the poor and deserving of the parish of Brewood at Christmas, as long as they were regular attendants of the Established Church.

In addition, there were bequests to the infirmaries at Stafford and Leeds, and the following Birmingham charities: the General Hospital, Queens Hospital, the Orphan Asylum for Infants, the Asylum for the Blind, the Asylum for the Deaf and Dumb, the Magdalen Asylum and the Blue Coat Charity School. Reverend Kempson also bequeathed money to the School for Clergymen's daughters at Casterton near Kirkby Lonsdale and to Clergyman's Widows and Orphans in the Diocese of York and Ripon. He ordered that the almshouses at Long Preston should be taken down and ten new ones built and the adjoining chapel, known as the Hospital of James Knowles in Long Preston, be rebuilt.

The three executors of Reverend Henry Kempson's will were his wife, Mary, Edwin Kempson, minister of Castle Bromwich who was his cousin, and Sir Richard Paul Amphlett, who had been a pupil at Brewood Grammar School. Mary Kempson died on 3 May 1870 at Holywell Toft, Giggleswick.

Reverend Kempson is remembered in Brewood as an excellent and steadying headmaster who left many bequests for the education of the children in the area.

Notes

1 Reverend Michael Ward had attended Worcester College, Oxford. He became a stipendiary curate at Clifton Campville with Chilcote in 1794 and became vicar of Lapley in 1806, presented to it by Mr Swinfen. He was then presented to the vicarage of Stiffkey with Marston by Marquess Townshend in 1836. He died in 1842, aged 72. *Gentleman's Magazine, January 1842, Vol XVII New Series*, p. 334; *Clergy of the Church of England Database.*
2 Edward Monckton of Somerford Hall was born at Fort St George, Chennai, India, son of Edward Monckton. He graduated at Christ Church, Oxford with a B.A. 1800, M.A. 1803. He was a magistrate and High Sheriff of Staffordshire, dying of influenza on 17 March 1848.

3 *Alumini Oxonienses.*

4 *Clergy of the Church of England database.*

5 *Wright's Leeds Intelligencer,* 6 November 1809, p. 1.

6 SRO, D1416/4/2/7; Will of Simon Kempson, proved 1832.

7 SRO, D1416/4/2/6.

8 *Staffordshire Advertiser,* 27 November 1813, p. 1.

9 *Staffordshire Advertiser,* 15 March 1817, p. 1.

10 *Staffordshire Advertiser,* 18 January 1812, p. 4; *Staffordshire Advertiser* 13 July 1816, p. 1.

11 *Staffordshire Advertiser,* 16 January 1836, p. 2.

12 *Staffordshire Advertiser,* 5 December 1807, p. 1; *Aris's Birmingham Gazette,* 10 December 1810, p. 1.

13 *Staffordshire Advertiser,* 29 March 1817 p. 1; *Staffordshire Advertiser,* 5 April 1817, p. 1.

14 *Staffordshire Advertiser,* 21 June 1817, p. 1.

15 WSL, Misc 706: A. J. Standley, *Imprisonment for debt at Stafford Prison 1725-1835.* Samuel Kenyon, formerly of the parish of Bolton-le-Moors in Lancashire, since of Stone and late of Brewood, schoolmaster, debtor prisoners *and Staffordshire Advertiser,* 21 April 1821, p. 1. Samuel was one of fourteen debtor prisoners whose case was heard at a Quarter Session meeting on 2 May 1821 at Shire Hall Quarter Sessions. Samuel Kenyon had been a Fustian Cotton manufacturer at Breighmet, Bolton, but the company was dissolved in 1796.

16 *Staffordshire Advertiser,* 18 January 1818, p.1.

17 *Staffordshire Advertiser,* 18 July 1818, p.1.

18 Richard Rhead's 73 acre farm with a good farmhouse was sold by auction in 1823. *Staffordshire Advertiser,* 25 January 1823, p.1.

19 *Staffordshire Advertiser,* 20 October 1838 – Assizes, p.2; *Staffordshire Advertiser,* 27 October 1838, p 4.

20 Wilday had bought the house from Thomas Bill in 1825. Originally it had been two houses but Bill had converted it into one house with garden.

21 SRO, D627/17/2.

22 SRO, CEG/2/1

23 Charles Hadfield, *The canals of the West Midlands,* (David and Charles, 1966); L.T.C. Rolt, *Thomas Telford,* (Longmans Green and Co, 1958).

24 Fleetwood lived at Wyre Hall, Penkridge.

25 Peter Brown, *Brief History of Belvide Reservoir, Journal of Staffordshire Industrial Archaeology,* No 25, pp. 25-28.

26 SRO, CEG/2/1, p. 559.

27 SRO, D1416/5/2

28 SRO, D1416/5/2

29 *Staffordshire Advertiser*, 14 May 1831, p. 3.

30 *Wolverhampton Chronicle and Staffordshire Advertiser*, 14 September 1831, p. 2.

31 *Hereford Times,* 22 September 1832, p. 2.

32 *Wolverhampton Chronicle and Staffordshire Advertiser,* 20 May 1840, p. 3; *Wolverhampton Chronicle and Staffordshire Advertiser* 30 May 1840, p. 1 and p. 3.

33 *Wolverhampton Chronicle and Staffordshire Advertiser,* 20 May 1840, p. 3.

34 SRO, D1416/2/2.

35 *Wolverhampton Chronicle and Staffordshire Advertiser,* 12 August 1840, p. 3.

36 *Wolverhampton Chronicle and Staffordshire Advertiser,* 19 August 1840, p. 3.

37 *Wolverhampton Chronicle and Staffordshire Advertiser,* 10 November 1840, p. 2.

38 Thomas Oldfield was deaf and dumb, but was able to read and make himself understood. He was employed by three headmasters of the school, firstly Reverend Harrison then Reverend Kempson for 27 years, and then Reverend Mason for ten years.

39 *Wolverhampton Chronicle and Staffordshire Advertiser,* 29 September 1841, p. 1.

40 *Wolverhampton Chronicle and Staffordshire Advertiser,* 12 July 1848, p. 2.

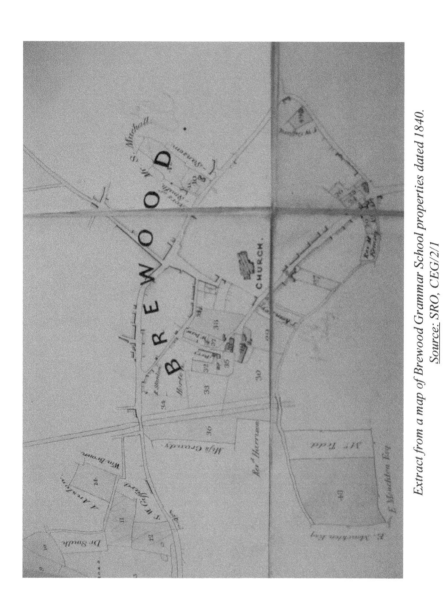

Extract from a map of Brewood Grammar School properties dated 1840.

Source: SRO, CEG/2/1

Reproduced courtesy of Staffordshire Record Office.

Chapter Eleven

Reverend Henry Brookland Mason

When Reverend Henry Kempson resigned as headmaster, the usual procedure for a replacement was followed by the Trustees of Brewood Grammar School.[1] A notice was put in the newspapers that any person wishing to apply for the vacancy had to be a graduate of Oxford or Cambridge Universities and would be in charge of the whole school. He, for the head of school was always a male master for the period covered by this book, was required to teach classics and mathematics to the Upper School scholars to university entrance standards. The headmaster would be expected to live in the "desirable residence" annexed to the office and be allowed to take boarders. His income, from land and property, was anticipated to be £300 per annum, from which a deduction would be taken for the first two years. Testimonials were to be sent to Mr Robinson of Wolverhampton, the Trustees' solicitor, by 28 September 1841.[2]

The Trustees agreed that before the new headmaster was appointed it would be beneficial to look at the conduct and management of the school. They formed a sub-committee comprising some of the most notable landed gentry in Staffordshire: Lord Hatherton, Lord Wrottesley, Major Chetwynd, the Honourable and Reverend Arthur Chetwynd Talbot, Mr Monckton and Reverend Haden. As the school was under the control of the Charity Commissioners, the Trustees had only limited powers, but they came to an agreement that 40 students could attend the Upper School, but only 20 could be boarders. They also made it a rule that no boy could progress from the Lower to the Upper School without the agreement of the headmaster and one or more Trustees.

The new sub-committee came to the conclusion that there should be a charge of 5/- per quarter per child, for the teaching of writing and accounts. This was a contentious decision as far as the parents of local children were concerned as the issue had not been resolved in 1840. Boys of school age who lived locally were entitled, under the Charity, to receive a "free education" but "new" subjects were chargeable to parents and provided much needed income for the efficient running of the school. The fee would cover the salary of a master, appointed by the Trustees, to teach these subjects. To placate local people, the Committee stated that at a later date, when the school funds were healthier, these charges could be dropped. The Trustees delayed any decision about the dormitories, which were badly in need of repair, until the new headmaster had been appointed.[3]

There were more than 30 candidates for the post, of which four or five were "double class" men.[4] The Earl of Dartmouth chaired the meeting, which was held on 25 October 1841, but also present were: Earl Talbot, the Earl of Bradford, Viscount Ingestre, M.P., Lord Bagot, Lord Wrottesley, Lord Hatherton, Henry Howard who was Dean of Lichfield, the Honourable and Reverend A.C. Talbot, the Honourable William Bagot, M.P., Edward Monckton, George Monckton, Reverend Richard Levett, Henry Hordern, Reverend Joseph Salt and Reverend Alexander Bunn Haden.[5]

The young Reverend Henry Brookland Mason was the chosen candidate. He was only 29 years of age, and English master at King Edward's School, Birmingham.[6] Whereas previous headmasters had usually been known as "Mr", Henry Brookland Mason always preferred to be known by his title of Reverend.

Mason was large in both stature and personality, a man of powerful physique, who in his later years, when rector at Navenby, Lincolnshire, managed to stop a prize fight by separating the two contestants.[7] He was an excellent teacher, skilled at delivering lectures, full of energy, popular, kind, thoughtful and had a strong belief in the importance of adult education. He enjoyed preaching and raised money for charity, at different parish churches.

Mason came from a close family. He was born on 13 September 1812 at Lymington, Hampshire, the eldest child of John Mason, an attorney from Plomer Hill, West Wycombe, Buckinghamshire, and his wife Elizabeth Ann née Richman, the eldest daughter of a Lymington attorney.[8] Mason attended Isaac Withers' Classical and Commercial Academy in Lymington which was situated in the High Street, opposite the church. It claimed to "embrace the most useful Branches of modern education adapted to the profession or business which the Pupils are intended to pursue…".[9] The strictest attention was also paid to the pupils' health and morals.[10]

Mason was an academic student and was admitted to Christ's College, Cambridge, on 27 June 1832 under Edward John Ash, who had been the tutor of Charles Darwin, a student at the college from 1828 until 1831. Mason obtained his B.A. in 1837, was elected a Fellow of Christ's College in 1839 and received his M.A. in 1840.

Mason was ordained deacon in Worcester diocese in 1837 and appointed priest in 1838 by the Bishop of Hereford.[11] These appointments were made whilst he was teaching at King Edward's Grammar School, New Street, Birmingham, having been appointed assistant master in 1837. In that same year his family home in Old Lymington was sold, and the day after the sale of the house Henry's brother, John, died in a boating accident on the way to Yarmouth on the Isle of Wight. The mail boat overturned in a squall and nine of the eleven people on board lost their lives.[12] In February 1838 Mason's father died at Honfleur in France leaving Henry Brookland Mason as head of the household.[13]

Mason and some of his family moved to Birmingham and, at the time of the 1841 census, the family were living at Trinity Terrace, Camphill. Here Mason carried out the duties of curate at Holy Trinity Chapel, Bordesley, but was only there for six months before he moved to Brewood. Such was the esteem in which Mason was held in this short time, the congregation presented him with books to the value of £50 as a definite and lasting expression of their regard for the efficient and exemplary manner in which he had performed his duties as curate.[14] This affection that the congregation had for him was to be a recurring theme wherever he went.

Reverend Mason could not take up his appointment immediately, as he needed to work a notice period at King Edward's School and so, with the approval of the Trustees, Edmund Clay, son of Reverend Francis Freer Clay, a master at King Edward's School, Birmingham, took on Mason's duties as an interim solution, boarding at the house of the retired usher, Mr Kemsey. [15]

Mason and Brewood

When Reverend Mason arrived at Brewood he became an active member of the community. The school that Mason inherited no longer exists, but in 1842, a drawing was made of Brewood Grammar School, attributed to John Buckler, and forms part of the Staffordshire Views Collection commissioned by William Salt, a banker, and brother of Reverend Joseph Salt, a Trustee of Brewood Grammar School at that time.

Examinations at the school

Reverend Mason's ability as headmaster is seen in the reports by external examiners who now made independent assessments of the pupils through school examinations. These reports are useful as some pupils are also named. In June 1842 the examiners were Reverend John Abbott M.A. and Reverend Charles Matthew Edward-Collins M.A., both masters at King Edward's School, Birmingham, where Mason had also taught.[16] The examiners were very satisfied with the standard of education that Mason was providing, and were particularly pleased with the proficiency in divinity, Latin and the Euclid. The student Walker of the Second Class was particularly singled out for his high examination marks in every subject. This was either Robert Walker, the son of Robert Walker, agent to Mr Giffard, who would have been 16 years old, or his brother, Thomas Andrew Walker who became a famous railway engineer, and would have been 13 years old.

Whilst it is possible that Mason may have known the first set of examiners, in subsequent years the examiners changed but all gave praise to the high standards at the school. They particularly liked the boys' competence and ability in the Latin and Greek languages, their knowledge of the classical books, their ability in history and divinity but also the pupils' knowledge of general "collateral information". The examiners were as much impressed with the standard of teaching in the Lower School.

Richard Shelton, received a special mention in 1845 from the examiners who felt that "in every subject, without exception [he] has done the greatest credit both to himself and to the school".[17]

In June 1848 the external examiner thought that three boys in particular were outstanding, including one named Cole who "evinced, in addition to his accuracy in the other subjects, an intelligence and mental power in his answer to the Historical question to be highly gratified and surprised the examiner".[18]

Mason was an excellent teacher but he also realised the importance of sport, especially for encouraging team work. The Grammar School boys regularly played cricket against Brewood Cricket Club. In September 1848 Reverend Mason's pupils played Brewood Cricket Club second eleven and won by just two wickets. The young players Shelton and James Underhill were commended for their good bowling. Reverend Mason and Reverend Rushton, the usher, also played cricket on the staff team.

Competition from other schools in Brewood

Although the Trustees had agreed that forty boys could attend the Upper School of whom twenty could be boarders, the number of pupils never reached the maximum number.

Date	Number of Pupils: Upper School	Number of Boarders: Upper School	Number of Pupils: Lower School
4 October 1844	30	19	28
5 October 1846	22	11	24
29 October 1847	20	7	21
14 December 1848	31	13	26
1849	30	13	18

Source: SRO: CEG 2/1

One of the reasons for the low number of boarders continued to be the provision of cheaper accommodation within the village for school-age children, who could then receive a free education at the Grammar School, as they were considered residents. Some accommodation was provided by enterprising local people, giving them extra income, but there were also private schools in Brewood, some of which competed with Brewood Grammar School. One example was Samuel Cholditch's Brewood Academy, a commercial school located in Dean Street. Samuel Stephens

Cholditch advertised in January 1844 that he charged £25 per annum for board and instruction in all the requisites for "a sound Commercial Education". Education in the classics could be obtained at the Brewood Free Grammar School and Mr Cholditch would let a few boarders into his house for this great privilege. He had the support of Reverend A.B. Haden, vicar of Brewood and one of the Trustees.[19] However, whilst Cholditch became insolvent in 1846, he did successfully continue his commercial school.[20]

Building work

The school, as with all buildings, needed continual maintenance and improvements, which were subject to the approval of the Trustees. The dormitories were in a bad state before the arrival of Mason and had been noted as such by the sub-committee of Trustees before Mason's appointment. Thomas Layton, a master builder living in Dean Street and parish clerk for Brewood, undertook some repairs to the School House before Mason arrived, maybe it was to the dormitories, but no details survive. Layton would only undertake the work if he received prompt payment. Reverend Mason understood the financial implications of this and was happy to pay Layton himself, and then reclaim the money from the school's estate manager, John Hay.

In 1846 the Trustees agreed that the Usher's House should have necessary repairs undertaken. Reverend William Rushton had been appointed as the new usher in 1842. He was a keen gardener and the Trustees agreed an exchange of gardens with the neighbouring Perry family in School Lane. Heber Perry, who had been the postmaster for Brewood, had recently died so Caroline Perry, his daughter, was the legal representative. The Trustees also gave their approval to the demolition of a cottage belonging to the school, which had been severely damaged by fire. This had been the home of James Mulloy, an organist at the church, who was blind, and is likely to have been at the southern end of Market Square, where James Mulloy was living with his family at the time of the 1841 census, near the churchyard, the vicarage and School Road.

In December 1848 a staircase was built which allowed the servants to get to their apartments from a back closet in the Headmaster's House. Previously they had needed to use a stepladder which had not only been awkward but extremely dangerous. Following the success of the staircase, Reverend Mason was given approval for a luxury water closet in the Headmaster's House. Edward Banks, who had been responsible for many of the prestigious buildings in Wolverhampton, was chosen for the work. His bill was not to exceed £65: the servants staircase cost £2 10s 0d.[21]

Reverend Mason and his religious work

When Mason moved to Brewood he was not appointed to the curacy at Shareshill, this privilege having ended, as mentioned earlier, with Reverend Hamlet Harrison, but he was never short of clerical duties and supported the clergy in local churches.

On 29 June 1843, for example, Mason officiated at Brewood St Mary and St Chad's church for the wedding of his sister Dora to Frederick William Wilson of Sheffield, a solicitor. In Brewood, flowers were thrown onto the churchyard walk by children when couples were married, and sometimes arches of evergreen were made. A few years later, on Tuesday 26 January 1847 and again at Brewood church, Mason also performed the marriage ceremony for his sister Ethel to John Bourne of Hilderstone Hall, Staffordshire.[22]

In 1846 Reverend Kemsey, who had been usher at the school for almost half a century, died. He was 73 years old. Kemsey had been an incumbent at the nearby St Nicholas's church, Codsall, and was buried there on 4 August 1846. Mason, who had given services at Codsall parish church on previous occasions, officiated at the service. In Matthew Kemsey's will, as a codicil, he wanted his nephew, Thomas Farmer Kemsey to purchase a piece of silver plate to the value of £10 and present it to Reverend Henry Brookland Mason as a memorial to his valuable church services. Later, in May 1847, a large group of people met in the National School room at Codsall and the "principal and most respectable inhabitants of the parish" presented Reverend Mason with a "very elegant and substantial epergne" manufactured at Soho, Birmingham, and which converted into a candelabra valued at eighty pounds. It was inscribed and presented to Reverend Mason to show the high esteem that the congregation had for him, and for the very great benefit that the parish had received from "his uniformly zealous and unwearied exertions for their spiritual and eternal welfare and happiness" during the three years that he had been their minister.[23]

Adult education

Reverend Mason was a firm supporter of adult education through evening classes, he gave lectures on a variety of topics, which not only captivated his audience but imparted a breadth of knowledge. He had an easy, earnest, conversational style which his audience enjoyed. He spoke from the heart, repeatedly pointing out the wonderous greatness of the Creator all around in nature, particularly in his talk about the "Instinct of Animals".[24]

In a series of historical, scientific and educational lectures organised by the clergy, at Wolverhampton, Mason gave one lecture on the French Revolution, and another on astronomy, which the newspaper reporter said was delivered in a "forcible and energetic manner". The reporter went on to describe how Reverend Mason was able to deliver an interesting lecture, and keep the audience's attention on what could be a very dry topic.[25] Mason's lectures were always very well attended and he taught a variety of subjects, not only about animals but also optics, the steam engine and hydrostatics, the poetry of Wordsworth and the Crusades. They were at different venues within Wolverhampton including the Wolverhampton Athenaeum, Queen Street. This encouraged John Hay, of Dean Street, Brewood, to also give lectures there.[26]

Brewood Cottage Garden Society

Mason may have been responsible for the instigation of Brewood Cottage Garden Society, or if not, helped it to thrive. The Society was set up in the 1840s and displays were held in the National School. Mason was a keen participant and, in a letter to Hay, tells him that he has a blue *lobelia gracilis* plant for him. Whilst this initially sounds insignificant as *lobelias* are common now, it may have been one of the first *lobelia* plants in Brewood. The plant was a native of New South Wales and introduced into the country by Sir Joseph Banks in 1801. This plant may have been provided by Reverend Mason's brother, Mashfield, who had strong connections with Australia, and lived there for a while. Alternatively, *lobelia* seeds were available from James Carter of High Holborn.[27]

An interest in flowers and vegetables and the improvement of gardens become a feature of Brewood's social life.

Mason's interest in gardening went beyond flowers. He tried an experiment with potatoes to help find a solution to the failed potato crop in Ireland and the famine that it caused. Information was urgently needed on either how to prevent potato blight or how to maintain a tainted crop. Some experiments had been done on planting potatoes on hillocks and the newspaper *The Downpatrick Recorder* of Northern Ireland, printed the results on 23 September 1848. They used extracts of letters which had been submitted to the *Gardener's Chronicle*. Henry Brookland Mason informed the readers that he had planted 10 tubers of Irish Lumper potatoes on a hillock of decayed turf, the produce of which was 76 lbs, "with scarcely one diseased".[28]

Reverend William Rushton, the new usher, was also a keen gardener, and a pioneer in the teaching of horticulture.[29] Rushton was Honorary Secretary of the Cottage Garden Society and he always exhibited flowers at the Brewood Flower Show, and similar societies at Wolverhampton and Birmingham. The Trustees agreed at their meeting on 3 December 1849, that the usher could extend his garden into the adjoining property of Mr Daw. The new boundary for Mr Rushton's garden was to align with the stable and the fence of Mr Daw's garden. The old buildings in the garden were to be removed as they had become unnecessary and the land adjoining the road was to also be enclosed. If hawthorn was to be used for a fence, Thomas Richards of the Malt Shovel Inn, Stafford Street, Brewood, had 100,000 very strong plants, for sale at £1 5s 0d per thousand.[30]

Railways

On Thursday 8 October 1848 Reverend Mason and Reverend Rushton both attended an "influential meeting" at the Lion and Giffard's Arms Hotel, Brewood, now known as the Lion, about the inadequacy of railway accommodation for people between the towns of Stafford and Birmingham. Numerous other people attended, including Trustees of the school such as Lord Hatherton. The inefficient train timetable prevented passengers who lived in Brewood from reaching Wolverhampton, Walsall or Birmingham until late in the day. This meant that the train service was impossible for use by farmers to attend market, but other forms of public transport, such as horse and carriage, had declined because of the competition of the trains. Reverend Mason continued to take an interest in the development of the railways, after he left the school.

Resignation of Mason

In 1850 Reverend Mason decided to resign his position at the school, no records show why. In his resignation letter to the Trustees, he expressed his sincere gratitude for the kindness that he had received from them. At the Trustees meeting the chairman, Lord Hatherton, praised Mason's conduct as headmaster during the nine years that he had held office and all Trustees expressed their sincere thanks for the assiduous attention that Mason had paid to the interests of the school. It was noted at the meeting that perhaps the dormitories should be repaired, as they were in quite a state. The Trustees had noted the dilapidation of the dormitories before Reverend Mason's appointment and nothing had been done about it.

In July 1850 there was an advertisement in the newspapers for the sale of the "excellent and genuine household furniture and numerous effects belonging to the Reverend H. B. Mason who is leaving the neighbourhood". There was to be no reserve price and the event would take place at Brewood Grammar School on Monday and Tuesday 8 and 9 July at 11.00 a.m. The auctioneer was Mr R. S. Walker of Red Lion Street, Wolverhampton.

The contents of the sale give an indication of what Brewood Grammar School was like at that time. The pupils of the Upper School had beds made of French birch, with mattresses, feather bolsters and pillows. There were also wash stands, dressing tables, chests of drawers, linen chests, one mahogany wardrobe and a mahogany secretaire.

The drawing and dining rooms included more than 24 chairs and a range of tables, as well as a mahogany sofa and a very superior Spanish mahogany sideboard. There was also a pianoforte and two eight-day clocks for sale. Amongst the other items were a four-wheel Phaeton, three store pigs, two hives of bees and a variety of gardening items.[31]

Reverend Mason travels around the country

After eight years in Brewood, and even longer in the Midlands, Reverend Mason left Staffordshire and moved around the country. In 1851 he became curate of St George the Martyr church, Queen Square, Holborn, and was officiating at marriage ceremonies. On the census return taken on 30 March 1851 Reverend Mason and his sisters Olive, aged 27, and Elizabeth, aged 16, were lodging at the home of William Lawson of 46 Great Ormond Street, Bloomsbury, London. The Mason's also lived at home at Dawlish in Devon. The town was a beautiful and very fashionable place "with picnic excursions and pleasure parties being a daily occurrence". A Reverend and Misses Mason were reported in the newspaper as being amongst the fashionable new arrivals to the town in 1850.[32] Reverend Mason, late of Brewood and now of Dawlish, Devon, is mentioned as a clerk in a document of February 1854 as the beneficiary of an inheritance.[33]

Reverend Mason continued his evening classes. On 27 February 1852 he gave a talk about the Crusades at Exeter Literary Society. The newspaper report praised his ability to deliver succinctly a talk about the Crusades and the character of Saladin, using "forcible language" and maps to illustrate the talk.[34] He then continued with lectures at Dawlish to the General Knowledge Society, eloquently covering a variety of subjects.[35]

In October 1852 Reverend Mason attended a meeting at the public rooms at Dawlish, for the purpose of establishing a standard measurement of time in the town. People were obliged to use both railway time and Greenwich Mean Time which led to confusion. Reverend H. B. Mason had done his research amongst the local eminent residents who, with him, supported Greenwich Mean Time as the local time. This had already been adopted at Bristol and Tiverton. The meeting was in favour of the proposal by Reverend Mason and this standard time was almost immediately put into operation. A subscription was opened to defray any expenses that would be incurred in the changeover, and people gave liberally to the fund.[36]

However, in late 1852, the Reverend Henry Brookland Mason accepted the curacy of Bishop's Itchington, Warwickshire.[37] It is not clear why he moved to Bishop's Itchington, but he only remained there for a short while. On Tuesday and Wednesday 24 and 25 October 1854, Mason auctioned off his household belongings ready for another move. The vicarage comprised nine bed and dressing rooms, a drawing room, dining room and a breakfast room. It is likely that he got to know his parish well, as there was a light phaeton to be auctioned, two strong and well-known six-year-old cob horses, and a brown pony. There were also eight pigs, a small rick of new and core of old hay and some outdoor effects.

It is unclear where Reverend Mason was living between 1854 and August 1857. In August 1856 he may have attended Teignmouth Archery Ball where a Reverend Mr Mason and Miss Mason were at the Assembly Rooms but a Reverend W. Mason was the curate for West Teignmouth.

In August 1857 Reverend Henry Brookland Mason was undertaking the clerical duties of Reverend Alexander Dawson Nowell, M.A., rector of the first mediety of Linton in Craven who was suffering from ill health. Reverend Kempson, the previous headmaster of Brewood lived at nearby Long Preston, but he died on 17 October 1857.

Reverend Mason continued with his lecturing work, which was always popular. On 3 November 1857 he gave a lecture on the history of the steam engine at Grassington Mechanics Institute. Again, there was a large audience who were captivated by the speaker. The talk was illustrated by numerous diagrams which showed the improvements of the steam engine by Captain Savery, Newcombe and Watt.[38]

Mason officiated at the marriage ceremony of his youngest sister, Elizabeth, to a family friend, Matthew Folliott Blakiston. The couple were married on 23 September 1858 at Linton. The Blakiston family had also moved from Lymington but Matthew, a solicitor and attorney, and Elizabeth made their home in Staffordshire. Although Elizabeth died young, Matthew Blakiston became a well-known figure in both Stafford town and the county.[39]

In October 1858 the Bishop of Lincoln instituted the Reverend Henry Brookland Mason to St Peter's church, Navenby, near Lincoln. He had been nominated by the Master and Fellows of Christ's College, Cambridge.[40] Reverend Mason had the Rectory House rebuilt in gothic style by the London architect, Henry Astley Darbishire, and it was said to have spectacular views of the Trent. The font, in "lavish Victorian style" was built by Charles Kirk, junior, and shown at the 1862 International Exhibition in London.

Mason did not leave Linton until May 1859. At a leaving party for him in the parish, Mason was thanked for the way in which he had performed his duties and the uniform kindness that he had displayed to all classes and all denominations. He was also praised for his work with the Grassington Mechanics Institute, organizing evening classes and delivering lectures free of charge. Mr T. Musgrove, one of the churchwardens, spoke for every family the length and breadth of the parish. He wanted to thank Reverend Mason for his soothing care in visiting the sick, his earnest solicitude for the parishioners' moral and religious improvement and summed up by saying that "His whole being seems wrapped up in the noble ambition of doing good." He wished him "a very long life, and may it be accompanied with every blessing to you and your amiable and kind-hearted lady". The parishioners presented Mason with a silver salad bowl inscribed: "Presented to the Rev. Henry Brookland Mason, M.A., by the parishioners of Linton in Craven, in conjunction with the members of the Grassington Mechanics Institute, as a token of their deep affection and regard, and as a tribute of a grateful people for his unbounded kindness, his earnest, faithful and unwearied labours during his sojourn in that wide parish May 22, 1859".

Reverend Brookland Mason was very happy with the speech given and was very self-deprecating. He also replied that whilst he was a firm believer in the Church of England, he respected the conscientious scruples of those who differed from him. However, he did not believe that any differences of opinion in religion should matter where there was sickness and sorrow.[41] The kind hearted lady referred to by Musgrove was likely to have been Sophie Caroline Du Bochet whom Henry Mason married on 5 May 1859 at All Saint's church, Blackheath near Greenwich. She had been born in Montreux, Switzerland, and was the daughter of the late George Edward du Bochet and his wife

Christiana Amelia.[42] It is not known how Henry Brookland Mason and Sophie Du Bochet met, but it may have been through Lord Hatherton, one of the Trustees. Sophie and her family did attend the same church, St George's church, Hanover Square, London, as Lord Hatherton and his wife, Hyacinth Mary Littleton.

Mason continued to work hard in Navenby and in early April 1862, a concert of vocal music was given by the Lincoln Music Union in the large school room at Navenby under the patronage of Reverend H. B. Mason, M.A. and the principal inhabitants of the neighbourhood.[43] Reverend Mason continued with his educational career and in 1863 was the examiner for Lincoln Grammar School. He spent four days at the school and enjoyed his task. Reverend Mason stated that the children had a good understanding of the French language and entered into the spirit of it. In fact, in his report to the school, he said that sometimes the task of examining a school was painful, but in this instance had been a pleasant one. He entreated the boys to work cheerfully and willingly, "like horses"![44]

Reverend Mason's high regard for humanity is reflected in the good deeds that he did for the community. In early 1864 he successfully helped one of his parishioners to get her poor relief increased from 3/6d a week to 4/6d.[45] In September 1865 he offered his help in an emergency situation. Mr Goodham, aged 60, of Navenby was conveying a ton of coal from Lincoln. He was walking alongside the cart when he tripped and fell. The wheel passed over his right arm and he suffered a compound fracture. Reverend H. B. Mason took the man to the County Hospital where he was reported to be doing well. The pain the poor man must have been in, is glossed over![46]

Henry Brookland Mason passed away on 23 July 1867 and was buried at Navenby four days later, aged 54 years old. His estate was valued at under £8000. The effects of his household were sold by Mr Richard Hall, of 38 Silver Street, Lincoln, by auction on 24 and 25 September 1867. The whole of the superior household furniture, included an oil painting by Nasmyth, engravings, 800 ounces of plate, 1000 books, linen, china, glassware as well as horse, wagonette, dog cart, harness, stable, utensils, two pigs and a lawn mowing machine. [47]

Sophie initially moved to Havant in Hampshire, but on 14 September 1874, she married the eminent physician Evan Buchanan Baxter, and returned to live in London at Portland Place. Sophie died in 1900.

Reverend Henry Brookland Mason was a compassionate and educated person, highly regarded by all.

Notes

1 SRO, CEG/2/1.
2 *Oxford University and City Herald*, 21 August 1841, p. 1.
3 SRO, CEG/2/1.
4 *Staffordshire Gazette and County Standard*, 14 October 1841, p. 3.
5 *Staffordshire Gazette and County Standard*, 28 October 1841, p. 3.
6 *Aris's Birmingham Gazette*, 1 November 1841, p. 3.
7 venn.lib.cam.ac.uk
8 Henry Brookland Mason was baptised with some of his siblings on 11 September 1817 at Lymington.
9 *Dorset and County Chronicle*, 10 January 1833, p. 1.
10 David William Garrow: *The history of Lymington and its immediate vicinity in the County of Southampton* (C. Baynes, 1825), p. 137.
11 venn.lib.cam.ac.uk
12 *Essex Standard*, 21 April 1837, p. 3.
13 *Ancestry* gives the following details from an original register of John Mason who died 12 February 1838 at Honfleur: wife Elizabeth Anne; parents Thomas Mason and his wife, Elizabeth Maishfield. John Mason was born near High Wycombe, Buckinghamshire.
14 *John Bull*, 21 August 1841, p. 5.
15 SRO, D1416/3/2/11, 30 June 1842. Edmund Clay attended Trinity College, Cambridge in 1843, and proceeded to become a well-respected clergyman.
16 Reverend Abbott, Fellow of Pembroke College, Cambridge, was assistant mathematical master at King Edward's School. Reverend Collins was also assistant master at King Edward's School, Birmingham, and was soon to be headmaster at Chudleigh Grammar School.
17 Richard Shelton became a solicitor in Wolverhampton. In later years, he lived with his brother, John, at Springfield House, Oaken, Codsall, close to Brewood. His law practices at the time of his death were at 47 Queen Street, Wolverhampton, and 3 New Court, Lincoln's Inn. He died on 7 January 1896, at 50 Weymouth Street, Portland Place, London. Richard Shelton was named as an executor of Henry Brookland Mason's will.
18 SRO, CEG/2/1.

19 *Wolverhampton Chronicle and Staffordshire Advertiser,* 10 January 1844, p. 2.

20 *Saint James's Chronicle,* 24 August 1846, p. 4.

21 SRO, D1416/3/2/11 16 June 1849.

22 *Aris's Birmingham Gazette,* 1 February 1847, p. 3. Witnesses at the wedding included Mashfield Mason, Ethel and Henry's brother. Mashfield Mason had been appointed in 1837 as secretary to the new Union Bank of Australia at Cornhill, London. He spent some time in Sydney before returning to England, settling in Hoddesdon, Hertfordshire, where he described himself as a merchant trading in the Australian Colonies, Cape of Good Hope, and Central America. From his home in Hertfordshire, he travelled frequently to London and had offices in various places in the City, but chose his brother-in-law, Matthew Folliott Blakiston of Stafford, to manage his affairs on his death. Mashfield Mason was an advocate for better passenger travel on the railways.

23 *Wolverhampton Chronicle and Staffordshire Advertiser,* 26 May 1847 p. 3.

24 *Wolverhampton Chronicle and Staffordshire Advertiser,* 18 April 1849, p. 3.

25 *Wolverhampton Chronicle and Staffordshire Advertiser,* 1 December 1847, p. 3.

26 *Wolverhampton Chronicle and Staffordshire Advertiser,* 3 October 1849, p. 2.

27 SRO, CEG/2/1; William Aiton: *Hortus Kewensis, Or, a Catalogue of the Plants Cultivated in the Royal Botanic Garden at Kew*, Volume 1, 1810, p. 359; hortscamden.com/plants/lobeliagracilis

28 *The Downpatrick Recorder*, 23 September 1848, p.2.

29 Charles Dunkley, *Brewood Grammar School and the Old Grammar Schools* (D. McGill, 1936), Appendix 1.

30 *Wolverhampton Chronicle and Staffordshire Advertiser,* 20 February 1850, p. 2.

31 *Wolverhampton Chronicle and Staffordshire Advertiser,* 26 June 1850, p. 2.

32 *Exeter and Plymouth Gazette,* 6 July 1850, p. 5.

33 Dorset Record Office, D1/KE/34 15 February 1854. Mason's uncle, Reverend William James Brookland of Netherbury with Beaminster, Dorset who had died in 1842, had been married to Ellen, also known as Eleanor, the sister of Reverend Mason's father, John. The couple had a daughter, Emma May Brookland who had made Reverend Mason her heir. Emma died in December 1845 aged 21, and Eleanor, her mother, died on 10 July 1847. Reverend Mason was not performing marriage ceremonies as either vicar or curate of St. Gregory's church, Dawlish.

34 *Exeter Flying Post,* 4 March 1852, p. 6.

35 *Exeter and Plymouth Gazette,* 9 October 1852, p. 4.

36 *Exeter and Plymouth Gazette,* 9 October 1852, p. 4.

37 *Worcestershire Chronicle,* 15 December 1852, p. 5.

38 *Leeds Mercury*, 10 November 1857, p. 4.

39 Blakiston became a partner in the solicitors' firm of Hand, Blakiston and Everett, later known as Hand, Morgan and Owen, Stafford He was also Clerk of the Peace for Staffordshire and Town Clerk for Stafford, before his death in 1906.

40 *Morning Herald (London)*, 25 October 1858 p. 7.

41 *Leeds Intelligencer*, 25 June 1859, p. 7.

42 *Wolverhampton Chronicle and Staffordshire Advertiser*, 11 May 1859, p. 4; Sophie, born September 1824 in Switzerland, had later been baptised in London at Old Pancras, in 1829. Her father, George Edward Du Bochet who died in 1847 was described as a "gentleman" in the baptismal records of his children. Sophie's grandfather, John James Du Bochet, a coal merchant, had written his will in Montreux, Switzerland, in 1818. His wife, Amelia had died in 1815, but although he had several children to succeed him, he left all his inheritance to his daughter Sophia Berwick, wife of Baron Berwick of Attingham, near Shrewsbury. He describes his London home as being in Queen Street, Mayfair. Probate was granted in 1826.

43 *Lincolnshire Chronicle*, 4 April 1862, p. 5.

44 *Lincolnshire Chronicle*, 26 June 1863, p. 6.

45 *Lincolnshire Chronicle*, 15 January 1864, p. 5.

46 *Lincolnshire Chronicle,* 9 September 1865, p. 5.

47 *Lincolnshire Chronicle,* 21 September 1867, p. 1.

Chapter Twelve

Reverend Henry Brown

The vacancy for headmaster of Brewood Grammar School was advertised in the newspapers after the resignation of Henry Brookland Mason. It was stated that Brewood Grammar School was situated in a delightful place with a desirable rent-free School House annexed to the office. An annual fund of £17 10s 0d was available for repairs to the School House and the headmaster's income would be approximately £275 per annum. The 20 boarders, allowed by the Charity Commissioners for the school, would provide extra income.

Trustees Lord Hatherton, Lord Wrottesley, the Honourable and Reverend Talbot, Major Chetwynd, the Reverend A. B. Haden and the Reverend Joseph Salt met on 14 May 1850 to discuss the testimonials received from the 61 applicants, most of whom had first-class honours degrees from Oxford or Cambridge, and had already been successful as teachers. The following were shortlisted: Reverend Frederick Samuel Bolton, Reverend J. H. Brown, Reverend George Moyle, Reverend John George Sheppard, Reverend W. C. West and Reverend W. Butler.

At the full meeting of the Trustees the following week, Reverend John Henry Brown was appointed as the new headmaster. There are no records as to why he was the preferred candidate. He was an experienced and conscientious teacher, but so were the other applicants.

Brown was born in 1810 at Norton, Derbyshire, the son of John Brown, a solicitor, and Sarah Brown, née Hopkinson. He attended Trinity College, Cambridge, where he did well academically, gaining first-class honours in his B.A. degree in 1833 and obtaining his M.A. in 1836. He was ordained a deacon in 1837, and a priest in 1838.[1]

Reverend Brown's first teaching position was at the new Kingston College, Kingston upon Hull, where he was appointed, in 1837, as

Vice-Principal of the College and Mathematical and Classical Tutor.[2] Henry Ralph Francis, who was the same age as Brown, was appointed headmaster.[3] The school aimed to provide the best education for the sons of the rising generation of "gentry, merchants and influential people in this part of the country". The school could accommodate 200 boys with accommodation for 15 boarders.[4]

John Henry Brown gained a reputation at the school for working hard and diligently for his pupils. He was oversubscribed with boarders but the headmaster and other masters had vacancies, which reflected the popularity and high esteem in which he was held.[5] In June 1838, John Brown married Emily, daughter of George and Emily Rudston of Newland, Cottingham, Yorkshire. She had received a privileged upbringing being described as a gentlewoman on the marriage certificate. Her father, George, had lived at Hayton Hall, Pocklington, Yorkshire, and been a very successful businessman in Hull but, due to some risky investments, had lost his vast fortune and was heavily in debt at the time of the marriage.[6]

The 1841 census records show that, at that time, the Browns had two children, Mary aged two years and Henry, or Harry as he was known by the family, just eight months old. They also had 13 children boarding with them and, to help with the boarders, a teacher, Bedo Boyes. Six servants helped with the household duties.

At the end of 1842, after five years at Kingston College, Brown changed schools to become headmaster of the Middle School at the new Collegiate Institution, Shaw Street, Liverpool. The school was officially opened by William Ewart Gladstone on 6 January 1843 and the ceremony was a grand affair in spite of the dreadful weather. Reverend Brown's Middle School had almost 200 pupils when it opened, the largest of the three schools: Upper, Middle and Lower. The Collegiate Institution was progressive, accommodating adult evening classes as well as regular concerts by the Liverpool Philharmonic Orchestra.

Brown's former pupils at Kingston College wished to give him a gift and chose a silver salver inscribed "Presented to the Rev. John Henry Brown, M.A. by the pupils, late of Kingston College, in grateful acknowledgement of his kindness and services to them while vice-president of that institution. Hull 18th January 1843".[7]

Reverend Brown also seemed to be held in high esteem at the Middle School, as the Principal, Reverend Conybeare, told the Lord Bishop at the prize giving ceremony in December 1844, that W.G. Wilks had refused his prize of moving up to the Upper School, in preference to remaining in the Middle School.[8]

Reverend Brown undertook church duties too. He was preaching Sunday sermons at St John the Evangelist's Chapel, Hope Street, Liverpool, but in 1845 Reverend Thomas MacGill, curate of the church, commented on the delicate state of health of his good friend. He added that Reverend Brown, a faithful minister of Christ, amiable and pious, had won the love and sympathy of all.[9] In November 1846 Reverend Brown was able to take on a temporary position as incumbent of St Augustine's church, Everton, but he may have already been doing some church duties there as, in August, he had christened three of his children at the church: Henry Francis, who had been born at Hull in 1840, Edith, who was born in 1843 and Walter Rudston Brown, born 1846.

After four years successfully teaching in Liverpool, Brown was appointed headmaster of the Royal Free Grammar School, East Retford, Nottinghamshire. At the final "Leavers Assembly" at Liverpool in June 1847, there were 2,500 people in attendance. Reverend W. J. Conybeare, the Principal, gave a speech reminding everyone that Reverend John Henry Brown had been at the school from the start, and during the whole of that time Reverend Brown's "deportment" had been endearing to them.[10] He was cordial, conscientious in the discharge of his duties to both staff and public, and he had many friends. Conybeare congratulated Brown on his appointment but wished he was staying with them. The speech received rapturous applause and Brown's pupils presented him with a very handsome piece of plate. Reverend Conybeare stated that it was the pupils' own idea for the gift, which reflected the high value they placed on his teaching, and the unceasing labours of Brown on their behalf.

Brown was very moved but replied: "It is true that the situation in which I have been placed has been an arduous one, and that the labours required of me have been great, and yet I feel that it is more than a reward for every exertion to know that these exertions have not been bestowed in vain". He added that he would look back with sincerest pleasure to that day, and the esteem and approbation of his colleagues, and the good will of his pupils and their trust.[11]

Brown had been selected from 41 candidates to become headmaster at East Retford Grammar School, also known as the Royal Free Grammar School. The position came with a house, and a salary of £240 per annum which was expected to rise to £300. When Brown left Liverpool, his post was advertised at a salary of £300, so this was less money, but he could supplement his income by taking boarders.[12] At the new school, Brown was expected to educate his pupils to prepare them for university and also for "Commercial Pursuits". The fees were 50 guineas for boarders under the age of 12 and 60 guineas for boarders over the age of 12, with an additional charge for laundry of 4 guineas. Each boarder was expected to provide two pairs of sheets, a silver fork and spoon, and six towels. Day pupils who did not live in East Retford had to pay a fee of 10 guineas if they were under 12, and 12 guineas if they were over 12 years of age. French, German and drawing were provided on the "normal" terms.[13]

Brown's headship at his new school was not trouble free as there were several on-going court cases at the school. In the first month, Brown's usher, James Holderness, was dismissed by the Trustees for failing to conform to the statutes of the school, and also failure to obey the instructions of the headmaster. This was presumably the previous headmaster, William Henry Trentham, rather than Reverend Brown. Holderness had been appointed in 1821 to teach solely Greek and Latin but in 1838, the Trustees expected him to take on extra duties without any increase in salary. Holderness refused to comply and the Trustees regarded this as a neglect of duties. Eventually, after threats of court cases, Holderness left the school in 1849 and Mr Bedo Boyes, who had been a master with Brown at Kingston College, became the new usher.[14]

In 1849, the Trustees proposed that there should be a new Grammar School outside the town centre. This was not popular with the local community and so the expense of building the new school was deferred.[15] In 1849 a Chancery Court case ruled against Cheltenham Grammar

School taking boarders as these pupils would have an advantage over day pupils.[16] Brown, now feared that his income would be depleted if this policy was applied to East Retford Grammar School.

To add to Brown's problems, there had been another ongoing Chancery case at the school, regarding the school estate rents, valued at between £500 and £600. The annual rentals provided part of the income for headmaster and usher. The former headmaster of the school, Reverend William Mould, the present headmaster, Reverend John Henry Brown, the late usher, William Parker, and the current usher, James Holderness, were all owed money, but received nothing until the dispute was settled in 1853.[17]

It was perhaps these various circumstances which motivated Brown to relocate to a more peaceful and pleasantly rural school at Brewood. The post of headmaster gave him a supposed income of £275 per annum, with additional income from boarders. The Upper School was to be rebuilt, with new dormitories on the upper floor, as the others were still in a bad state of repair. The "desirable School House" was ideal for his family now comprising Mary Helen aged 10, Henry Francis aged 9 who attended the school, Edith aged 7, Walter Rudston aged 3, Rudston Calverley aged 1 and baby Madeline Rosa. The family continued to flourish in Brewood with William John being born on 24 April 1851, Percival on 10 December 1852 and Herbert Rudston on 21 May 1855. All the children were christened at Brewood church by their father.

The rebuilding of the school and dormitories

Reverend J. H. Brown and his family arrived in Brewood during the summer holidays and the headmaster wasted no time in announcing that the school would open on Wednesday 14 August 1850. The building work for the promised new school had already begun. William Daw of Brewood removed the roofs, walls and ceilings in the 'Old Schools', cleared the timber and old lathes in the fould yard, removed old quarry and brick tiles and the rubbish in the garden. The builder, Thomas Layton of Dean Street, and his men worked with Daw and stacked 20000 bricks and over 10,700 tiles. They also moved five barrows of mortar which were used to build the wall and fix tiling on the house. Thomas Layton charged £7 16s 5d and William Daw, £2 10s. 0d.[18] Three firms had tendered for the building work and at the next Trustees meeting the respected builders Messrs Higham of Castle Street, Wolverhampton, were selected submitting the lowest bid of £406 7s 10d.[19] George Robinson was chosen as the architect. He was responsible for the Wolverhampton Baths, the Corn Exchange, Christ Church at Gailey, St John's church at Bishop Wood, and the Town Hall in Burslem, amongst other buildings.[20]

The building work was to be financed from a fund bequeathed by a former pupil, Mr Hurd, Bishop Hurd's nephew. As the interest from the fund alone would not cover the costs, some capital would have to be used, which needed the approval of the Charity Commissioners. The Trustees hoped though that this would be an insignificant amount, as they planned to sell the sand belonging to the school, which was still piled high on the canal banks, left over from the construction of the canal in the 1830s.[21] John Hay, the school receiver, was confident that the sand would fetch a good price.

The money from the sale of sand was not as remunerative as Hay had expected. Prior to John Hay's appointment as receiver to the school, some of the sand had been bought by Messrs Hoof, Hill and Moore, railway contractors, for use on the construction of the new Stour Valley Railway. Paul Taylor, a "very steady and respectable man", who lived close to the sand bank at High Green, supervised the work when Hoof, Hill and Moore needed supplies. The firm had agreed 10/- a boat load with payment when their work was complete. Hay monitored the accounts by comparing the number of boats Paul Taylor claimed with those received by the lock keeper at Autherley Junction. The character of the firm was, Hay believed, as good as that of the Bank of England. However, the prompt payment Hay was expecting, was not forthcoming. Hoof, Hill and Moore refused to pay the bill of £248 10s. 0d claiming that they did not owe any money. On 11 September 1850 George Robinson, the Trustees' solicitor, was instructed to start legal proceedings against the company but this needed to be done quickly as Messrs Hoof, Hill and Moore had almost finished work on the Stour Valley Railway and were now selling their boats.[22]

In January 1851 Brown put an announcement in the newspapers that the school room and dormitories had been rebuilt and he could accommodate a limited number of boarders. The school would re-open on Wednesday 29 January.[23] Upper and under housemaids were employed who needed to be proficient in a number of jobs including cleaning plate, waitressing and needlework. A nurse was also employed and a person to do the laundry which, in 1856, was Ann Simpson of Dean Street, Brewood.[24]

Standard of education at the school

Reverend Brown strived to maintain the high standards of education expected of a prestigious school. Henry Turner of Brewood Hall, a previous pupil at the school, claimed that the standard of classical education at Brewood Grammar School had been so high that even Dr Samuel Johnson had been unsuccessful in his application for the post of usher and, under Reverend Kempson's headship the school was like a "little University".[25] However, Brown was struggling as the education system was changing, and the Trustees no longer sent their own children to the school. A commercial education for the pupils was preferred by most parents in Brewood to that of the classical one needed for university.

The number of boarders had declined, and even with the new dormitories, there were only four boarders listed on the 1851 census, taken on the night of 30 March. These were: John Thurstans from Wolverhampton, aged 15, who in later life became a solicitor; Robert Ginders aged 11, son of Samuel Ginders, a land agent to the Earl of Shrewsbury for the Ingestre and Shrewsbury estates; Joseph Spencer, aged 11 from Bilston, who became a grease manufacturer in Birmingham; and William Rudston Garthorne, (although the name is given as Walter on the census return) nephew of Reverend Brown who later became a ship owner and shipping agent.[26]

There were other teachers at the school including: assistant master John Emery, born in nearby Walsall, who had attended Trinity College, Dublin and taught writing at the school; Monsieur Willenboard Buscot, who lived at Wolverhampton, and described himself as a Professor of French; the drawing master, Mr Docker of Dean Street, artist and professor of drawing. There was also a drilling master at the Grammar School, Sergeant Major Smith.

Under Reverend Brown's headship the school received good reports from the examiners, who thought that the children were taught well.

On 17 June 1851 the examiner, Reverend W. C. White, reported that he was pleased with the work of the children. Ginders was described as an excellent student and William Rudston Garthorne was noted for his knowledge in geography and history. In the summer of 1854 Reverend William Lewis Page Mercier, headmaster of Birmingham and Edgbaston Proprietary School, was the examiner for the Upper School. He tested the boys in Greek, Latin, mathematics and French. Reverend Mercier thought that the results of the examinations were perfectly satisfactory and one class, the year below the university entrance scholars, showed considerable aptitude for the classical languages as well as French. Mercier also noted that the behaviour throughout the school was respectful.[27] Reverend Mercier was fluent in French, and so it would have been quite an accolade for the boys to have had such a good education at Brewood in that language, which would have been to the credit of Monsieur Buscot. In 1872 Reverend Mercier translated into English, *Twenty Thousand leagues Under the Sea, From the Earth to the Moon* and *Around the Moon* by Jules Verne.

The praise continued with the examinations in December 1855. Reverend John Edwards of Sheriff Hales, Shropshire, was impressed with the careful manner in which the boys were prepared for their examinations. Their answers, he thought, were accurate and scholarly and it was obvious to him that this standard of education had been going on throughout the year. Commendation was particularly given to the two head boys, Brown and Hay, sons of the headmaster and the estate manager, who were a credit to themselves and the school. In addition, the behaviour of all the boys was, without exception, quiet, orderly and gentlemanly. Edwards agreed with a suggestion by Reverend Brown to make public the overall marks of the boys but only in the Upper School, not the Lower School.[28]

At the end of 1855, John Emery, the writing master, left the school,[29] so Brown took the opportunity to suggest to the Trustees that the tuition fees for writing should be paid directly to Mr Hay, the receiver, before the student received the lessons. Under the system in place, the fees were paid directly to the writing master after the lessons had been taught. The current fee of 5/- per quarter Brown found insufficient to cover the master's salary. This was partly also due to lack of demand and partly because the parents often refused to pay the fees for those pupils who did want to learn the subject. The latter may have been because the parishioners felt that the subject should be taught for free. Brown claimed that he had reimbursed John Emery £120 owing to him from the students, but this was the equivalent of almost £10,425 today.[30] Brown also suggested raising the fees to 10/- per quarter, which although double the amount that parents had been paying was substantially less than the cost of £1 a quarter paid at Wolverhampton Grammar School. There were many candidates for the vacant post of writing master which was filled by James Beaumont Bolton.[31]

The school examiner in 1856 was Reverend Thomas Harris Burn, from Kinnersley, Shropshire, who again congratulated Reverend Brown on his work. The pupils had a highly creditable knowledge of divinity and English history and particularly had an excellent knowledge of dates.[32] A satisfactory report of the students was also given in 1857 by Reverend Henry Erskine Gedge, a master at Birmingham School, who became a curate at Brewood in 1857. He spent two days at the school and his only complaint was that Ward in the Lower School should be promoted to the Upper School as his work was equal to the senior boys.[33] Any boy moving to the Upper School, had to have the approval of at least one Trustee, it was not up to the headmaster.

In 1858 examiner Reverend Thomas Price, assistant master at King Edward's Grammar School, Birmingham, also reported that the boys had all received an excellent education.[34] In November 1858 there were 23 pupils at the school, 14 of whom were day pupils but there were only eight boarders.

Records of the school at Staffordshire Record Office give some names of pupils attending the school in 1857 and 1858. These included: Henry Burgess, nephew of Esther Jones, dressmaker of Stafford Street, Brewood; Corser, possibly John Corser, son of Francis Corser, attorney, living at Harvington Birch, Kiddemore Green, Brewood;[35] Thomas William Littleton Hay aged 8, son of John Hay of Dean Street, the receiver for the school; William and Henry Nightingale, sons of William Nightingale, head gardener at Stretton; John A. Ward, of Bargate Street, Brewood; Alfred Gilbert son of W. Robert Gilbert, builder of Clay Street, Penkridge; John Smith, son of Mrs Sarah Smith of Stafford Street, Brewood;

William Davenport of Hawkshutts Farm, Kiddemore Green; Henry Arnold, son of Edwin Arnold, locksmith of Willenhall; and W. Morris, son of Thomas Morris of Dean Street.[36] The children were now younger than in previous years with pupil 15 year old Brookes being the eldest.

In October 1859, Reverend Brown's 16-year-old daughter, Edith, suddenly died. It was a terrible shock for the headmaster and his family as she had only been ill for a few days. A doctor certified that her death was due to an effusion on the brain brought on by sow fever.[37] Her father was by her side at her death. On the gravestone in Brewood churchyard are the words that Edith was "most tenderly loved" and "deeply lamented".

Financial insecurity and Willenhall

At the time of Brown's headship, and for the period covered by this book, headmasters were not given an annual salary by the Trustees. Their salary was based on rental income from school property, land and dwellings, and additional income from boarders. Any improvements to houses rented out to tenants was deducted from the promised income. The headmaster received two-thirds of the rental income, the usher one third, less certain deductions for costs of managing the estate. Reverend Brown was, until 1853, already owed money from the Trustees at East Retford Grammar School, due to the ongoing Chancery court case, but he was then owed a substantial amount of money from the Trustees at Brewood Grammar School, connected with the sale of some school land at Willenhall.

In July 1842 the Trustees had been successful in their application for an Act of Parliament, to be able to sell or lease school land at Willenhall for mining coal and ironstone.[38] However, it was not until 22 April 1847, that the Trustees accepted an offer from ironmaster, Walter Williams, to receive a royalty of one tenth on the produce of their mines from New Invention, Willenhall. [39]

The school minutes of 1848 state that the Trustees had a claim against Walter Williams, and suggested that Williams consult with Mr Thorneycroft to resolve the matter. This may have been in relation to an offer that George Benjamin Thorneycroft, ironmaster and first Mayor of Wolverhampton, is supposed to have made for the same land.[40]

Then, in 1850, John Hay reported to the Trustees that the amount of Capital Stock from the sale of the Willenhall land was £3879 6s 0d and interest was £116 7s 6d which gave the headmaster and usher a combined increase in their income of £32 7s 6d, over the previous farm land and property rentals. However, the headmaster and usher did not receive this money for many months due to cumbersome legal processes and even lost out on dividend payments at times. The receipt of the promised money was completely out of their control and in the hands of the legal profession and the Trustees. The constant delay and difficulty in receiving any money put immense financial strain on the masters, resulting in both Brown and Rushton having to borrow from friends and family.

In 1853 the Trustees sold some land at Willenhall to Philip Williams of Wednesbury Ironworks, Tipton, brother of Walter Williams, in a sale that was not made public.[41] Henry Turner of Brewood Hall, former pupil of the school, a solicitor and attorney, believed that the Willenhall land had been sold at below market value and should have been sold on the open market. Turner complained that when the Trustees applied for the Act of Parliament to mine the land they claimed that the land was valuable, but despite the growing importance of the Staffordshire Coalfields they had not got a new valuation of the land ten years later. In fact, there was a distinct lack of interest in the matter from the 30 Trustees. Only two had attended the initial meeting about the sale so the meeting had to be adjourned, and then only six Trustees attended a meeting to authorise the sale of the land.

Turner also believed that between £200 and £300 relating to the sale of some school land had never been invested and was now lost. He also claimed that another £600 of Trust money had not been properly sanctioned for the discharge of a large debt contracted by Trustees for, amongst other things, the rebuilding of the new school. Turner believed that the old school had been pulled down without the consent of the Charity Commissioners and had been perfectly adequate for the education of the number of boys attending the school.

Finally, Turner complained that there was a debt of between £600 and £800 to the Wolverhampton and Staffordshire Banking Company, of which £580 was a loan from the bank for the legal costs of the Act of

Parliament relating to the Willenhall lands. The masters had to pay £29 per annum for the accruing interest of this loan which, Turner argued, was in contravention to an Act of Parliament which stated that salaries of the masters should not be less than the salaries that they received at the passing of the Act.[42] The loan of £580 had been obtained in 1843, when Richard Wedge was receiver of the rents. The interest was to have been paid half-yearly to the bank from the ordinary proceeds of the school estate. However, this was neglected until 1847 when the bank manager asked for the arrears of £115 11s 0d. Hay negotiated the interest owed to be added to the original amount, meaning that the debt then rose to £695 11s 0d, but none of the capital was paid off. A new bank manager arrived who was not happy with this arrangement. Hay suggested to the Trustees that they sold some consols and reduced annuities which had been acquired from the sale of Grammar School lands to the canal company thus releasing £720 and enabling the Trustees to pay the bank the money that was owed to them. It would also mean that the masters would be better off by £7 8s 0d per annum. This did not happen.

Turner continued to try to stop the sale of the land at Willenhall and get a higher price for the school. He even tried to borrow money to buy the land and work it as the Brewood Coal Coke and Gas Company.[43] The whole affair was written about publicly in the newspapers, not helping the reputation of the school.

On 21 May 1853 Phillip Williams agreed to relinquish his purchase of the Willenhall property but put his side of the argument. He had initially heard about the sale of the Willenhall land during a conversation whilst at Stafford Assizes. He inspected the land, made an offer which was rejected, and agreed a new price which was accepted. Williams had been unaware of any problem at the time. He now, out of goodwill, would re-sell the land to the Trustees for the amount he paid of £4560, plus his expenses. Any profit that he made from the re-sale he would give to the school.[44]

Turner wrote to George Robinson, the Trustees' solicitor, demanding that the mismanagement at the school and the sale of the school estate be investigated by two unbiased parties, such as the solicitors Mr Hand of Stafford and Mr Charles Corser of Wolverhampton. The Trustees declined to do this but promised a full enquiry at the Trustees meeting of

21 June 1853. However, not only did the Trustees not meet on this date, but they completed the sale on the 30 May 1853 at £67 per acre, which Turner believed was the "bare surface value of the land".

Turner then put the matter before the Charity Commissioners for their investigation. Instead of being pleased, Brown and Rushton were horrified! They wrote immediately to Philip Williams about his kindness and hoped that "any irritating remarks" made by Turner would not interfere with the fulfilment of Mr Williams "liberal intentions" towards the school and that the re-sale of the land would proceed. Brown and Rushton could not afford to wait any longer for financial reimbursement. Their salaries had already taken a sharp fall and they were struggling financially. The masters realised that any court case would be expensive and drag on, which would not be in their interests.[45]

Turner was not happy that Rushton had complained about his "irritating remarks" and wrote a letter to the newspapers, claiming that Rushton had complained loudly and frequently to anyone who would listen, about the mismanagement of the School Charity. Like Turner, Rushton also believed that the old school was perfectly adequate for the number of pupils and that the Trustees were wrong to pull it down and rebuild it.

The farmer of the land in question, Joseph Hemingsley, was also unhappy that he was going to be forced out of his home at Ashmore Lake, and wrote to the Trustees that he was devastated that, at the age of 84, he and his wife, also 84, were being forced out of their home and off the land that he had farmed for 40 years, as well as building a barn, stable and cow house at his own expense.[46]

Williams kept his word and there was a resale of the Willenhall land. The event took place at the Swan Hotel, Wolverhampton, on 2 November 1853. Robinson, the Trustees' solicitor, began the proceedings by reading out a document stating that the land had been unsuccessfully offered for sale in 1843, and again in 1846. Philip Williams' brother, Walter, had taken a lease of 20 acres of land, but after boring had abandoned the workings. Philip Williams denied any knowledge about his brother having any interest in the same estate. The land was bought by a Mr Venables of London for £6,400 which was £1,840 more than Mr Philip Williams had paid.

Turner, publicised the details of the second sale in the newspapers. He believed that when Reverend Kempson was headmaster, he valued the land to be worth at least £17,000, but it had increased even more in value since then.[47] As Turner also claimed that no investment of the money had been made from the sales of Willenhall land, George Robinson now demanded to see the school accounts.[48]

Turner was now short of cash himself and in February 1854, asked the Trustees for financial help on the basis that he had brought more income to the school from the additional sale of the Willenhall land. The Trustees, not surprisingly, refused his request. Turner then appealed to the public via the *Staffordshire Advertiser*, detailing what had happened.[49] In May 1854 Williams made his own statement to the public. He would give the school the promised money but he was unhappy with the accusations against himself, the Trustees, the solicitor and the agents. He claimed that mine agents had been consulted and the price came up to their valuations.[50]

Williams then asked the public how they would like his donated money spent, his own opinion being that the Lower School room was a most wretched place, unfit for purpose. He wanted to rebuild it and proposed an annual public examination at the school with prizes for children's improvement and good conduct. He also offered additional financial assistance for the day pupils which would meet the needs of the local inhabitants. The new Lower School room was re-built at a cost of £633 7s 0d.

Financial strain on the Headmaster and Usher

Hay, perhaps trying to help the masters, was admonished by George Robinson for paying Brown and Rushton some rent money received from the elderly Mr Hemingsley. They were not entitled to it, as it now belonged to Mr Venables who had bought the land, and the money had to be returned to him. Robinson did admit though that the masters were suffering financially from, "the delay of the Commissioners" and suggested that Hay should approach Lord Hatherton to try and resolve the situation by making a personal visit to the Charity Commissioners. Robinson also admonished Hay for "importing Brewood feelings into the matter".[51]

In February 1854 Rushton threatened to contact the Charity Commissioners to inform them of the amount of money owed to Mason, Brown and Rushton. Cleverly, Rushton wanted Hay to provide the figures for the Charity Commissioners, even though Rushton was known for his good accounting skills and was actuary at Brewood Savings Bank. The financial strain continued for the masters and Reverend Rushton was forced to ask James Hicks Smith for a financial loan. James Hicks Smith, better known now as historian of Brewood, was a lawyer in Sergeants Inn, Fleet Street, London, and lived at Dawscroft, Bargate Street, Brewood. Smith wanted Hay to explain why the masters were under so much financial stress. He had already lent Rushton money and wanted security from the income of the school property rentals before lending any more as he did not feel that he would be reimbursed. Rushton claimed that he needed an extension of his loan in order to pay tailors bills and "other circumstances too tedious to go into". Previous ushers had been able to barter their tailoring bills for a reduction in the school fees for the son's education, but this was no longer the case.[52]

The October dividends were late again so Brown and Rushton were forced to highlight their financial situation to the Trustees. The planned Trustees meeting for November 1854 was cancelled so they wrote a letter. Brown and Rushton claimed that the sale of the Willenhall estate to Philip Williams in 1853, and the consequence of the representations made by Mr Turner to the Charity Commissioners, had caused considerable difficulties for them. Although Mr Williams had paid £4,560 for the property, not only had the masters received no money but their salaries had been reduced as they were no longer receiving rent from Mr Hemingsley. Brown had written to the Charity Commissioners in June but they could not give an immediate reply as they were inundated with papers relating to the Willenhall case. The Commissioners had issued a certificate which gave permission for an application to the Court of Chancery for the investment of the purchase money, but that had been six months ago and the masters had received nothing. Brown wrote that he and Rushton could not regard the lack of this income with financial indifference, and the income they were expecting to receive was much smaller than they had been led to believe when they were both appointed. The Willenhall money needed to be invested immediately, if not, the masters would have no claim to the dividends payable next January, and consequently for another six months at least, and no arrears of interest would be paid to them. [53]

Robinson replied that the Charity Commissioners had only given him permission to go to the Court of Chancery, not for the investment of the money. He trivially picked up that it was a five-month delay and not six. In fact, it was two weeks short of six months, and the masters had written "nearly" six. Robinson pointed out that three months of the court delay was due to the court's long vacation. This was frustrating to Brown as his father, a lawyer, had pointed out the matter needed sorting before the court holidays, which he, in turn, had pointed out to Robinson. The solicitor claimed that he was also very anxious to resolve the matter. When the case finally went to court, the Vice-Chancellor ordered the case to be held over for a special affidavit respecting the Bank advance. This rendered it impossible to get any of the owed money to the masters.

By February 1855 neither Brown nor Rushton had received any dividend money, in spite of their request for help from the Trustees. The delays were due to niggling legal requirements, for example, a new power of attorney was required, signed by five Trustees, and the required affidavit was not accepted. In April 1856 John Gibbons Low, the assistant bank manager at the Wolverhampton and Staffordshire Banking Company, paid out too much money to Reverend Brown by 10/-, based on the previous dividends, so that money had to be returned. Josiah Wiley, manager of the bank, then wrote to Hay to make him aware of a payment made on Brown's life policy. Wiley, then refused Brown any more loans so Brown was borrowing from other people in Brewood such as Hay, and also a Mr Fox, who wanted his debt repaid, probably John Fox of the Angel Inn at the corner of Stafford Street and Bargate Street. On 6 November 1856 Brown could not even pay the £2 laundry bill to Mrs Simpson, and several staff had left. Brown continued to blame his poor finances on the Trustees for their indifference to the situation, which, he felt, had been brought on by the lack of regular income.

Philip Williams kept his word and in 1855 plans were made to build a new schoolroom for the usher, with dormitories above. William Godfrey of Birmingham, who had built St Paul's church, Coven, agreed to build the new school according to drawings and specifications provided by

Edward Banks a respected Wolverhampton builder who built the Royal Hospital, Wolverhampton.[54] Whilst the new school was being built, Reverend Rushton also had the gulley end of his house replaced and a culvert made, the brewhouse with the chimney was taken down and rebuilt, a new staircase was constructed from Rushton's entrance with a new hall floor, and the cellar windows were improved. There was also a door step made from Brewood stone, the garden wall was repaired and a new iron fence and gate were provided. [55]

The Charity Commissioners finally, on 8 February 1855, made their report about the sale of the Willenhall land. They did not believe that the Trustees had been negligent in their duties "even though the purchaser realised a considerable profit by the resale of the property, and maybe the last purchaser will do so too". Robinson was very happy with the report.[56] Although the Charity Commissioners did absolve the Trustees and their agents from any wrong doings, George Griffith in his report of the *Free Schools and Endowment of Staffordshire* published in 1860 did not agree. He believed, like Henry Turner, that the sale of the land had been carried out with unnecessary haste and that there should have been a proper valuation. He also added that there was a ridiculous rule that no boy could be moved from the Lower to the Upper School without the sanction of one or more Visitors or Trustees. When George Griffith wrote his report only 18 pupils were at the school, and no boarders at the Headmaster's House. The usher, Reverend Rushton, had one boarder and eight day scholars. Griffith blamed the decline in the school to two factors: firstly the parishioners had no say in school matters, and secondly the Trustees all lived too far from the school. Griffith felt that such indifference by the Trustees should not be tolerated, and the parishioners should have some power.[57] Immediately after the Charity Commissioners report, the Trustees did give instructions for the headmaster and usher to receive their rents on a regular basis.

School rentals and repairs

Hay was responsible for improving the school estate, and properties that belonged to the school were not only in Brewood, but in different parts of Staffordshire. The headmaster and the usher received rental income of two thirds to the headmaster and one third to the usher, but had to pay for improvements and repairs, not decided by them, but by the estate manager and Trustees. Mr Hay, as the estate manager, wanted the school estate to be thriving. Hay was so successful in his work that at the meeting of the Trustees on Tuesday 4 November 1856, he was appointed secretary in addition to receiver. His salary increased from 10 guineas per year to £20.

The Trustees wanted Hay to improve the school estate but the measures that Hay implemented began to impinge greatly on the masters' income. Reverend Rushton was now, for the first time, being billed for repairs to the Headmaster's House. This had never happened in the 11 years that he had been at the school, and he felt that it was not only unfair but the extra cost had been imposed on him without prior notice.[58]

An example of the improvements that John Hay made to the cottages in 1850 was the removal of thatch from one cottage, replacing it with tiles, which cost £20. The same cottage had no water supply, so he agreed with the owner of the adjoining cottage that a well could be sunk and a pump erected. The rent could only be increased a little, as the owner, a widow, was paying a high rent anyway. The impact that this would have on the masters was more expense but little additional income, but John Hay was doing his job, improving the school estate.

The new National School was built in 1859 and Hay wanted to convert the old National School premises, which belonged to the Grammar School, into five good cottages at a cost of between £250 and £300. He then wanted to make substantial improvements to three cottages and a stable in Dean Street which Hay believed were "absolutely necessary to preserve the condition of the estate". The largest of the cottages was next door to Samuel Cholditch and his school. It had been occupied by Jane Wallers, an elderly widow, who had been averse to any alterations or repairs on the house. Following her death Hay wanted substantial improvements made: a thorough repair of the range, the removal of some offensive outbuildings near to the back doors of the houses, privies and pigsties to be provided, and the gardens re-divided. Hay wanted to convert the stable into a house, and the main cottage into two homes. In this way the rental income from the premises would increase and the cost would only be £6. Reverend A. B. Haden approved of the idea but Major W. F. Chetwynd of Brockton Hall was more cautious. He believed that for such a large number of improvements a meeting of the Trustees would have to be convened. Chetwynd felt that the masters would also strongly object to having to pay more money for improvements out of their incomes. The masters had no control over the decision though.

Chetwynd suggested an interim measure of spending £15 on general repairs to the cottages. Lord Wrottesley gave Hay his approval for the improvements but did not see the point of dividing the principal cottage into two as it would be very small and after the alterations would not provide much more rent, but he allowed Hay to use his judgement. Lord Hatherton also gave his approval but added that he thought that the masters did not need to be consulted as it was the duty of the Trustees to make improvements to the estate. However, he did advise spreading the expenses over three years, through the incidental fund, rather than burdening Brown and Rushton with the expense in one outlay. This confirms that the Trustees had some awareness of the financial difficulties of Reverends Brown and Rushton.

Hay suggested to the Trustees that the headmaster and usher should receive the first Ladyday rents without deduction for the building work. This initially shows some empathy towards the financial struggles of the masters until Hay added that he had agreed to pay the contractors interest on the amount owed at a substantial rate of 5% per annum, and the payment would come out of the Michaelmas rents. Hay did suggest that the payment should be made over two years. The masters would have an increased rent from the properties, but would have had the bill for the work and the high interest rates to pay too. With fewer pupils boarding at the school and the maintenance required at the school, which came out of their own finances, life was hard. [59]

The new road and the larger churchyard

During Reverend Brown's headship there was a plan to enlarge the churchyard, opposite the school and demolish some houses on the south side of Market Place, allowing a new road, now known as Church Road, to be built connecting Dean Street with Market Place. The Grammar School was close to the proposed new road and instead of having the safe cul-de-sac which the boys often used as a playground, in addition to their allocated ones, the area would be a thoroughfare for traffic, and no longer safe for a play area. Whatever the views were locally, Brown could not have been entirely happy with this proposal as it meant curtailing the playground for his pupils. The building of the canal through the school lands in the 1830s had already reduced the play area.

Whatever Brown's opinion, the proposals for the enlarged churchyard and the new road met with the approval of Brewood Grammar School Trustees and that was the end of the matter. They approved the exchange of some land between Charles Corser, a solicitor, and Henry Underhill and James Edward Underhill, former pupils at the school.[60] Corser wanted to exchange with the Trustees the house and garden at that time in the occupation of Mr Pearson "with two cottages and building land in front", for two cottages and gardens in Sandy Lane held by Mr "Makins" [Machin] and a field of arable land occupied by Mr Handley of Leafields, Shutt Green, which adjoined Charles Corser's land on Kiddemore Green Road, and through which Charles Corser had a right of way.[61]

Schools in competition with Brewood Grammar School

Samuel Cholditch still provided his Commercial School at Dean Street and there were schools available for the education of girls, not a Grammar School though. A new and larger National School in Brewood was also underway to provide an education for both boys and girls.

More of a problem for the Grammar School was Broadgate School which also opened in 1859 at Market Place, now marked by a plaque showing where Thomas Andrew Walker, the famous civil engineer, had been born. This school was in direct competition to the Grammar School. The principal, Henry Smith advertised that his school provided a "first class mercantile education". Smith had been to a teachers' training college in London, known at the time as "Normal College" and had an impressive teaching record. Amongst his employers were Thomas Milner Gibson, M. P., who later became President of the Board of Trade, and T. W. Giffard, esquire of Chillington Hall, Brewood. Just two years after it had opened, Broadgate School claimed to have many local pupils, but also some from Gravesend and Manchester. The pupils received education in English, French, German, physical sciences, drawing, classics, mathematics, music, dancing and gymnastics. A preparatory department was also provided. Discipline was mild but firm and corporal punishment was not allowed.

Henry Smith advertised that the rooms were lofty and well ventilated. This was in contrast to the Grammar School where the rooms had low ceilings and were a source of complaint by the next headmaster, Reverend Wall. The Broadgate House premises had a large playground attached to the school and there were regular walks to Boscobel, Somerford Hall, Stretton Hall and Chillington, illustrating that Smith was trying to appeal to the students that would normally have attended the Grammar School. Smith also undercut the boarding costs at Brewood Grammar School. This school posed a threat to the Trustees, being in competition with the Grammar School, and may have been one of the reasons why the Trustees thought they needed a change of headmaster.

Dismissal of Reverend Brown

Just before Christmas, on 23 December 1859, Lord Wrottesley, Lord Shrewsbury and Lord Hatherton had an informal meeting and decided that the state of education at Brewood Grammar School was unacceptable and that a Trustees meeting should be convened at the Judges House, Stafford, on Saturday 21 January 1860. A month earlier, they had received a letter from Henry Vane of the Charity Commission clarifying that a master could only be sacked if there was sufficient reason to do so but every precaution should have been taken to prevent this at the time of his appointment. Reasons for dismissal were negligence or being unfit or incompetent in his duties either from immoral conduct, age or any other cause. The Trustees tried to dismiss Reverend Brown for financial embarrassment and drunkenness.

Initially, the Trustees wanted both masters to attend the meeting but, in the end, they were never invited. Reverend Haden tried to avoid the meeting by stating that he was in poor health and old. He offered to write a statement about the state of the school though. Lord Wrottesley tried to pressurise Haden to attend so instead he resigned as Trustee, claiming that a new name would be more efficient, given his age. Haden also wrote to Hay reprimanding him for implying that he, Haden, had known about the "unhappy case" of Reverend Brown. Haden did not wish to be either "an accuser" or "a witness" to the state of affairs, and could not substantiate the charges against Reverend Brown any better or worse than anyone else. Hay had written to Reverend Haden about the almost habitual intemperance of Reverend Brown but Haden replied that he was "not aware of the Evil having reached such an extent till your letter informed me". [62]

Reverend John Buckham of Bishop's Wood, also refused to give evidence against Reverend Brown and suggested that servants, pupils and parents should be asked for their opinion, instead. Reverend Rushton was also supportive of Reverend Brown and wanted to help him remain in post.

At the special meeting of Trustees, the minutes of the meeting held on 4 November 1859 were read and the lack of pupils at the school was brought to the notice of the Trustees. They were also made aware that the pecuniary affairs of the headmaster were in a very embarrassed condition, but this should not have been news to them as Brown himself had brought it to their attention. The Trustees concluded that they would send a letter to Reverend Brown saying that there would be a formal investigation into his conduct unless he resigned.

Hay wrote the letter to Brown, saying that the Trustees were aware of the "present lamentable condition of the School" and as the School had declined under Reverend Brown's management then his conduct as headmaster would be questioned.

Reverend Brown replied on black edged writing paper, in remembrance of the death of his daughter, Edith. He needed to give Hay's letter careful consideration and he needed to obtain advice, presumably legal advice from the solicitors within his family. Once he had done both, he would give his reply. Reverend Brown felt that the state of his affairs had been misrepresented to the Trustees, and although he had been in a little financial difficulty, his debts were not large.

Brown's response, both to the Trustees and Hay, stated that he felt that his work as headmaster of the school had been conscientiously carried out. As the Trustees letter to him was vague, he wanted a distinct statement of the charges brought against him with the dates of any offences supposedly committed by him. He sent a copy of the letter to Lord Wrottesley.

Hay responded on 28 January 1860 that he did not have permission from the Trustees to give the headmaster any details of the charges that the

Trustees wished to bring against him, and he had no details himself. The Trustees believed that the present lamentable condition of the school compelled them to make a searching enquiry into the causes of that condition, his general conduct during the whole period of his mastership would be given in a public enquiry where he could hear and rebut any evidence.[63] Mr Hay was now managing the Littleton estate and living at Teddesley Farm.

Brown again asked Hay for the details of the charges and the date of any alleged offence. He had the right to know as the Trustees wanted his resignation or would submit him to a public investigation into his affairs, on the grounds of certain "representations" which had led them to believe that his pecuniary affairs were in a very embarrassed condition. The Trustees had already condemned him and prejudiced his case, by giving him the alternatives of resignation or public investigation. It was only fair that he knew the charges to obtain advice. If he had been allowed to speak to the Trustees he could have given them an explanation, but they had not done him that courtesy.[64]

In the end, on 9 February 1860 Reverend Brown submitted his letter of resignation to take effect from midsummer. Lord Wrottesley was immediately informed and was happy with the outcome and quite willing to accept Brown's resignation on his terms. Reverend A.B. Haden was also happy with Brown's decision to resign: "the poor family as well as the whole neighbourhood are spared the pain of the disclosure which must have been made had the unfortunate man been obstinate".[65] Henry Chetwynd-Talbot, 18th Earl of Shrewsbury, Reverend John Buckham at Bishop's Wood, Major William Fawkener Chetwynd of Brockton Hall were also pleased with Brown's decision, as it avoided an investigation of both the headmaster and Brewood Grammar School.

Reverend Brown was keen to pay his debts and receive any money due to him too. He paid Hay the half-yearly sum that he owed him for his life assurance on 17 February 1860, but there were delays on some school rents due to him. Brown reminded Hay that any arrears in rent were against the instructions of the Trustees who had ordered that on no account should any tenant be allowed to get into arrears. On this basis Reverend Brown thought he was well within his rights to expect the rent money to be paid to him three months ago, when he should have received it. Hay complained to Brown that he was being unjust in his "murmurs of non-receipt of Rents" which he should have a clear knowledge about, but Brown retorted that any criticism was all in Hay's imagination, and that he could not think it was wrong to expect prompt payment of money.

On 27 April 1860 Reverend Brown wrote again to the Trustees about his forced resignation and how the falling school numbers had been unfairly represented to them. He felt that they had been led to believe that the state of his finances had impacted, in part, on the school and they should have given him the opportunity to refute the claims instead of condemning him at Stafford in his absence. He believed that the Trustees had been intentionally misled. He did not deny that the death of his daughter and his son, Henry's, departure for India was an expensive time for him but he believed that it was the intention of the Trustees, weeks before the meeting, to remove him from the school. In fact, he had since been told this personally, and later realised that everybody in Brewood seemed to know but himself. In Reverend Brown's opinion it was impossible that the rumours of his resignation could have originated with the Trustees, and in fact, he had no doubt as to who had spread the rumours, referring to John Hay.

Reverend Brown was upset that the Trustees offered him two options: resignation or investigation. The one would throw his family homeless into the world, the other would bring his name before the public, blighting his future prospects which is why he chose the option to resign. In view of the fact that he had not been given the opportunity to defend himself, Reverend Brown felt that it was only fair that the Trustees should grant him some compensation. Mr Kempson, a retiring previous headmaster, had been given an amount of money by the Trustees when he left. Brown had been headmaster of Brewood Grammar School for ten years, and had during that time taught an average of 40 pupils, faithfully and conscientiously. He could produce the testimonies of both boys and parents on that point. He felt that his success with his pupils could be proved as they attended some of the largest public schools in the country and the examiners, appointed by the Trustees, had confirmed the soundness of his teaching. He regretted that no examination was held last year. He believed that the standards of education had not fallen, even though the number of boys at the school was low.

In March the advertisement for a replacement headmaster quoted the salary arising from rents and dividends as averaging £280 per year with ample room for 20 boarders. When Reverend Brown left Brewood Grammar School, he was presented by the masters and Fellows of Trinity College Cambridge, with the vicarage of North Holme and the perpetual curacy of Langford, Nottinghamshire. This only gave him a small income of £84. John Hay must have realised that the fluctuating salary that the masters received through rentals contributed to the financial problems of both Brown and Rushton. He wanted the Trustees to appoint a new headmaster on a fixed salary, but Wrottesley replied that the Trustees did not have that power.

Brown finally presented his case to the Trustees on the day of the interviews. He wanted the Trustees to read the letters of Dr Benjamin Kennedy, headmaster of Shrewsbury School, and Reverend Henry Highton, D.D., headmaster of Cheltenham College as they had found no fault with Reverend Brown. On this basis, he wanted the Trustees to give him a testimonial which would allow him to obtain another appointment. Reverend Brown wanted the money from the dividends due to him and his entitlement of rents. With regard to the alterations of the three cottages in Dean Street, Reverend Brown wanted the Trustees to repay some or all of the £35 that he had been required to spend on the renovations, as his successor would gain from the increased rent, and he would receive no benefit, only cost. Finally, and importantly, Reverend Brown wanted the last ten years of the school accounts to be audited by a competent person, and wanted permission to see the results.

The School accounts

In 1860, after Brown had left Brewood, John Hay came under scrutiny of Mr W. G. Hayter for the Charity Commissioners, who queried some anomalies in the accounts. Hay had left Brewood in 1859 to work for Edward Littleton, Lord Hatherton at Teddesley Hall, but remained as secretary to the Trustees. One query by Hayter related to some charges on the accounts made in 1859. Hay explained that this related to the Trustees changing the power of attorney to Mr Capes, a solicitor of Gray's Inn,

London, from Messrs Glyn and Co, the latter firm having failed to give the headmaster and usher a regular income from the dividends.

Mr Hayter also wanted clarification of anomalies in the accounts for 1854 and 1855, when an additional 16 acres of land belonging to the school appears in 1855 and disappears in 1856. He also wanted clarification over the prize money awarded by Mr Philip Williams when he resold the Willenhall property in 1853. Williams had paid over £900 to the Trustees and the interest on that money was to be used for prize money for the boys. This money was not traceable in the accounts. There were several other problems with the accounts which were not clear and open enough for Hayter's liking. Mr Hay wrote to Hayter on 9 November 1860 from Teddesley and apologised for the inaccuracies in the accounts but he had given them to an accountant and thought that they were accurate. He now had no copy of the accounts. With regard to the prize money, the number of prizes was reduced in 1857 and 1858 as so few boys attended the school, and in 1859 no prizes were given as the headmaster was called upon to resign.[66]

In addition to the Charity Commissioners investigation, Lord Wrottesley also scrutinised the sale of the Willenhall property and the resulting investments, so now the Trustees could only be more knowledgeable of the situation.

Reverend Brown leaves Brewood

Reverend Brown and his family, like his predecessor Mason, sold their goods by auction on Thursday and Friday 12 and 13 July at 11 a.m. at the Grammar School. The whole of the "superior household furniture" was to be sold including oil paintings, water colours and engravings, glass, china, earthenware, a fine toned grand pianoforte by Broadwood and Sons, brewing utensils, ale casks, an almost new mangle, a single barrel gun, and a shower bath with a force pump. There were also rosewood tables and chairs, Brussels carpets and a telescope, amongst other items. Catalogues of the goods would be available at the Lion ten days before the auction. [67]

When Reverend Brown left the school there was an inventory of the items that remained. The pantry kept the slate table, the boys' dining room was furnished with deal tables and book shelves. There were three passageways one for the hats, another passage for the shoes and one which contained cupboards. There was a linen chamber, washstand and wardrobe. The drawing room contained a lady's rosewood work table fitted with a chess top. The garden contained four cucumber frames and flue. The brewhouse had three boilers, two of copper and one of iron. There was also a larder with a hanging shelf for the meat, a water tub in the yard, and the water closet, which had been installed during Reverend Mason's time as headmaster.

Reverend Brown asked John Hay to pay Charles Docker, the art master, the sum of almost £20 that he owed him from the rent due in November. Mr Docker clearly thought that he was entitled to it sooner, but agreed to wait. Brown requested that his portion of dividends and of the rents due in November from the school should be sent to his temporary lodging at South Collingham, Newark, Nottinghamshire.

There is no record that Brown, who had for so long appeared to be a good, kind and conscientious teacher, continued in this profession. He was not the same John Henry Brown who was appointed to Nottingham School Board. Reverend Brown's personality was perhaps not the public outgoing figure who could bring in new students and maintain flourishing numbers of pupils, especially in a time when educational needs were changing, in contrast to Reverend Mason who was always out in the community and travelling, giving lectures.

In 1861 Reverend Brown and his family lived at Holme Hall, whilst their new parsonage at Langford was being built. On the night of the 1861 census, John and Emily were living with their children Mary Helen, Walter Rudston, Rudston Calverley, Madeline Rosa, William John, Percival and Herbert Rudston Brown. Harry had gone to India, and was doing very well in his career. In 1862 the newspaper described Reverend Brown as assisting at the wedding of Miss Burnaby of Langford Hall to Edward Finch Dawson of Launde Abbey, Leicestershire. Reverend H.F. Burnaby, the bride's brother, married the couple. The church was described as being beautifully decorated by Reverend Brown's family with white roses, geraniums and evergreen.[68]

The family moved from Holme Hall to Langford at some time before May 1863, when Reverend Brown was officially declared bankrupt.[69] In 1870 and 1871 he was paying dividends on his debts and his children married or moved away from home for work or school, only his wife and daughter Mary Helen remaining at home. His son William John, who was only 21-years-old, was lost at sea travelling home from Calcutta. He had boarded the ship, *Arcot*, at Calcutta on 10 April 1871 bound for London. The last that was heard of the ship was on 11 June at Algoa Bay, on the Eastern cape of South Africa. It was believed that the ship then caught fire. The family were devastated and did not confirm his death in the papers until 9 February 1872, when it was reported in the *Stamford Mercury*.

Reverend Brown died on 2 November 1872 and was buried five days later at St Bartholomew's church, Langford. He was only 62 years old. His death certificate recorded his death from albuminuria heart disease. A local story has a different version that Reverend Brown went to the cellar for a bottle of port, fell down the stairs and broke his neck.[70] After Reverend Brown's death, Emily went to stay at 4, The Crescent, Filey, near her sister Sophia, also known as Sophy.

The children were successful in their careers. Harry, who had received a lot of his education at Brewood Grammar School, did particularly well, becoming a merchant with the East Indian Company. In 1877 he was appointed Consul General at Calcutta for His Majesty the King of Denmark. A year later Harry was with his mother when she died at Filey. He had travelled from Calcutta to be at her side. Harry had a large mausoleum built as a memorial for his parents and siblings at St Oswald's graveyard, Filey. The monument was of white sandstone with fretwork and lancet shaped windows carved in India with pillars of tinted marble.[71] In November 2018 the Diocese of York approved a grant of up to £1,900 for a conservation report for its repair. The monument has a plaque saying that it was erected by the eldest son in honour of his father and mother. It was also erected as a testimony of affection for his eight brothers and sisters and for other members of his family whose names were inscribed. During the 1880s Harry moved back to Britain, and by 1885, was a partner in Messrs Kilburn, Brown and Co of Orient House, New Broad Street, London, merchant and shipping agents. He died in 1920 and bequeathed, even after debts, about £86,000.[72] The other children of John and Emily were also successful, mainly working in India then settling in Scotland, or sheep farming near Nelson and Picton, South Island, New Zealand.

Notes

1 venn.lib.cam.ac.uk

2 *Globe*, 12 January 1837, p. 4.

3 Henry Ralph Francis was born 11 July 1811 and educated at Brentford, then St John's College Cambridge. After he left Kingston College, he became a private tutor before studying law at Inner Temple. He emigrated to Sydney, Australia where he became a judge. https://www.records.nsw.gov.au/person/193

4 Speech by Mr J.R. Pease, Chairman of the Building Committee when the foundation stone for Kingston College was laid in August 1836. *Hull Packet*, 5 August 1836, p. 4; *Hull Packet* 10 February 1837, p. 3.

5 *Hull Packet*, 19 January 1838, p. 1.

6 www.eastridingmuseums.co.uk Rudston family.

7 *Gore's Liverpool General Advertiser*, 2 February 1843, p. 4.

8 *Liverpool Standard and General Commercial Advertiser*, 17 December 1844, p. 10. This is probably William George Wilks, born in Hull but moved to Everton. He was the son of John Wilks, a flax and hemp broker, and became an actuary.

9 *Liverpool Mail*, 18 May 1844, p. 3.

10 Reverend William John Conybeare, M.A., a preacher at Chapel Royal, Whitehall in 1843, had been a Fellow of Trinity College, Cambridge.

11 *Liverpool Mercury*, 22 June 1847, p. 4; *Liverpool Mail*, 19 June 1847, p. 3.

12 *Oxford University and City Herald*, 14 February 1846, p. 1.

13 *Stamford Mercury*, 23 April, 1847, *Stamford Mercury*, 1 June 1847; *Liverpool Courier and Stamford Mercury*, 30 July 1847, p. 1.

14 *Clergy of the Church of England database*; *Leeds intelligencer*, 18 September 1847 p. 5; *Stamford Mercury*, 14 July 1848, p. 2; *Nottinghamshire Guardian*, 15 February 1849, p. 3; *Stamford Mercury*, 9 November 1849, p. 2. Mr James Holderness, brother of Reverend William Holderness clergyman of the Thames Church Mission accompanied the Bishop to give religious instruction to seamen on a voyage to Hong Kong and Whampoa. In 1851 James Holderness was teaching classics and literature in East Retford.

15 *Nottinghamshire Guardian*, 1 February 1849 p. 3.

16 *The Lincoln, Rutland and Stamford Mercury*, 28 December 1849, p. 2.

17 *Staffordshire Advertiser*, 25 May 1850, p. 5.

18 SRO, D1416/5/8.

19 SRO, CEG/2/1 p. 4.

20 George Robinson moved from Heath House, Wombourne and lived at Manchester, Leamington Spa and Kensington, London. He had been a pupil of John R. Hamilton and James Medland. In 1848 he began his own firm with Henry John Paull and known as Paull and Robinson. He was also a journalist and art critic for the *Manchester Guardian*.

21 The canal was originally known as the Birmingham and Liverpool Junction Canal, but became known as the Shropshire Union Railways and Canal Company in 1850.

22 *Birmingham Journal*, 15 June 1850, p. 1.

23 *Staffordshire Advertiser,* 11 January 1851, p. 1.

24 Ann Simpson was the wife of Lewis Simpson, a carpenter, and daughter of William Daw, locksmith.

25 *Staffordshire Advertiser,* 11 March 1854, p. 2.

26 William Garthorne's brother Walter was not born until 1852.

27 SRO, CEG/2/1.

28 SRO, D1416/5/8 and CEG/2/1.

29 John Emery married Anne Payne of Coven at Brewood church in May 1855.

30 www.bankofengland.co.uk/monetary-policy/inflation/inflation-calculator 2023.

31 SRO, D1416/5/8. Bolton attended Clare Hall, Cambridge and obtained a Bachelor of Law degree in 1859. He was later to become Reverend Bolton.

32 SRO, CEG/2/1.

33 SRO, CEG/2/1.

34 SRO, CEG/2/1.

35 John Corser, son of Francis Corser, attorney living at Harvington Birch, Kiddemore Green Road, Brewood. Francis Corser put his property up for auction and moved to Manchester in November 1858. In 1859, Francis Corser was living at the Hurst, Lapley, when his daughter Elizabeth married Reverend George Monckton, incumbent of Coven.

36 SRO, CEG/2/1 and D1416/4/2/13. Thomas Morris left Brewood in June 1859.

37 Death certificate for Edith Brown.

38 SRO, CEG/2/1.

39 SRO, CEG 2/1; Walter Williams lived at Oxhill house, Handsworth as an ironmaster in 1841 then, in 1851, lived at Summerfield House, Bratt Street, West Bromwich. He was the brother of Philip Williams.

40 Henry Turner claimed that G.B. Thorneycroft made an offer for the land of between £10,000-£12,000, but the Trustees had rejected the money as being insufficient.

41 SRO, D1416/2/2.

42 SRO, D1416/1/4/7, Letter from Turner to George Robinson, 7 May 1853.

43 SRO, D1416/1/4/7.

44 SRO, D1416/1/4/7.

45 SRO, D1416/1/4/7, Letter from J. H. Brown and W. Rushton, to Philip Williams, 11 July 1853.

46 SRO, CEG/2/1, Letter from Joseph Hemingsley to Trustees, 29 June 1853. Although on the 1851 census a Joseph Hemingsley is listed as aged 70 and a farmer of 160 acres at Ashmore Lake, Willenhall. The enumerator may have only guessed his age.

47 *Wolverhampton Chronicle and Staffordshire Advertiser,* 9 November 1853, p. 4.

48 SRO, D1416/1/4/8, Letter from George Robinson to John Hay, 20 January 1854.

49 *Staffordshire Advertiser,* 11 March 1854, p. 2.

50 SRO, D1416/1/4/7, Letter from Philip Williams to the inhabitants of Brewood, 8 May 1854.

51 SRO, D1416/1/4/8, 13 June 1854.

52 SRO, D1416/5/7.

53 SRO, D1416/4/2/8, Letter from Brown and Rushton to Hay, 16 November 1854.

54 SRO, D1416/5/8.

55 SRO, CEG/2/1, 24 March 1856.

56 SRO, D1416/4/2/8, Letter from G Robinson to John Hay, 10 February 1855.

57 George Griffith, *The Free Schools and Endowments of Staffordshire and their Fulfilment*, (Whitaker and Co., 1860).

58 SRO, D1416/5/7.

59 SRO, D1416/5/8 Repairs of Dean Street cottages.

60 SRO, D1416/1/4/9; SRO, D590/790/27.

61 Charles Corser, born 1816 married Mary Thorneycroft at St Peter's church, Wolverhampton, in 1839. Mary Thorneycroft was the daughter of ironmaster George Benjamin Thorneycroft, who had put in an offer to the Trustees for the Willenhall land for mining. The couple were married by Reverend A.B. Haden of Brewood parish church.

62 SRO, D1416/5/9, Letter from Haden to Hay, 6 January 1860.

63 SRO, D1416/4/2/8.

64 SRO, D1416/4/2/8.

65 SRO, D1416/4/2/8.

66 SRO D1416/5/9, Letter from W.G. Hayter to John Hay, 8 November 1860.

67 *Staffordshire Advertiser*, 30 June 1860, p. 8.

68 *Nottinghamshire Guardian*, 26 September 1862, p. 3.

69 *Nottinghamshire Guardian*, 8 May 1863, p. 6.

70 Jenifer Roberts, *Where the wind blows*, 2020, p.165.

71 Jenifer Roberts, *Where the wind blows*, 2020, p.166.

72 British India Office Wills and Probate: Bengal: date of death of Henry Brown, 22 July 1920.

Chapter Thirteen

Reverend Richard Wall

Now that Reverend Brown had been ousted from his post as headmaster, the Trustees needed a new and dynamic replacement. The new headmaster had to be able to embrace the rapidly changing education system. There was a belief, across the country, not just in Brewood, that the education of the middle classes, "the pith and marrow of the country", was being neglected.[1] Universities were raising their standards of teaching but their students were predominantly from the upper classes. The masters at the National Schools received regular government inspections of their work and knew what they were expected to teach. There was a growing belief that the National Schools were giving a better education than could be obtained from schools with "much higher pretensions".[2] The masters of the endowed grammar schools were more restricted in their curriculum, and classics had to be included in the syllabus. The residents of Brewood, in common with the rest of the country, wanted their Free Grammar School to provide free education for their children, and embrace a curriculum covering science and industry. However, the endowed grammar schools were tied by the rules and regulations of their charitable status.

On 18 June 1857 the Delegacy of Local Examinations was established by the University of Oxford. Its purpose was to test the children of school leaving age who were not going to attend university and aimed to raise the standards of education. The first examinations were held in June 1858 at Oxford, London, Bath, Bedford, Birmingham, Cheltenham, Exeter, Leeds, Liverpool, Manchester and Southampton. Examinations in religion were now optional. There were Junior Examinations for children under 15 and Senior Examinations for children under 18. The University of Cambridge quickly followed with its own public examinations and this then paved the way for the current examination system across the country.[3]

With the changing education system in mind and the needs of Brewood Grammar School, the Trustees met at Teddesley Hall, Penkridge, the home of Lord Hatherton, to shortlist five candidates for the position of headmaster from the 71 very impressive applications that they had received. Those selected would be interviewed at the school on 25 May 1860 and elected to office a few days later. The chosen interviewees were Reverend Wall, M.A., an experienced teacher and incumbent of St Anne's church, Birkenhead; Reverend Percival Richard Renorden Sandilands, M.A. who had graduated from Jesus College, Cambridge, and was a classical master at Cheltenham College; Reverend W. Cleeve, M.A., master at Bromsgrove School; Reverend W. Gurney, M.A., headmaster of Stockport School and Reverend G. Perkins, M.A., a master at Manchester School. An additional candidate, Reverend J. Dixon, was also interviewed at the request of the chairman of the Trustees, Lord Wrottesley.[4]

It was a difficult final choice between Wall and Sandilands but Wall was selected. Perhaps this was not surprising in view of the numerous positively worded testimonials he had obtained from influential people, and the tactics he used to impress the Trustees. He had asked additional questions about Brewood School even before submitting his application. He had enclosed some pamphlets and printed papers along with his testimonials and, as an "afterthought", provided a copy of his religious plan which had been adopted by Cambridge University, and soon would also be adopted by Oxford University. His pamphlet, entitled *The Religious Education of the Middle Classes: Considerations on the Effects of the Oxford Regulations for 1858* had been well received by the *Chester Courant*, whose reporter described it as a "remarkably vigorous and clever pamphlet" and went into great detail. Wall certainly provided a balanced view, supporting prizes and competition but believing that too much stress would be placed on pupils if they were put in class order of merit for each subject.[5] Wall had in depth knowledge of the new Oxford and Cambridge examination system and his students at Birkenhead had achieved excellent results.

Testimonials for Wall were provided by the Archbishop of Canterbury and Reverend Arthur Rigg, a former employer, who was the dynamic and forward-thinking Principal of Chester Training College, the first Diocesan Teachers Training College. These testimonials showed that Wall was a good school master, very able and knowledgeable, even tempered and had boundless energy. His ability as a teacher had been publicly acknowledged in the newspapers in May 1847 by the Venerable Archdeacon John Rushton.

The glowing testimonial from Rigg was more important than first appears. Wall had been dismissed from his position as Vice-Principal of the College, for reasons unknown, and requested that Chester Training College Committee investigate the matter. Archdeacon Rushton publicly stated that Wall had been completely vindicated and they were sorry that the "event" meant that, after three years, they were losing someone as "able and valuable" as Mr Wall.[6]

Reverend Thomas Ridhead of St Peter's church, Rock Ferry, Birkenhead, informed the Trustees that Wall was headmaster of the best school in Birkenhead. He educated the elite of the locality in classics, mathematics and modern languages, and pupils from his school went on to universities at Oxford, Cambridge and Dublin. He added that whilst Reverend Wall was a "sound" churchman, he did not hold extreme religious views. Reverend John Saul Howson, Principal of the Collegiate Institution at Liverpool,[7] also emphasised Wall's energy and industry as headmaster. Howson then wrote to his aunt, the philanthropist, the Honourable Mrs Edward Cropper of Dingle Bank, Liverpool, asking her to recommend Wall to her friend Lord Hatherton, a Trustee at the school.

Wall's own determination to impress and assert his suitability was evident from a letter he wrote to John Hay on 14 May 1860, before the interviews took place, inquiring about the Headmaster's House. He made it known that he planned to rebuild the school and restore it to the position "which so fine a foundation ought to hold".

In his application for the post of headmaster, Wall stated that he was finding the workload of combining both teaching and preaching too much at Birkenhead. His school was expanding fast. He had already built the school up from zero to 75 pupils, with a high number taking examinations. The population of Birkenhead had already doubled and was likely to increase even more. He needed to give up either his incumbency or the school, but the incumbency was insubstantial so he needed to teach to support his income. He was loathe to give up his position in the church and just keep the school, and so Brewood provided the ideal combination.[8]

This new dynamic headmaster was praised in the *Staffordshire Advertiser* of 25 August 1860. The article stated that the selection of such a teacher as Mr Wall was a great step towards restoring the faded reputation of Brewood Grammar School. When Brown resigned, the school had only 2 boarders and 25 day pupils.[9] During Mr Mason's time as headmaster, between 1844 and 1850, the average number of boarders had been 14 and there were, on average, 38 day pupils.

Wall had been born on 28 February 1820 at Chatham, Kent, the son of Sarah and John Wall, a coal merchant and brewer. He had attended St John's College, Cambridge, where, in 1844, he was awarded his B.A. degree, he was ordained a deacon at Chester and appointed Vice-Principal of Chester Diocesan Training College. Here, the Principal, Reverend Rigg, realised the importance of science and technology in the curriculum.[10]

Wall stayed at Chester Training College for three years before becoming Principal of Hamilton Square Academy, Birkenhead, and incumbent of St Anne's church, Birkenhead. Many affluent people lived in Hamilton Square including John Laird, the shipbuilder, whose son Henry, was a pupil at Wall's school.

On 17 December 1850 Wall married Elizabeth Sophia Higgins Salt at St George's church, Bristol. Elizabeth's father, Reverend Francis Salt, was also a headmaster. He had been Principal of King's Collegiate School at Windsor, Nova Scotia and then returned to England as headmaster at Wem Free Grammar School, Shropshire.[11]

Wall was successful in his career and in January 1852, relocated to a new and spacious school at Birkenhead Park. The school's new modern premises aimed to provide for the health and comfort of the pupils, helped by being adjacent to 100 acres of parkland. Lewis Hornblower, a Liverpool architect, designed the impressive entrance gate to the park, and his son, Alfred Lewis Hornblower, came with Wall to Brewood to continue his education with the headmaster.[12]

Every December at Birkenhead Wall organized a prize-giving ceremony for his pupils. This was an opportunity not only to celebrate examination successes but also gave pupils the opportunity to perform plays and give recitations in front of an audience of parents and friends.

In 1857 Monsieur Charles Jean Delille was one of the external examiners at the school. He was an esteemed teacher and academic as well as an author of popular French text books. Delille set the questions for Wall's pupils in the same style as he anticipated for the new University of Oxford examinations. These examinations were to provide a form of standardisation across the country for the middle classes. Delille was very impressed with the high level of education in French which Wall provided at his school, and regarded the school as one of the best in the country. The top students wrote French well and spoke it fluently, as well as having an understanding of French history, geography and literature. He felt that credit for this had to go to both Reverend Wall and the French teacher, Monsieur Durlach.[13]

In 1860 the Liverpool examination results for the Oxford examinations were published in the newspapers. Wall's school had by the far the greatest success rate. Reverend Wall had 15 boys pass out of his 75 students, whilst the next highest was the Collegiate School, which had a pass rate of 14 boys out of 750.

A state-of-the-art school at Brewood

Wall had done sufficient research to know that Brewood Grammar School had great potential but needed a new and well-designed Headmaster's House to meet modern standards. He wanted to increase the number of boarders at the school, because they generated income for both school and locality. Wall believed that 30 boarders was the optimum number for running a successful school, lower numbers would mean that the school would operate at a financial loss. There was capacity to increase the number of boarders in the Lower School although the Upper School had been limited to 20 boarders by the Charity Commissioners. Wall suggested that the lack of boarders with Mr Rushton, the usher, was because he was a bachelor with no wife to help him with the welfare of the pupils. However, Wall failed to tackle the key problem that had plagued many of the previous headmasters, that of reducing the number of pupils boarding in the village at lower rates than the school could charge.

Boarders' fees provided income for extra staff which, in turn, gave the opportunity to provide a higher level of education, essential for the new examination system. The more individual tuition helped the boys achieve good places at universities, the civil service and the army, which helped enhance the school's reputation. An increase in boarders would allow the pupils to play a good team of cricket or football and so, in Wall's words, raise the "esprit-de-corps" amongst the pupils. As many of the day boys lived a long distance away, and many were farmers' children who were also needed for work on the farm, Wall believed that only the very enthusiastic pupils would want, or be able, to return to school to play cricket or football. He felt that sport should be actively encouraged at Brewood, as Wall mistakenly thought that Brewood was such a "quiet place" and "boredom and lethargy" might be a problem.

The Trustees must have been looking forward to the arrival of a new headmaster with such a successful teaching career, but when Wall took possession of the Headmaster's House on 20 July and then commenced teaching on 2 August, he confirmed his belief that in order for the school to be successful the House would have to be entirely replaced or have extensive improvements. The low ceilings throughout the buildings were oppressive. There was no separate passage from the kitchen to the boys dining room. Instead, the meals had to be taken down the hall and across the front room to the dining room. The large school room had two fire places, but one was so close to the door that it did not heat the room as the door was continually in use. The dormitories needed to be redesigned and the floors all needed replacing. The school stables and coach-house were also in a poor state of repair.[14]

Wall immediately started the process of reconstruction of the school by providing several plans to the Trustees. Plan E was adopted and Edward Banks of Wolverhampton, was again chosen as the architect for the school. It was not until 30 March 1861 that the specifications for the plans were agreed. The cost of the building work was expected to be £1530–0 –0d. These costs made provision for all new materials to be of the best quality but when the old buildings were taken down any good material would be cleaned and reused. The ground was to be dug to a depth of 8 feet for the cellars, to which there would be steps down. The floor would be of common blue bricks and there would be cast iron windows three feet by three feet. New eight-inch square red quarry tiles were to be used in the kitchen, larder, passage and porch, but re-cycled old quarry tiles would be used on the floor of the scullery. The best quality Brewood stone was to be used, but Darlaston stone would be used for the hearths in the attics. The wooden floors of the attics and chambers were to be made of red deal but the vestibule and hall would have oak boards from the old School House.

There was a dining room, drawing room, study, master's room, china room, pantry, butler's pantry, larder, housemaid's closet, lavatory and boot house. Doors which needed to be locked would have a good seven-inch mortice lock, Brewood having an excellent reputation for its plate locks. There would be five additional rooms for the expected 24 boarders, six fewer boarders than Wall had wanted. He insisted that "the most hideous porch" be removed, the fireplaces in the large School Room repositioned and the water supply and drainage system at the school improved.[15]

Wall was unhappy with the financial plan provided by John Hay, secretary to the Trustees, to pay for the work. He felt that Hay's plan would permanently injure the school estate. He pointed out that the Hurd Fund had already been lost when Brown's redevelopments at the school had taken place and no provision had been made for its recovery. Wall's calculations showed that Hay's scheme would involve a loss of £1300 which he did not believe would be approved by the Charity Commissioners.[16] The correspondence shows that Wall was a proficient financial manager of the school, as well as an excellent teacher.

Hay was not happy with Wall's criticism and queried the headmaster's opinion of him. The energetic Mr Wall replied that he had good cause to doubt John Hay's "earnestness" because on the 3 January 1861 Hay had received instructions from Lord Wrottesley to proceed with the new school but he had done nothing until he received a prompting second letter on 20 March from Lord Hatherton. It then took Hay another 12 days to arrange and meet with certain of the local Trustees, known as the Visitors,[17] to discuss the matter and another 12 days for him to meet with the Charity Commissioners. Wall thought that this time gap was far too long and complained that if Hay had been in equal earnest in January, then work would have commenced on the new building and the Headmaster's House would have already been demolished. "I repeat had I not cause to doubt your earnestness? However, let bygones be bygones ......"[18]

Discussions continued about the funding of the building work. Finally, Wall wrote to the Trustees on 9 December 1861, stating that if the Court of Chancery did not agree to the submitted plans, he would pay for the agreed alterations to the school himself. However, if they were approved then the cost of the alterations would be included in an agreed price of £1490. Reverend Wall would then add to the Reserve Fund with the accumulations of interest to £600 consolidated stock. He added that Mr Rushton, the usher, was not to suffer any loss of income and he, Wall, would bear the whole loss from the diminished income arising from the stock.

Meanwhile, Rushton wanted to know exactly what Vice-Chancellor Sir John Stuart had decided about the rebuilding of the Headmaster's House. He had doubts about all the costs and the effect on his income from this dynamic headmaster. It is not surprising that Rushton was so cautious given what had happened with regard to his finances in the preceding years. Rushton asked his Brewood friends, James Hicks Smith, barrister at law in London, or his assistant, Harry Daw, to attend the Court of Chancery and report back to him.[19] James Hicks Smith had already been involved with the case of the sale of the Willenhall school land during Mr Brown's headmastership. Rushton explained that whilst Mr Manby, the local solicitor, would tell him the outcome, he would not go into the detail that he wanted.

Rushton wrote again to Smith on 13 January 1862 worried about the Trustees application to the Court of Chancery for more boarders at the school. Mr Wall had 35 boarders when he should only have had 20, and Rushton believed that Wall wanted to increase the number of boarders still further, but it was to be kept secret from the court. He thought that this would be a radical change for the school and neighbourhood and should be openly and carefully considered, and sanctioned by the Court of Chancery.

On 16 January 1862 the application for the new Headmaster's House was turned down by the Court because the monetary side of the Charity Trust had been agreed by an Act of Parliament and could not be altered. Wall was unhappy with the decision and wanted to appeal to the Vice-Chancellor. Lord Wrottesley agreed with Wall. An urgent meeting of the Trustees of Brewood Grammar School was called by Lord Hatherton for the following day. Wall attended but Rushton was not invited, which upset the usher who believed that the Trustees and headmaster wanted the opportunity to discuss his opposition to the new building, without his presence.

The new school was important to Wall, and on 28 January 1862 he provided Hatherton with some alternative options for financing the rebuilding of the Headmaster's House. One possibility was using the Royal Insurance Company, Liverpool. Percy Dove, general manager of the company, was willing to loan the Trustees £1100 which they could pay back at an annual rate of £71 3s 8d over 30 years. His son, Henry Percy Dove, was a pupil at Brewood Grammar School. There was also the possibility of borrowing the same amount of money from Wall's father-in-law, the Reverend Francis Salt, at 4½ % interest over 30 years, but it would need the approval of the Charity Commissioners which would involve a delay. A third possibility, suggested by Hatherton, was to raise £1100 by subscription. If the amount was increased to £1500, the extra £400 could be used as a contingent fund for an exhibition. Wall was happy to contribute £200, in addition to the payment of over £270 that he had already made for alterations to the school. The Monckton family of Brewood also offered to contribute some money.

Rushton was still not happy and instructed his solicitors, Edwards and Edwards, to write to Henry Vane, secretary to the Charity Commissioners, informing him that the Vice-Chancellor had ruled that the Court of Chancery did not have the power to alter the application of funds other than as decreed by the Act of Parliament. Edwards and Edwards believed that the proposed rebuilding of the Headmaster House would increase the accommodation for boarders and so was an alteration to the scheme. They highlighted that the present number of boarders already exceeded the number of boarders allowed. If the school was enlarged, and the masters had to re-pay a loan, it would reduce their salaries and make it difficult for them to keep the buildings maintained to prevent permanent deterioration. If in the future the number of boarders declined, as Rushton correctly predicted did happen, then the masters' income would be reduced. Edwards and Edwards also brought to Vane's attention that most of the noblemen, clergymen and gentlemen who were Trustees, were not legally entitled to be so, as only two were qualified by residence within the parish of Brewood, and only one by property, the requirements needed to be a Trustee.

At the Trustees meeting on 31 January 1862 Reverend Francis Salt's offer of financial help was accepted for building the new Headmaster's House. Any additional costs would be paid by a mortgage. Rushton was summoned to the meeting and admonished for his conduct towards the Trustees. They were unhappy about his contact with the Charity Commissioners and especially annoyed as he had previously prevailed on the Trustees to insert a guarantee that his interests would not be affected. Rushton retaliated saying that the headmaster was undermining his authority but the Trustees reminded Rushton that Wall had their approval for complete authority over the management of the whole school. Lord Wrottesley was particularly furious.

The legal work commenced. John Simons carried out an inspection at the school on behalf of the Charity Commissioners and agreed that the Headmaster's House was in a very dilapidated condition and insufficient for its necessary purposes and approved the plans for the new school. On 14 March 1862 Wall and the Trustees held a meeting in the school room to explain to leading local people why there was a need for the new building. John Hay, secretary to the Trustees, Mr E. Banks the architect, John Simons and Reverend Rushton also attended in an official capacity. Amongst the local people in the audience were James Hicks Smith, Mr Brooke Chambley of Coven Lawn Farm, Mr Keeling of Somerford, and Mr Holles of Horsebrook.

Wall explained why he needed a modern new Headmaster's House to be built on the site of the existing one even though it was only going to be three feet longer and three feet six inches wider. The cost was to be £1,490 which would be repaid in under 30 years. He had already made improvements to the school and added some buildings. At a later date, he anticipated rebuilding the old stables and coach house. School numbers had increased since he became headmaster. There were only a small number of pupils at Brewood Grammar School when he took over the school, but 37 of his pupils from Birkenhead had come with him and were boarding at the school. He now also had 28 day pupils.

James Hicks Smith, representing the churchwardens, queried why there were more than the permitted number of 20 boarders. He added that Mr Mason, a previous headmaster, had offered to rebuild the school if the number of boarders could be increased but this had been refused informally by the Trustees. Lord Hatherton and Major Chetwynd denied any knowledge of this but whilst Mason had been headmaster the number of boarders at the school had fluctuated between 30 and 40 pupils. Major Chetwynd confirmed these figures and added that when he was a pupil at the school there were eight boys sleeping in his dormitory, two in a bed. Mr Brooke Chambley of Coven Lawn Farm supported the headmaster's wishes and firmly said, "The house did then, but it won't do now"!

Simons felt that the day boys would benefit with the increased number of boarders elevating the standard of education. It would be unacceptable if the boarders and foundation boys, or day boys as they were also known, were kept apart but as the foundation boys had access to the same playgrounds and had the same rights as the boarders, they benefitted by "contact with the master's superior grade of boys".[20]

James Hicks Smith claimed that he was not opposed to the new building but wanted the whole business to be made more open and public in Brewood. Lord Wrottesley replied that the Charity was not for Brewood alone but for any part of the Kingdom, and Lord Hatherton added that none of this was the churchwarden's business. The matter became more agitated when Mr Ward, the other churchwarden, claimed that James Hicks Smith had been using his name, as if he, as churchwarden, was in agreement with Smith! Ward had lived in Brewood for seven years and had two sons, one of whom had been taught by Mr Brown. He had needed to send this son to another school, at great expense, when Brown was headmaster, but the child returned to Brewood Grammar School when Mr Wall arrived, and in that one year he had learned more with Mr Wall than any other master. Ward added that Wall was a credit to Brewood helping the parishioners both parochially and clerically: "a man and a gentleman".[21]

As the meeting drew to a close, Rushton joined in the discussion raising his concerns about a reduction in his income and wanting to be allowed more boarders too. He reminded everyone that as his appointment had been made before the Charitable Trusts Act was passed, no decisions could be made which would prejudice him. Rushton taught an average of 20 boys each year. Wall confirmed that Rushton's position and interests would not be affected and cleared the way for a decision to be taken. Thus, finally, the plans for the new school building were passed after nearly two years of argument. Construction work began after the Reverend Francis Salt, Elizabeth Wall's father, had provided a loan of £1100 and Mr Wall had provided £386 6s 5d.

The new school was completed by 1863. Each boy who boarded had a separate bed, and an area of 470 cubic feet of space in the room.[22] However, two popular and hardworking Trustees died before they saw the new school, the Reverend A.B. Haden and Lord Hatherton.

A view of the Reverend Wall's new school, on the left, and the Usher's House and school, on the right-hand side of the photograph. The photograph is undated but was taken before 1904.[23]

Reproduced courtesy of Brewood Civic Society.

The success of Brewood Grammar School under Wall

Reverend Wall soon built up the school's reputation even before the new state-of-the-art building. In 1861 the school was thriving. On the night of the 1861 census, 30 children were listed as boarding with Wall, most of whom had transferred from his school at Birkenhead Park, which reflects the high esteem in which he was held. There were also two young teachers living at the school, Charles F. Delany from Switzerland and John Jenkins from Aberystwyth. Reverend Rushton was listed on the census as having nine pupils boarding with him, and most of those had also moved with Reverend Wall. Wall and his wife, Elizabeth, now also had a family: Anne Elizabeth, born 1852, who died Christmas 1864; Charlotte Sophia born 1854; Walter George, born 1859 who later became mayor of Birkenhead; and John William born just before the April census was taken.

A few months later, at the time of the November 1861 examinations, there were 61 students, 38 of whom boarded with Mr Wall and two with Mr Rushton. There were also 21 day pupils: seven from Brewood, six from Bishop's Wood, two from Coven, four from Chillington, one from Codsall and one travelling the much greater distance from Trysull.

The 1861 school examinations were conducted by Reverend J. Moore, Fellow of Queen's College, Oxford and Monsieur H. Durlach, who had taught French at Mr Wall's school in Birkenhead but now taught the subject at the High School in Dundee. Frank Marshall from West Bromwich, who had been a pupil of Mr Wall's at Birkenhead Park School before moving with Wall to Brewood, excelled in mathematics and scripture in the examinations. He also played rugby and went on to become a well-respected referee and author of the book *Football - the Rugby Union Game*.[24]

With the increase in the number of boarders at the school, Mr Wall needed more pews to be allocated to the pupils at Brewood church. The pews at the parish church at the time were the box type, and as soon as Wall had arrived at the school the churchwardens had allocated an unused one to him for his students. It belonged, though, to Henry Holles, a farmer at Horsebrook. This did not cause a problem until April 1862 when Henry

Holles wanted to attend church and sit in his pew. Two boys, Augustus Mongredien Watson, son of a ship broker and ship owner, and James Torrance Wood, son of an American Cotton merchant, believed the pews belonged to the school and would not allow Holles into the area, locking the pew door. Holles tried to climb over the back but was pushed out by the boys.

Mr Holles was not happy and raised the matter at the church vestry meeting but James Hicks Smith the churchwarden, said that both parties should have informed the churchwardens as soon as they realised that there was a problem. Not satisfied with that decision, Holles raised the matter of assault with the magistrates, who were holding a court locally at the Lion Inn. It was eventually decided that there was blame on both sides and the case was dismissed.[25]

The school continued to flourish under Wall. The November 1862 examination report, recorded 72 boys at the school, 28 day boys and 44 boarders aged between 10 and 17 years old but six pupils were in quarantine after an outbreak of scarlet fever. Reverend Norris, the University of Cambridge external examiner, stayed three days at the school. He was impressed with both the Upper and Lower Schools. He was particularly positive about the standard of teaching for mathematics, modern languages, English and the classics. Norris also thought that the number of teachers was "abundantly adequate" for the number of pupils being taught. He was a little disappointed in the standard of map drawing and the teaching of Greek, but the boys were all moral, obedient and truthful and played "heartily" at recreation time.

Reverend Norris noted a lack of punctuality and precision in the school "arrangement". Wall felt that this was unfair as not only was Brewood Grammar School the first school to be visited and examined under the new University of Cambridge external examination system, but the new School House was still being built on the site of the previous one so the regularity of the timetable was disrupted out of necessity. Wall also complained that some of the subjects had only received a moderate amount of the examiner's attention, both orally and in writing. The Trustees were very pleased though and, at the awards ceremony in December, complimented Wall on his dynamic energy in running the school.

Ever progressive, in January 1863 Mr Wall started a new class for chemistry. The teacher was John Jones, secretary of the Dudley Geological Society. Wall also wanted to set up a competition exhibition for a scholarship for Oxbridge for two years. It was to be for boys under the age of 16 so that anyone struggling financially could go to university, in this he had the support of the Trustees. In the November examinations of the same year, the boys at Brewood Free Grammar School gained more external examination passes than any other school in the district. The boys also achieved five out of the eight honours against all the schools in the district, and Augustus Mongredien Watson, obtained the Liverpool Scholarship of £40 per annum.

Brewood Grammar School went from strength to strength. In December 1863, at the Cambridge Examinations for under 16-year-olds which were held at Wolverhampton, most of the successful candidates who obtained honours in the exams again came from Brewood Grammar School. In order: E. Banks of Wolverhampton, Brewood Grammar School; C.W. Blease of Liverpool, Brewood Grammar School; T.W. Browne of Brockton, Shifnal, Brewood Grammar School; T.W.L. Hay of Teddesley, Brewood Grammar School; T. Hill of Wombourne who attended Wolverhampton Grammar School; G.E. Pratt of Malvern who attended Cannock Grammar School then A. Shuker of Trysull who attended Brewood Grammar School.

Those from Brewood aged 16 years and under who did not obtain honours also did extremely well, as did the Juniors, of which five out of the six pupils who passed their exams came from Brewood Grammar School and were mentioned for their ability in religious knowledge, English or chemistry.[26]

In 1865 Mr Henry John Chaytor, an assistant classical master who excelled at sports, was living at Speedwell Castle, and supervising the extra boarders who could not be accommodated at either the Headmaster or Undermaster's Houses. Cricket was a popular sport with the pupils and an extra field was rented for the game.

Mr Wall's pupils continued to achieve excellent examination results, and the number of students had now increased to close on one hundred.

The existing school room was too small to accommodate the five resident masters and three visiting masters so Mr Wall had a new classroom built. Two other rooms had to double as dining rooms for both Mr Rushton's boarders and his own. Mr Wall also rented part of the Working Men's Institute, previously the old National School, which belonged to the Grammar School.

Friction between Reverend Wall and Reverend Rushton

Wall was an extremely successful headmaster but he consistently felt that he was being undermined by Mr Rushton, the usher, who had been a popular teacher at the school since 1842 and also had a Cambridge degree, technically qualifying him to be headmaster. Rushton may have felt that he understood Brewood Grammar School better than the younger newcomer, but he was also of the opinion that Wall was not as well qualified to teach the classics as previous headmasters. However, the classics were becoming outmoded as mathematics and the sciences grew in popularity.

There were also financial reasons for the disagreements between the two masters. Wall would have liked Rushton to incur more of the expenses of the school as Wall's outgoings were substantial. Wall needed his new school room, but he was also paying the debt on the Headmaster's House, the salaries of extra masters, £10 for an outside classroom at the old National School and six guineas rent for a cricket field. Rushton was having to do more work with this new headmaster, teaching more pupils and accommodating more boarders. On the other hand, his pupils were receiving the benefit of the extra masters and he was not paying any of the expenses. However, it had already been agreed in 1862, before the new school was built, that Mr Rushton's income would not be reduced.

The ill-feeling between Wall and Rushton was so bad that Dr Frederick Temple, headmaster of Rugby School, was asked to mediate. The well-respected Temple had improved Rugby School's reputation both in the classics and natural sciences and on 23 November 1865, came to his conclusions in this dispute. [27]

Temple began with the facts. When Wall became headmaster, the school was organized into two departments, the headmaster taught in the Upper

School and the usher in the Lower School. The headmaster was allowed to take 20 boarders on his own terms and the usher eight boarders on his own terms. Mr Wall had united the schools, but Dr Temple believed that the limitation of the numbers of boarders had reduced the school's efficiency and reduced the income of the headmaster too much, which limited the quality of applicants. The Trustees had allowed Mr Wall to exceed the number of boarders and given the headmaster control of both schools.

Wall had employed additional masters and proposed that the fees for boarders should be sufficient to cover their salaries. Mr Rushton, the usher, did not want to teach more boarders than Mr Wall or his assistant were teaching. The headmaster and usher were each receiving a proportion of income dependent on estate rental income, not the number of students, so there was no encouragement to take boarders from a financial point of view. Dr Temple felt that Mr Rushton could claim that he was being overworked but not that his work depended on how many boarders were lodging at which part of the school. Mr Rushton had an average of three boarders, which had increased that year to seven boarders. The extra teachers at the school, Dr Temple believed, had increased the school's reputation from which Mr Rushton was gaining the benefit and also reducing his workload. Rushton's negative attitude was not in the pupils' best interests, nor the school as priority had to be given to the boys' welfare and education.

Dr Temple concluded that he understood why Mr Rushton was anxious to protect his own interests, having had authority over his own school for so long, but he felt that Rushton's attitude was to the detriment of the school. Rushton should now concentrate on throwing himself heartily into the duty of doing his best to make the school thoroughly efficient.

Mr Rushton did not respond. Lord Dartmouth and the Trustees believed that if Mr Rushton did not change his attitude, he should resign and a letter was sent to this effect on 15 January 1866.

On 22 January 1866 Rushton sent a letter to Wall, who was only in the next building, saying that he had carefully considered Wall's proposals about what he ought to pay and how much income he should receive.

However, after studying the Public School Commissioners Report relating to Harrow, Rugby and Shrewsbury Schools he found that the second masters in these schools, in common with all the other masters who took boarders, paid a fixed sum into a School Instruction Fund for each boarder and then received a fixed proportionate share of its aggregate.

Wall wrote back promptly at 4 o'clock on the same day that Rushton's suggestion was not acceptable as he had done nothing to raise the standards of the school but had done much to impair his authority, increase his expenses and "weaken the esprits-de-corps of the whole school". Wall also complained to Rushton that he belittled the school prizes but Rushton replied that he was defending one of his boarders, Tom Brown from Beckbury, who he believed deserved a prize but had not received one, in favour of prizes received by Shaw, Kempson and Shuker.

In October 1866 the first Hatherton scholarship presented by Lord Hatherton in memory of his father, and open to all boys in the area, was awarded to Abraham Shuker of Brewood Grammar School. Abraham Shuker also obtained a first in the Cambridge University Local Examinations and received the Wolverhampton Borough prize, as well as a scholarship from the Oxford Local Examinations.[28]

At the speech day held in September 1867, Mr Wall was able to report that he now had a new school room which was "large, lofty and very light" as well as a new classroom, a new laboratory, a covered gymnasium and a fives court. The school now received 33 day boys and 66 boarders. The 16 students who had entered the Cambridge Local Examinations had done exceedingly well, being awarded 15 special distinctions, five in English, three in French and Greek, and one each in Latin, German, religious knowledge and zoology. William Hay had also taken second prize in chemistry and botany awarded by the Royal Agricultural Society.

The programme for the April 1868 sports day indicates that Wall placed as much importance on sport and exercise as he did on examinations. The event took place on a field adjoining the cricket ground and a large number of former pupils and spectators attended. The flat race of 100 yards was won by William Hay in 11 seconds. The under fifteens flat race was won easily by E. White in 12 seconds with Gilpin second, and the mile flat race was won by Newbold senior in 5 minutes and 49 seconds followed by Mills then Owen. Mr Percy Churton of Birkenhead gave a cup as did Mr Gilpin of Wedges Mills, Cannock, the edge tool manufacturer. A half mile race followed, won again easily by E. White in 2 minutes and 30 seconds, with Gilpin again second and Marsh in third place. Mr Parke, bookseller of Wolverhampton, gave a cup for that race. There were many other races including hurdles, high jump, long jump and pole jump. The broad jump was open to all under 5 feet tall. The flat race of two miles was open to all, strangers, old boys and those present. There was also a sack race and a three-legged race. Mr H. J. Chaytor was the judge.

The Taunton Commission Report and Brewood Grammar School

At the 1868 Speech Day Wall reported that the school numbers had again increased. There were now 105 pupils on the school role in August, of which 72 boarded, and 33 were day pupils. Mr Wall believed that there would be even more day pupils if there was more housing in the village. He went on to outline the key findings of the School Inquiry Commission's Report about Brewood Grammar School. This Commission had been established by the Government to report on the standard of education in England and Wales and make recommendations. It was now complete and published in 20 volumes. Mr Thomas Hill Green of Balliol College, Oxford, the Assistant Commissioner for The School Inquiries Commission, or Taunton Commission as it was also known, had visited Brewood School in 1864 and 1868, and given the school a very favourable report.

Mr Green had stated that Mr Wall had raised Brewood Grammar School from a declining school to a thriving one. He was particularly impressed with the standard of education of the boys wanting to go to university. Mr Wall gave Mr Chaytor the credit for the high standard of teaching in the classics, but there was an additional qualified English master, with a teaching training certificate from Edinburgh. The French master received a fixed salary and a bonus for every boy who passed the local examinations and a further sum for every boy who was placed in the first class for French. The pupils also had the chance to learn German instead of Greek. Green noted that Wall encouraged his students to take the local examinations which were held at Wolverhampton, particularly those of the University of Cambridge, and that the boys were driven there by a special omnibus.

Green praised the education that the boys received for entering business too. In fact, he wrote positively about almost every subject, and was impressed with the general ethos of the school. He noted that whilst many of the boarders had followed Mr Wall from his school at Birkenhead, the day boys were the sons of parents who were living in Brewood because of the education the school provided, or were the sons of the "better sort of farmers", of which eight travelled a distance of five miles every day. The farmers who had less land and the traders, did not use the school because of the "genteel or semi-genteel character of most of the boys" and because the education was not exclusive to English and arithmetic. These parents sent their children to either the National School or a small private school in Brewood.

Mr Green, in his first visit to the school in 1864, had thought that Brewood would benefit from the establishment of an elementary school to give the pupils an education for business. Latin would only be taught to the highest class who could then go to the Grammar School. A separate school would be required for this proposal and it could be headed by the undermaster, but only when Mr Rushton had left the school. Mr Green changed his opinion on his second visit to the school in 1868, and was impressed with the way the headmaster had integrated the boarders and day pupils, and maintained a high standard of teaching.[29]

With regard to religion, Mr Green noted that on Sundays the boys who boarded received some religious instruction on Sunday at school as well as attending the parish church service. The school was opened and closed daily with prayers and the boys were taught the bible and the catechism. Punishments included detention during play hours and caning in public. Birching was very rare and done in private by the headmaster only. Monitors were also allowed to punish the boys by setting impositions and fagging.

The report also commented on the physical activities available for the children. There were two playgrounds, one of two acres and another of four acres, both close to school. Cricket and football were played and the masters sometimes joined in the games. Drilling was also taught.

Mr Wall continued his speech by saying that the Taunton Report wanted the re-election of Trustees every five years, which neither Wall nor the Trustees thought was a good idea. The Trustees joked that it would be "Vote for Hatherton and Geology", "Vote for Shrewsbury and Technical Education", "Vote for Dartmouth and German". Wall concluded his address with reflections on the lives of two of the Trustees who had recently died, and had helped the school so much over many years: Lords Shrewsbury and Wrottesley. The headmaster then gave a dinner party for 100 people.[30]

In the academic year of 1867 /8 for reasons unknown, there was an analysis of the occupations of the fathers of the students. Of the day boys, the highest achiever was the son of a clergyman, and the second was the son of retired Captain John Thompson, magistrate, who lived at Ivetsy Bank, and the third child was the son of an agent of the school estate. The day boys considered to be low achievers, were the children of farmers at Shareshill and Ivetsy Bank, and the son of a merchant's widow who lived in Brewood. Distance from the school was also noted. However, of the boarders, the highest achievers were sons of farmers from Trysull and Shifnal, followed by an architect's son from Wolverhampton. The lowest achieving boarders were the son of an iron broker from near Wolverhampton, a civil engineer's son from Mitcham, London, and a Shanghai merchant's son from Liverpool.

The day pupils were travelling from as far away as Shareshill, Bushbury, Ivetsy Bank and Chillington, and some of the boarders came from homes at nearby Wolverhampton, Cannock and Stafford. Several children had their homes though at Liverpool and Birkenhead, and other localities were Bridgnorth, London, and Omskirk in Lancashire.

At the September Speech Day of 1869, the Trustees and their guests included the Earl and Countess of Shrewsbury, the Earl and Countess of Dartmouth, the Earl and Countess of Bradford and Lord and Lady Hatherton, as well as prominent members of the locality. A lavish lunch was again provided at the school, catered for by Mr D. Miller of

Wolverhampton. Mr Wall reported that there were 34 day boys and 59 boarders at the school, so the numbers of pupils were still very high for the time. Students had done extremely well in their exams including, amongst the many, William Wills who had obtained an open scholarship to St John's College, Cambridge,[31] Abraham Shuker who had obtained a 7th in First Class at St John's College, Cambridge, and Richard Thompson of The Hurst, Lapley, son of Captain Thompson, who came 5th out of 141 in his Woolwich Academy entrance exams. Contrary to some similar schools where the teaching of English and English literature was neglected, the pupils at Brewood Grammar School received a good education in both subjects as well as the classics. In fact, of the 26 hours given to teaching 12 hours were given to English, six to Latin, and eight to writing and arithmetic.

Mr Wall believed that Brewood Grammar School provided an education to suit all local needs, whether the pupils wanted an education for business or university. In line with the Taunton Report, Wall believed that Brewood Grammar School was providing an education for three levels of students: those that left school at 14, those who left at 16 years old and those that stayed on until 18 or 19 and progressed to university or a profession. Wall rejected the statements made by Mr Griffith in the *Staffordshire Advertiser* about the day students being neglected, in favour of the paying boarders, a statement which, in the newspaper the week later, Griffith firmly denied.[32] He also disputed Mr Griffith's analysis of the finances of the school, which had failed to take into account the expenses incurred by both masters.[33]

Samuel Bate of Springfield, Newcastle-under-Lyme, gave a detailed argument about the inaccuracies in Griffith's statement in the same newspaper.[34] He wanted to defend the honour of the school that he had attended as a pupil. Bate informed the readers that when Lord Hatherton was a pupil at the school it was well renowned in the Midlands and the sons of nearly all the gentry were educated there but, for no apparent reason, this no longer happened. He continued that before Reverend Wall was appointed headmaster at the school there were fewer than 24 pupils, and day boys were not allowed to mix with the boarders who tended to be the wealthier schoolchildren. The boarders and day pupils had a separate classroom and a separate playground. Under Mr Wall there was no such differentiation. The school numbers had risen to over 100, and the school was now top of the county for its standard of education. It was the leading school for the Cambridge examinations held at Wolverhampton, and in 1868, the school was the centre for the Oxford examinations. In the years from 1861 until 1867, 116 boys from Brewood Grammar School passed the entrance exam, honours or otherwise, 28 were day boys and, of these, eight gained distinctions in English, which included geography and history, two in religious education, five in Greek, two in chemistry, four in French, two in Latin and two in German. If 28 day boys seemed a small number, Mr Bate reminded the readers that Brewood was a small village within a farming community and naturally there were more boarders than day boys. In 1864 a scholarship was provided, and out of the five recipients boys three were day boys. In 1865 the Hatherton scholarship had been introduced for boys educated anywhere in Staffordshire. It had already been awarded to three boys, of whom two were day boys from Brewood.

This all proved, continued Mr Bate, that the day boys did not receive an inferior education and all boys had the benefit of the beautiful scenery around the school with its historical connections. The school had an extensive playground, there were several large fives courts, a magnificent cricket field, and a bathing place in the river Penk. The Albrighton pack of hounds met nearby with which the boys had many runs on foot, "so the body was not sacrificed to the mind". The school buildings were large and spacious, and more classrooms had recently been added. The headmaster and his staff, aimed to educate the children in being "Englishmen and Christians".[35]

At the meeting of the Trustees on 3 March 1869, the Trustees remembered John Hay who had died, and sent their condolences to Mrs Hay and her family. Mr Robert Hay Walker was appointed secretary and receiver to the Trustees in his place at a salary of £20 per annum.

The Endowed Schools Act

In 1869 the Endowed Schools Act brought in by Gladstone's government aimed to restructure the Grammar Schools across the country. This Act encompassed recommendations of the 1868 Taunton Report.

The Commissioners had envisaged three grades of secondary education: first-grade schools to prepare boys for university and certain professions; second-grade schools to prepare boys for the army and civil service and third grade schools for boys who were expected to become tenant farmers or tradesmen.[36] It was without doubt a class orientated system. Local residents were to have a say in the education system that they wanted for the school, and the Trustees were ready to listen.

The majority of residents wanted a good commercial and agricultural education for their boys. Brewood community were worried about the higher capitation fees that a first-grade school could charge, which would prevent many parents being able to afford to send their children to school in Brewood. There were 58 signatures to this letter including Fred Keeling, farmer and miller, Somerford, J. H. Heatley, farmer of Engleton, H. Holles, farmer of Horsebrook, Thomas Shemilt, farmer of Hyde Farm, John Brewster of Stretton Mill, farmer and miller, S. S. Cholditch, gentleman, William H. Lees, maltster, E. J. Wrottesley, vicar of Brewood, and John F. Speerhouse, surgeon.

The Trustees had taken notice of the petition and, on 25 January 1871, wrote to the Endowed Schools Commissioner, Henry John Roby.[37] They were very pleased with the School's Inquiry Report which had deemed Brewood Grammar School as "classical" in reference to its instruction and "first-grade" in respect of the scholars. The Trustees wanted the school to be one of the chief country boarding schools in Staffordshire. There were no similar boarding schools for miles. However, the Trustees wanted the Commissioners to retain the present education system as any material change would seriously damage the interests of the headmaster who had done so much to raise the educational standard at the school and at his own expense.

The Trustees were happy for any day boys to attend the school who could walk or ride from their own homes; there was not a geographical limit for this privilege. However, the Trustees stressed that Grammar School boys should not be allowed to lodge in houses in Brewood and then be allowed to use the school on the same terms as the day boys. The Trustees wanted the Commissioners to provide clear regulations to support them in this matter.

Mr Wall had produced a workable plan for the school to remain essentially as it was, and it had the backing of the Trustees. The plan suited the educational needs of the local boys and was financially viable. The Trustees were concerned that whilst the county could take the benefit of Dr Knightley's endowment, the boys of the neighbourhood found "themselves denied even the crumbs from the Founder's tables".[38]

Mr Rushton, on the other hand, was once again not in agreement with either the headmaster or the Trustees and sent a letter to the Endowed Schools Commissioners. He stated that he did not believe that Brewood Grammar School needed to be a first-grade school. The parents of his pupils were in trade or agriculture and he felt that they wanted their children to continue in the same trade and leave school at the age of 16 or 17 years. The parents of Mr Wall's pupils tended to be in mercantile and manufacturing careers rather than agriculture. Rushton believed that this had not changed in 29 years. Rushton also added in his letter that whilst Wall had been headmaster at the school there was an average of 80 boys each year with eight boys attending university. However, only three of these eight boys were from Brewood or surrounding area. In the last 30 years, Rushton did not remember any pupil becoming either a barrister or a physician. The School Inquiries Commission had also reported that in May 1867, there were only three undergraduates at Oxford or Cambridge who had been educated at Brewood and attended university. The Commissioners wanted a first-grade school to have at least sixty per cent of their pupils aiming for university.[39]

The Endowed Schools Commissioners believed Brewood Grammar School to be a successful school under the influence of Wall, an energetic and efficient headmaster. They were worried that Brewood was so rural with a small and scattered population. There were only 3,399 people in Brewood parish which covered an area of 11,832 acres. The school had an endowment of only £500 a year gross. They had cautiously agreed to a probation period to test out Reverend Wall's scheme whilst he remained as headmaster and also to "avoid any unnecessary annoyance".[40] The school was doing first-grade work with a good success rate and fulfilling the requirements of the district but, since the autumn of 1871, both Wall and the Trustees had noted that the number of pupils attending the school was beginning to decline for the first time in Wall's headmastership.

This, they believed, was solely because the Commissioners would not come to a decision about the future of the school.

The Trustees told the Commissioners that the School had always provided an excellent first-grade school education and they had a promise from an old scholar that if the first-grade status of the school was made permanent, he would increase the Kempson Scholarships immediately to an amount that would make up three scholarships, each of £50 per annum. The Trustees also complained that they had not been allowed to see the report written by Mr Stanton, the Assistant Commissioner, a stranger to the locality, which was having so much effect on the school's future, and the uncertainty was damaging the school.

Resignation of Wall

In June 1872 Reverend Wall decided to resign his position as headmaster at the school. His wife was in ill health and needed to be relieved of her heavy work, but there were other reasons relating to the new education system. Mr Wall wrote his resignation letter to Lord Dartmouth and Lord Hatherton on 7 June 1872 and told the boys on the last day of term, but several had already gone home due to an outbreak of scarlet fever. Wall had accepted the position of vicar of St James church, Hill Top, West Bromwich, and needed to be there at the end of July.[41]

In another undated letter, Wall wrote that the school needed younger blood and if Brewood people could work together for the improvement of their school some good might come out of it.

Reverend Wall had built the school into an extremely successful establishment, provided a new Headmaster's House, new classrooms, laboratories and gymnasium to meet the needs of a modern successful school, and the building still stands today. The Endowed Schools Act brought a period of instability but Wall left a school which was thriving.

Wall continued as a school examiner, for example at Chester Middle School in 1873 and St James's School, Almondbury, under the headship of Reverend Frank Marshall, a past pupil of Wall's at Brewood Grammar School.

Wall also worked hard in his new position as vicar of St James church, Hill Top. When he left in 1889 to become rector at St Peter's church, Drayton Bassett, the parishioners presented him with 100 guineas in recognition of the work he had done in their parish during the last seventeen years, with regard to public health, religion and education. He had also been on West Bromwich School Board for seven years where he had advocated religious education for the school children.

Reverend Wall had lighter duties at Drayton Basset, but in May 1895 he officiated at the funeral of Sir Robert Peel, 3rd baronet, son of the former Prime Minister, Robert Peel and, in 1896, Wall dedicated a new splendid organ in St Peter's church, the service being attended by many people, including the Bishop of Lichfield and Sir Robert Peel, 4th Baronet.

In 1897 Reverend Wall with his wife and daughter, Charlotte, moved to Dunraven Road, West Kirby, Birkenhead. He had left Drayton Bassett for health reasons and died on Wednesday 24 May 1899 aged 79 years. His wish was to be buried at St Peter's church, Drayton Bassett and his funeral there was attended by friends and congregation from both Drayton Bassett and West Bromwich.[42]

In his obituary in the *Cannock Chase Courier* the reporter noted that Reverend Wall had rebuilt Brewood Grammar School for modern needs, he worked with untiring energy and his cricket team was well known in the county. Wall had been a fluent and powerful preacher and sometimes preached at Brewood, Shareshill and Wolverhampton amongst other places when he was at the school. In 1873 he and some other clergyman spoke out against the "extreme Ritual" practised by Reverend F. Willett of West Bromwich, Reverend C. Bodington of Christ Church, Wolverhampton and Bishop Selwyn, a Trustee at Brewood Grammar School.[43] Reverend Wall was well respected by all who knew him, and always ready to support good or charitable causes relating to Brewood.

Wall's legacy of a thriving school was written about in the newspapers for many years afterwards. Again, the *Cannock Chase Courier* reported on 10 November 1900 that a memorial was to be placed in Brewood church by his old Brewood pupils. It went on to say that when Wall was headmaster of the Grammar School it was in a "more flourishing condition than it has been since he left about 25 years ago". In 1902, the *Cannock Chase Courier* reported that Wall had raised the school from a very low level to a high one with many of his pupils gaining "high honours" at the university, and his school cricket team were renowned in Staffordshire. The *Courier* also noted, as did other newspapers, that Wall had taken a great interest in parochial matters. He was well respected.[44] The *County Advertiser and Herald for Staffordshire and Worcestershire*, as late as 9 April 1904, also reported that the school had flourished under Wall's headship and its reputation had fallen away after he left.

The school still remains as Wall's legacy. The brass memorial in Brewood parish church was presented by over 50 of his students who had outlived Wall. It is situated under the memorial for Kempson and adjacent to the memorial of Rushton. It reads that he had presided over the Grammar School assiduously, pleasantly and diligently. Wall had certainly left a legacy that was difficult to surpass.

Notes

1 Dr Richard Lynch Cotton, Provost of Worcester College in *Morning Advertiser*, 6 June 1857, p. 4.

2 Sir Thomas Dyke Acland, *Middle-class education: scheme of the West of England examination prizes, for June, 1857*, (J. Ridgway, 4th edition, 1857), Letter from Reverend F. Temple, late Fellow of Balliol College, Oxford, H.M. Inspector, to Reverend Dr Jeune, master of Pembroke College, Oxford, formerly headmaster of King Edward's School, Birmingham, April 1857. p.13. Frederick Temple became headmaster of Rugby School in 1858.

3 University of Oxford Delegacy of Local Examinations (UODLE) (1857-1999) | ArchiveSearch (cam.ac.uk)

4 The candidates had to present themselves to seven Trustees: Lord John Wrottesley, an active astronomer and one of the founders of the Royal Astronomical Society; Honourable Reverend Howard, Dean of Lichfield; Honourable Reverend Arthur Chetwynd Talbot, Rector of Ingestre; Major William Fawkener Chetwynd of Brocton Hall; Walter Giffard of Chillington; Reverend Alexander Bunn Haden of Brewood and the Reverend Joseph Salt of Standon Rectory.

5 *Chester Courant*, 3 March 1858, p. 2.

6 *Chester Chronicle*, 7 May 1847, p. 3.

7 The Collegiate Institution was where Reverend Brown, the previous headmaster at Brewood, had been headmaster of the Middle School.

8 SRO, D1416/4/2/9, 3 May 1860.

9 Douglas Thompson, *A History of Brewood Grammar School 1553–1953* (Brewood Grammar School, 1953), Chapter V, p. 47.

10 F.E. Foden, *The Rev. Arthur Rigg: Pioneer of Workshop Practice: The Vocational Aspect of Secondary and Further Education*, (Routledge, 1959), pp. 105-108.

11 Elizabeth Sophia Higgins Salt was sister to Reverend George Salt who was the first curate of St Anne's church, Birkenhead and Reverend Francis Gardner Salt who became vicar of St John's church, Bishop's Wood, Brewood.

12 Alfred Lewis Hornblower, died in 1863, at Birkenhead, soon after his seventeenth birthday. Birkenhead Park was the first public park of its kind and became inspiration for Central Park in New York. Open to the public in 1847, the park was designed by Joseph Paxton.

13 *Liverpool Daily Post,* 26 December 1857, p. 3.

14 *Wolverhampton Chronicle and Staffordshire Advertiser*, 19 March 1862, p. 6.

15 SRO, D1416/4/2/10, Letter from Wall to Hay, 3 April 1861.

16 SRO, D1416/4/2/10, Letter from Wall to Hay, 6 April 1861.

17 The Visitors were Trustees who usually lived locally and had the power of 'Visitation' to the school at any time.

18 SRO, D1416/4/2/10, Letter from Wall to Hay, 6 April 1861.

19 WSL, M790, Letter from Rushton to Smith, 10 January 1862.

20 *Wolverhampton Chronicle and Staffordshire Advertiser,* 19 March 1862, p. 6.

21 *Wolverhampton Chronicle and Staffordshire Advertiser*, 19 March 1862, p. 6.

22 Roy Lewis, *Grammar Schools in Staffordshire, 1868,* Schools History Sourcebook S14 (Staffordshire County Council Education Department, 1984), p. 23.

23 A postcard of the same view was advertised for sale in 2023 by www.worthpoint.com, with a Brewood postmark of 1904.

24 Frank Marshall became headmaster of Almondbury Grammar School later known as King James's Grammar School.

25 *Staffordshire Advertiser*, 24 May 1862, p. 4; Augustus Mongredien Watson became a graduate of St John's College, Cambridge, Fellow of Jesus College, Cambridge and an Inspector of Schools. He died on 19 May, 1879, aged 33. James Torrance Wood became a cotton broker of Liverpool and New Orleans.

26 *Staffordshire Advertiser*, 13 February 1864, p. 3.

27 Thompson, Chapter VI, pp 59-62 and SRO, D1416/4/2/11.

28 Abraham Shuker was born at Stockton, Shropshire, graduated at St John's College, Cambridge and then taught mathematics at Trent College, Derbyshire. He was highly respected there, and considered one of the best teachers, and cricketers, of his time. He also played football for Derbyshire County Football Club.

29 Roy Lewis, *Grammar Schools in Staffordshire,* pp. 21-22.

30 *Wolverhampton Chronicle and Staffordshire Advertiser,* 7 October 1868, p. 7.

31 William Wills was the son of William Ridout Wills and his wife Emily of Edgbaston, Birmingham. He had attended King Edward's School, Birmingham before coming to Brewood. He was very successful at St John's College, Cambridge and joined the Inner Temple in 1874. In 1908 he became a commissioner for the prevention of diseases in the Brass Foundries. Source: www.venn.lib.cam.ac.uk

32 *Staffordshire Advertiser,* 11 September 1869, p. 3. George Griffith published many books including *"The Free Schools and Endowments of Staffordshire, and their fulfilment",* (Whittaker and Co,1860).

33 *Staffordshire Advertiser,* 2 October 1869, p. 5.

34 Samuel Bate was an estate agent and surveyor, born in Moreton Say, Shropshire.

35 *Staffordshire Advertiser,* 2 October 1869, p. 5.

36 education-uk.org/documents/taunton1868 Derek Gillard, *Education in the UK: the history of our schools, colleges and universities.*

37 Henry John Roby had been born in Tamworth, Staffordshire and educated at Bridgnorth Grammar School and St John's College, Cambridge.

38 SRO, CEG/2/1, Letter from R. H. Walker to C.H. Stanton, 28 January 1871

39 SRO, CEG/2/1, Letter from H.J. Roby, Endowed Schools Commission to R.H. Walker, 22 December 1871.

40 SRO, CEG/2/1, Letter from H. J. Roby, Endowed Schools Commission to R. H. Walker, 22 December 1871.

41 SRO, D1416/4/2/15, Letter from Wall to R. H. Walker, 7 June 1872.

42 *Tamworth Herald*, 3 June 1899, p. 5.

43 *Cannock Chase Courier,* 3 June 1899, p. 8.

44 *Cannock Chase Courier,* 12 July 1902, p. 5.

Brewood Grammar School: the tennis court at the back of the
Headmaster's House and School, circa 1900–1905.

Reproduced courtesy of Brewood Civic Society.

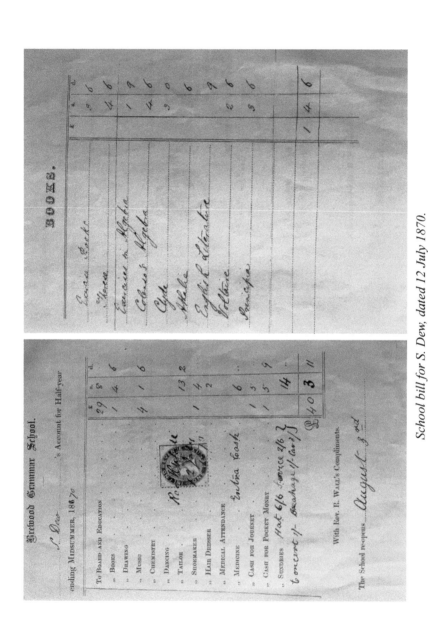

School bill for S. Dew, dated 12 July 1870.

A bill from Reverend Wall

S. Dew is likely to have been Samuel Richard Dew who became a respected solicitor, head of the firm S.R. Dew. This person was born in 1853 at Llangefni, Anglesey, son of William Dew, auctioneer and estate agent, and Alicia his wife. The family moved to Bangor. On the night of the 1871 census, Samuel, now a solicitor's articled clerk, and his father, William Dew, were staying at Queen Street, Wellington, Shropshire. Samuel died in 1933. In his obituary notice the *Western Mail and South Wales News* 1 November 1933, reported that Samuel had been a renowned solicitor in North Wales, a prosecutor for the police, a Captain in the Caernarvonshire Volunteers and had been an excellent athlete. In his will, Samuel Dew's own self-belief was different. He felt he had been an" absolute failure" and had been selfish, obstinate and unwise. Whilst there are grammar schools closer to Anglesey, Brewood Grammar School may have been chosen, not only for the standard of education due to Reverend Wall, but also because William Dew would have known Henry Paget, 4th Marquess of Anglesey and 5th Earl of Uxbridge, who was one of the Trustees of Brewood Grammar School. Paget owned Beaudesert in Staffordshire as well as Plas Newydd on Anglesey, and also had links to Staffordshire through his wife, Henrietta, the daughter of Charles Bagot of Blithfield Hall, Staffordshire.

Chapter Fourteen

James Heber Taylor and the end of an era

In the summer of 1872, the Trustees of Brewood Grammar School had to consider the appointment of another headmaster in entirely new circumstances determined by the twenty-volume report of the Taunton Commission, the Endowed Schools Act of 1869 and the policies adopted by the Endowed Schools Commission. The scheme of work that had been agreed by the Commission, the Trustees and Reverend Wall, a hard-working, popular and very successful headmaster, was not necessarily permanent. Wall's successor had to prove that the new scheme to maintain a first-class status for Brewood Grammar School would work and guarantee the future of Brewood Grammar School.

The Trustees invited applications for Wall's replacement from graduates not only of Oxford and Cambridge universities but now from any university within the British Empire. They complied with the Endowed Schools Act by confirming that the headmaster no longer had to be in holy orders.

The advertisement for the post claimed that there was accommodation for 45 boarders and that the school and class rooms were both excellent.[1] The school also had a large and productive garden.

There were 38 applications, almost half the number that had applied in 1860 when Wall had been appointed. The local Trustees, Major Chetwynd, Henry Charles Vernon of Hilton Park and Walter Peter Giffard of Chillington, chose five applicants to attend for an interview which was to take place at the School House at midday on Friday 2 August.

The short list was impressive but the Trustees unanimously chose James Heber Taylor, aged 32, who had been educated at both Oxford and Cambridge, receiving honours in the examinations and several other prizes. He also felt it necessary to note the academic achievements of his brothers: William Wilberforce Taylor[2] and Henry Martin Taylor too.[3] Noting the achievements of siblings was unusual in any application for the post of headmaster. The Taylor brothers were the sons of Reverend James Taylor, D.D., headmaster of Queen Elizabeth Grammar School, Wakefield, and Taylor informed the Trustees that he had the advantage of witnessing the management of a school where the pupils had been very successful in gaining university honours.

James Heber Taylor had been born at Bristol on 31 January 1840 and received his initial education under Reverend Penny, headmaster of Milton Abbas Grammar School, Blandford, Dorset. It was a successful school and the headmaster was friends with Reverend Taylor. Later, the young Taylor returned to Wakefield and attended Queen Elizabeth Grammar School under the headship of his father.

Taylor achieved his M.A. at Queen's College, Oxford as well as many other prestigious awards. At Trinity College, Cambridge, he became a Chancellor's Classical Medallist and was awarded his M.A. from there in 1871. He claimed to be the first Chancellor's Classical Medallist not to have obtained a Fellowship and that was because he had chosen to marry. His wife, Mary Elizabeth Pearce, was the daughter of an inventor and civil engineer from Stourbridge, John Charles Pearce. When James Heber Taylor applied for the post at Brewood the young couple had a two-year-old son, John Charles, and a baby daughter, Mary Ethel.

James Heber Taylor also had teaching experience. He had been a college tutor at Cambridge University and then, for three years, he had been second master at Mill Hill School, Hendon, a leading Nonconformist school. Taylor told the Trustees that he believed that teaching at a Nonconformist school had prejudiced his career. Lancaster Grammar School had interviewed Taylor, and invited him to meet the Governors, but Taylor was convinced he had not been offered the headship there because he had not been teaching at a Church of England school.

Marriage did not deter Taylor from continuing with his studies and, whilst teaching at Mill Hill, and just before he moved to Brewood, he was awarded a Bachelor of Science degree from London University, a subject that he was happy to teach if the Trustees provided the scientific apparatus.

254

The Trustees probably felt that Taylor was the ideal candidate because he seemed to perfectly fit the needs of the school. A young family man with an impressive classical and scientific background, he could continue to run the school in the way that Reverend Wall had planned rather than as a second-grade school under the new Education Scheme. Without some recognition of first-grade status, as defined by the Endowed Schools Commission, the Trustees and Wall, believed that the school would decline. If more pupils went on to achieve university places, Brewood Grammar School stood more chance of continuing under the dual scheme proposed by Wall and the Trustees. As Taylor's father was a successful headmaster of a prestigious school, the Trustees must have agreed with James Heber Taylor that he had gained some management expertise, and would receive useful advice from his father. Taylor, was also happy to take religious orders if the Trustees wished him to do so.

The fixtures, fittings and general state of the school

After the new head's appointment, Reverend Wall kindly invited Taylor to stay at the school, for two weeks, so that he could understand the management system of the school and his duties as headmaster. During this fortnight, or shortly afterwards, the new headmaster's father, Reverend Taylor, arrived in Brewood, to give his son advice. He suggested that the Inspector of the Charity Commissioners should provide an inventory and price for the fixtures and dilapidations, and detail all legalities of the system. As the buildings had been funded by money raised by mortgage and subscription, anything in excess of the amount raised could be claimed as belonging to the freehold. He advised his son to refuse any fixtures that he did not want or need.

James Heber Taylor opened negotiations with Reverend Wall and the Trustees for the hand-over of the school property by saying that he did not like the school desks. They were to be repaired or taken away. Wall replied that he had inherited them in that state from Mr Brown, his predecessor but Taylor retorted that it was Wall's fault for accepting them in that condition.

The Headmaster's House had been built less than ten years but had not, Taylor complained, been maintained very well. All dilapidations needed to be made good before Taylor took possession. The wooden window sill of the drawing room window was decaying for want of new paint, and water was leaking into the room when it rained. The cracked panes of glass needed replacing too.[4] There were several places in the large school room where the rain came in through the roof and a bad leak in one of the dormitories. The rain also came through into the passage by the chemistry room. Other items that needed attention were the mantelpieces in the upper classroom above the chemistry room and in the old school room, and the gate at the corner of the playground near the canal bridge.[5]

To resolve matters Taylor was invited to attend a Visitors Meeting at the School House to discuss the fixtures.[6] Wall had spent £500 of his own money on the house so felt that he had an equitable, if not strictly legal, claim to the fixtures. Taylor told the Trustees that he had not been informed at his interview that the fixtures and fittings were Mr Wall's but, in Mr Taylor's opinion all fixtures and fittings should have been paid for by subscription, and this was Wall's mistake.

At Brewood Grammar School it was the tradition that the headmaster paid his predecessor for the fixtures in the Upper School House. Mr Wall had paid Mr Brown, the previous headmaster, who in turn had paid Reverend Mason. The Trustees agreed that an Inspector from the Charity Commissioners could inspect the school premises and state which of the fixtures Mr Taylor should pay for, and which would then belong to him. The Trustees also confirmed with the Charity Commissioners whether it was compulsory for Mr Taylor to take any fixtures that he did not want.[7] Mr Taylor had his own views on the subject. He started to alter the school to his liking and removed the dining and drawing room cornices, sending them to Mr Wall at his home in Hill Top, West Bromwich. Wall was away at the time and the cornices were left outside in the back yard, without his permission. Reverend Wall was furious.[8]

The Charity Commissioners advice was that the Trustees should pay Mr Wall for all his claims relating to the school, but that the fixtures should belong to the headmaster. The Trustees did not have the funds available to comply. Instead, at the Trustees meeting in January 1873, Lord Wrottesley and Augustus Leveson Vernon, the only Trustees that attended, wanted to look at the original building specifications to see if they could find a way forward.

When Wall was updated on the state of affairs, he could not see that knowing the specifications would solve the problem. Wall believed that the fixtures were his, as he had replaced them from the old School House with better ones, and more besides. Wall now wanted to involve his solicitor.[9] Taylor had concerns that the cost of any fixtures and fittings would be a heavy charge on the income of any future headmaster, as it was an additional charge to the £70 per annum made known to the candidates.

The Trustees wanted the matter settled by arbitration: Lord Hatherton for Mr Taylor, and Rupert Kettle, of Merridale, Wolverhampton, a famous judge and arbitrator, for Reverend Wall. A licensed valuer would be appointed to fix the amount to be paid. Arbitration, Taylor argued to Lord Hatherton, in this case meant the freedom for the arbitrators to do anything they please.[10] At the end of September 1873, over a year since Reverend Wall had left the school, £100 was agreed by both parties for the fixtures. Wall was unhappy that he had not been reimbursed a higher amount of money as no account had been made for any improvements or replacement costs that he had financed nor was there a financial allowance for the number of boarders that were staying at the school when Taylor arrived.

Wall's opinion of his successor was not glowing. In a letter to Hatherton, Wall wrote that bad workmen blamed their tools and Mr Taylor may have blamed his alleged want of knowledge but when Taylor stayed with him for two weeks, Wall had told him all about the school in the minutest detail. Wall added that Mr Taylor had serious faults including believing that the fact that he had a Chancellor's Medal has relieved him of the need for reasonable diligence and common sense.

In the meantime, during April 1873, Edwin Taylor, a builder who lived at High Green by St Mary's bridge, worked on the maintenance of the front of the School House, the drawing room window and the playground wall.[11]

Taylor rightly had serious concerns about the safety of the large spoil bank of sand by the canal and was continually asking Robert Hay Walker, the secretary to the Trustees, to remedy the situation.[12] The canal had been built 40 years previously, so had been an ongoing issue for headmasters for decades. Walker tried to sell the sand but had the problem of getting the sand into the boats without trespassing on land belonging to the canal company. Walker wrote to Messrs. Higham, the builders at Castle Street, Wolverhampton, giving them permission to use the school sand from any part of the spoil bank by Edwin Taylor's house. Mr Higham was interested, but only wanted the sand by the cricket ground, which would suit their needs better.

The spoil bank continued to worry Taylor, and after waiting a few weeks, he again complained about it to Walker, who now made an agreement with the Shropshire Union Railways and Canal Company, the owners of the canal, for access to their land to load the boats. The first sand taken out of the slope would belong to them.[13] There was not much demand, but George Holford, a brickmaker, born in Brewood but now living at Stretton, agreed to take ten cart loads of sand, at 1/- per horse cart load, which helped a little. James Fellows and Co, Canal Carriers at Tipton, later Fellows, Morton and Clayton, declined.

Mr Taylor changes the routine of the school

Mr Taylor had been at the school less than a year before he wanted to change the school hours. He wanted the school day to commence at 8 a.m. and finish at 1 p.m. with only half an hour's break for the children. This would mean the boys would be working harder as the school week would be 27 hours instead of 26, not including homework. It would also give the boys an incentive to listen and do their best work as quickly as possible so that they would be allowed to play sport, or have a free afternoon, if they had learnt their lessons. If they had not, they would have to stay in school and complete their work. Taylor had already stopped between 15 and 18 boys from having three half holidays "with the best possible results". He wanted the new hours to begin immediately.

Mr Walker, both in his role as secretary to the Trustees and a parent of a pupil at the school, did not approve of the 8 o'clock start as he thought that the day boys who lived a distance from the school, and had to walk, would not be able to arrive on time. Mr Walker's own son, Frank, had a difficult walk, initially across fields, of about a mile and half each way every day from their home at Whitemore, Chillington.

Walker told Taylor he could start the day at 8.30 for a trial period but Taylor took no notice and began the school day at 8 a.m. anyway. As a consequence, Walker raised the matter with the Trustees. Taylor belatedly then agreed to alter the morning time of school to 8.30, but the Trustees ordered the school times to be 9 a.m. until noon, throughout the year, but afternoon school would be 2.00 p.m. until 4.30 p.m. in spring and autumn, until 4.00 p.m. in winter and until 5 p.m. in summer.[14]

Taylor then refused to allow day boys to study French, unless their parents paid higher fees. Taylor had more than doubled the fees from 2 guineas per annum to 4½ guineas without any authority to do so from the Trustees. He also wanted payment in advance, which was normal in many schools, but not at Brewood Grammar School. Lord Wrottesley ruled that the day boys must be reinstated in their language class until the Trustees gave a ruling at their meeting in May. The Trustees did not allow the fees to be raised, and Taylor did not allow the day boys to attend the French class, until forced to in July 1873.

Unhappiness at the school

At the same time that the cost of French lessons was in dispute, there was another very different and serious issue relating to the headmaster's excessive use of punishment. James Henry Heatley, a farmer at Engleton, complained to the Trustees about the severe caning his son, James Edward Heatley, had received from the headmaster. Teddy, as he was known, was only nine years old, and a new pupil, having previously attended a school in Waterloo Road, Wolverhampton. Teddy's fellow pupils had played a joke on him saying that he was not needed for afternoon lessons. Taylor sent two boys to his house to bring him back to school where he received a severe caning from the headmaster, and was then sent to Rushton for the same punishment. The usher refused, the boy's back from the first caning described as being like jelly.[15]

A few months later, Teddy was in trouble again with Mr Taylor, and again for not returning to school in the afternoon to finish some work. The boy said that his mother had sent him to get the doctor as one of the servants had been taken ill. Taylor caned the boy again, believing it to be an excuse, but it was the truth. Two weeks later, Teddy was again in trouble for losing his homework which he had done, not in his exercise book but on a piece of paper, and lost it. Taylor expected all homework to be written in an exercise book, one book for each subject. It was unacceptable to write the homework on paper and unless the work was done the boy would not be allowed to attend the school sports day.[16] Heatley now consulted his solicitor, Richard Nock Hearne, at Newport, Shropshire, and added the complaint that the headmaster was still charging extra for French lessons rather than the lower fee authorised by the Trustees.

Thomas Griffin, a farmer from Preston Vale, Penkridge, had tried to pay the extra money for his son to attend French, but Walker, secretary to the Trustees, had returned his money, advising that the extra should not be paid until there was a firm decision from Mr Heatley's legal case. Mr Griffin also wrote to Walker about a school desk that had been damaged by the boys. He believed that the unpleasantness between the day boys and boarders was solely due to them having lunch at different times, so they could not intermingle. The school hours were such that the boarders finished their school day at 1.30 p.m. and then went for dinner. The day boys had their lunch from noon until 2.00 p.m. so the two groups did not have the chance to mix. Griffin's eldest boy, Frank, enjoyed being captain of the cricket club, and the school was renowned for its cricket prowess. However, now the day boys could only find five or six boys to play cricket at lunchtime, not enough for a game, whilst the boarders had enough cricketers to play cricket most afternoons.

Mr Griffin continued that he quite understood that the boys naturally preferred to be out playing rather than studying in the afternoon but Mr Rushton, usher of Brewood School, had kept the same hours for boarders and day pupils. The pragmatic Mr Griffin continued that Taylor did not even teach the boys, but just walked through the room sometimes making a remark and sometimes not. He regretted that the "nice friendly kind feeling that ought to exist between 'Master and Lad' will never be in Mr Taylor's day". Mr Griffin's own boys were not happy at the school. The Trustees should not have been happy either, as one of the reasons for the experimental two-tier system being allowed at the school by the Endowed Schools Commission was because Reverend Wall had an integrated timetable for day pupils and boarders, there was to be no separation.

Taylor undeterred by complaints about punishments and timetable, continued to make changes at the school. Every new boy was to fill in an application form stating which books he was reading in Latin, Greek, English, French, German, mathematics and natural science. He would then be examined in proficiency in reading, handwriting, four rules of arithmetic and an outline of the geography of England. The Trustees agreed that each child should have an admission slip giving details of name, date of birth, previous schools attended, books being read in the subjects to be studied, proposed destination in life, any relevant additional information and the name and address of parent or guardian. Taylor complained that the proficiency of the pupils was low but he did not add that now less than 40 boys attended the school. He saw no reason for an examiner to be present for the school examinations in July, but he was happy for the examination papers to be sent to the school.

News about the state of the school reached Reverend Wall at Hill Top, West Bromwich. He was in correspondence with several people who had connections with Brewood, including Reverend Arthur Chetwynd Talbot and Edward Fernie, grandson of the Congregational Minister of Brewood.[17] The Brewood residents were not happy about the amount of "thrashing" going on at the school. Wall realised that he might be receiving an exaggerated version of events as the stories relating to the headmaster were passed on, but felt that "Taylor's powers seem all dispersive and none attractive". In Wall's opinion 34 pupils was the optimum number of pupils, with the present number of staff. Numbers of pupils, he had heard, were declining. If the number of pupils fell to 33, Taylor would be compelled to reduce staffing levels.

On Thursday 5 June 1873 there was a special meeting of the Trustees to consider Mr Heatley's complaints against the headmaster. The Trustees examined the charges, firstly of excessive or undue punishment to Teddy Heatley, secondly for suspension of the boy without sufficient authority and thirdly for making a charge for instruction in French in excess of his authority. Mr Taylor claimed, in a detailed speech, that young Heatley had used obscene words to a school nurse. According to Mr Walker, the Trustees tried to stop Taylor relating the words in detail, but he persisted. Lord Wrottesley dismissed this story as hearsay.[18] The Trustees concluded that Heatley had deserved some form of punishment but as the alleged severe punishment had been given seven months ago and as no complaint had been made at the time, they declined to express any opinion about the quality of the punishment administered. No boy was to be suspended though, without the matter being first brought to the attention of the Trustees. The headmaster could not charge extra for French, the £2 per annum had been agreed when the headmaster was appointed. Finally, the Trustees decreed that the school hours should be identical for both day boys and boarders, there should be no differentiation, not even for play times.

In September 1873 the Trustees were now aware that Taylor did not have either the temperament or ability of his predecessor. They tried to influence Taylor's teaching methods by stating that public examinations would be held in the last week of July every year and the examiner would be appointed by the very capable and tenacious George Selwyn, Bishop of Lichfield. Taylor had to present his school report to the Trustees in September, and recommend which scholars should receive prizes. It was to be a big event with friends and relatives attending, and recitations and speeches made by the scholars, just as it had been when Mr Wall was headmaster.

Public opinion

Throughout Taylor's headship the parishioners of Brewood were not happy with the way that he ran the school. Most parents at the school wanted a professional education for their sons, but this meant that the school would be graded as a second-class school under the new educational system. The school had thrived under Wall because he understood the needs of both parents and pupils, and kept up to date with the changing educational system. Under Taylor, there were now only seven day pupils and the parents felt that the boys of Brewood were not receiving the education to which they were legally entitled. On 23 October 1873 there was a public meeting about both headmaster and school. The parents were particularly unhappy about changes to the school terms and hours which they believed had been put into place by Taylor without the Trustees approval and against the regulations.

The school year had been divided into two half years with holidays at Christmas and midsummer and ten days either at Easter or Michaelmas, in line with most schools in the County. Taylor wanted the school year to be divided into three terms of equal duration with three equal intervals of holiday.

The school day, ruled by the Trustees to be both morning and afternoon, starting at 9 a.m., had not been implemented by Taylor, and he continued to teach mainly in the mornings, starting at 8 a.m. The parishioners felt that Taylor's new timetable was detrimental to both the health and the studies of the day boys, particularly for those who had to walk three miles or more to school. Parents had spoken to Mr Taylor about the problem but to no effect.

The state of the school was so bad that it was discussed publicly at a meeting of the Staffordshire Chamber of Agriculture held at the Swan Inn, Stafford, on 1 November. Mr Masfen, probably Robert Masfen who farmed at Pendeford, was not sure if it was the fault of the headmaster or the Trustees, but Brewood Grammar School was a declining school. In Mr Masfen's opinion the school received a good endowment for the education of the middle classes. Within the last four years 120 boys had been educated at the school but now there were only 25 of which only seven were day boys, but the masters were receiving all the privileges that the endowment afforded. In other words, the masters were receiving a set income regardless of the number of day boys that they taught. The fewer pupils they taught, the higher the rate of pay per pupil. The audience agreed with Mr Masfen that this was not acceptable. Mr Masfen stated that he was a Trustee of two schools and in his opinion the subject of middle-class education in rural districts needed further consideration.[19]

The Trustees held a special meeting very early in December to discuss the complaints made by the residents of Brewood which was almost certainly spurred on by the public comments made about the school at the Chamber of Agriculture meeting at Stafford. They listened to a deputation of three people from the parish. The Trustees agreed with the parishioners that the school should be conducted for the benefit of the day boys as was the intention of Matthew Knightley, founder of the school, and they would pass this resolution to Taylor.

Taylor, the Brewster family and the future of the school

A Trustees meeting was held on 30 January 1874, but as only four Trustees attended, the meeting was adjourned until 11 February 1874. Matters of the school could still be discussed at the January meeting, but not legally agreed. The Trustees who attended: Lord Wrottesley; Orlando Bridgeman, Earl of Bradford; Augustus Leveson Vernon of Deansfield, Brewood; and the Honourable Edward George Littleton of Teddesley, believed that the number of scholars had decreased so much that at the next meeting the question of Taylor's resignation should be discussed.

A large number of Trustees attended the special meeting held on 11 February 1874. They first considered a letter from Mr Taylor who wanted to amend the present scheme of work. This was declined. In their view, as Taylor had undertaken to manage the school with the present scheme in place there should be no amendment. The scheme had been successful under Reverend Wall but under Mr Taylor there had been such a decline in numbers over the last 15 months by both day scholars and boarders that the efficiency Taylor wanted at the school could not be restored. If Taylor felt that he could not run the school successfully without a new scheme, then he should resign. No decision was made about Taylor by the Trustees at that meeting.

The 1874 summer examination reports from Bishop Abraham and Dr Edward Bolston were not good. They reported that the pupils were receiving an indifferent education, with no subject being taught really well, including Latin. Spelling was very defective, except in dictation.

Matters became worse when Edward Brewster of Stretton Mill was dismissed from the French lessons by Taylor. On 2 October 1874 Taylor wrote to Mr Brewster that he could not possibly let the two eldest Brewster children learn French, as requested. In Taylor's view, the eldest son, Edward, was idle and had fallen materially below standard for his age, and Frederick, the younger brother, was also not achieving the standard for his age. Taylor would not let Edward learn a language until he had shown a competent knowledge in his other subjects. However, in the opinion of Mr Rushton and the examiners, Abraham and Bolston, Edward was a very competent student.

Mrs Brewster went to see Mr Taylor at the school, her husband could not accompany her as he had to go to Stafford Market. Mrs Brewster asked the headmaster if he would help her children but Taylor replied that he had never been so overworked in his life as he was last term devoting his time to teaching her two boys to read, and all the parents were the same in their expectations.

Lord Hatherton, Chairman of the Trustees, was being kept up to date with the problems of the Brewster family. The headmaster had the right to withdraw a pupil from the school only if he was idle or incapable of being educated to the standard for his age. When Bishop Abraham supervised the examinations, he placed Edward Brewster, aged 13, substantially above other boys of his age and top of the year. Edward had achieved a similar position with Mr Bolston's examination papers, so Taylor could not be justified in withdrawing the elder Brewster from school for idleness or incapacity. The problem, Walker believed, was nothing to do with the educational standard of the Brewster boys but solely because Mr Brewster was not paying the higher fee for French lessons demanded by Taylor.

On 10 October 1874 Hatherton wrote to the Charity Commissioners explaining that for some time the Trustees had been "painfully aware" that Mr Taylor had lost the confidence of the inhabitants of the neighbourhood for whose benefit the school was originally endowed as was shown by the small number of day pupils attending the school. Taylor refused to teach the scheme which Mr Wall had successfully taught, and had not sent the pupils for the Oxford and Cambridge Local Examinations, at which Wall's pupils had excelled.

The Charity Commissioners reply in November 1874 did not address the issue and was not helpful to the Trustees, but was more helpful to Mr Taylor. They advised that the matter could be put on hold "without any material inconvenience" as an improved scheme for the effective working of the school, in line with the Endowed Schools Act 1869, would be introduced by the Charity Commissioners in 1875.

Meanwhile, the Brewster children had still not been reinstated in the French class, so Edward's father, John Brewster, spoke to Lord Hatherton about the matter when they both attended the December Board of Guardians meeting at Penkridge. Taylor had under-estimated the power and friendship of the local community. Following the meeting, Hatherton again wrote to Taylor asking him to reconsider reinstating Brewster's son into the French class. Lord Hatherton again stated that Edward was not backward in his learning which was the only reason the headmaster could use for him not to study French. If the boy was not reinstated the matter would be raised at the Trustees meeting.

Taylor replied to Lord Hatherton that he had thought about the matter of the boy's withdrawal from French for six months and was extremely surprised and much grieved to find that his Lordship could be "led to believe" that he would require a boy's withdrawal from the school because he would not teach the boy French on "certain terms". Taylor felt that he had given Edward a chance of improving but he was well below the standard of French required for his age, and similarly with Frederick, the second son, who Mr Taylor believed was also not sufficiently of an academic standard to take French. The third child, the younger Percival, was likely to overtake both children academically.

Taylor wanted Lord Hatherton to benefit from his explanation of the difference between "dismissal" and "expulsion". "I suppose, my Lord, that by "dismissal" you mean "expulsion" which is public. My letter to the father was private and he had the opportunity of withdrawing his son without any publicity". Taylor wrote that the Brewood scheme was "unmistakably plain" that he had the right to withdraw a pupil from the class.[20]

The ill-health of Reverend Rushton

In his letter to Lord Hatherton, Taylor also questioned why the Trustees were expecting Mr Rushton to teach when he needed medical attention for tongue cancer and was clearly unwell. Mr Rushton had been at the school for 32 years, and both his health and teaching were suffering. Rushton had consulted Sir James Paget, one of the best surgeons in the country, but was advised that the illness was too far advanced. The letter from Taylor was written with very little empathy for Mr Rushton. Lord Hatherton agreed that Rushton was too ill to teach but also felt that Taylor should have shown some sympathy for Rushton's condition and, as there were not many pupils at the school, taught the lower school boys himself as a temporary measure, out of kindness and compassion. Mr Reusch, the French master, had, in fact, been taking Rushton's classes to help, his salary being paid by Taylor.

At the Trustees meeting on 29 January 1875, it was readily agreed that a deputy should be appointed to do Rushton's work during his illness, and that he could remain in his home, which they hoped would put Mr Rushton's mind at rest with regard to school matters. Mr Rushton passed away a few days later, on 9 February. A memorial is erected to him in the parish church, subscribed by his old scholars and carved by John Taylor of Brewood.[21]

Dismissal of Mr Taylor

Mr Francis Monckton of Somerford Hall and Mr A. L. Vernon met at Mr Walker's estate office at Chillington to discuss the best way to secure Taylor's dismissal. They wanted as many Trustees as possible to attend the meeting on Friday, 29 January 1875. The Trustees would be told the seriousness of the state of affairs at the school before the official meeting. Mr Brewster was also asked to attend the meeting.

Mr Taylor wrote to the Trustees the day before the Trustees meeting, stating that he wanted Brewood School "to be on an equal footing" with other schools. He reminded them that he had a very unusual depth of university education and when he applied for the headmastership, he believed that the job was for a Classical first-grade school and that his qualifications and experience would be useful. However, he found no boy who had a competent knowledge of classics, mathematics or physical science. He felt that the Trustees had placed him in a false position if they did not intend to have a scheme for a first-grade school in place, only an inferior school.

Lord Hatherton was not able to attend the meeting as he had suspected whooping cough, but he did not want Taylor to remain as headmaster at the school and thought that Taylor could be dismissed for failing to conduct the school in accordance with the school scheme, and also because the school under his management provided no advantage to the neighbourhood. Hatherton wanted the Trustees to be aware of the legalities in evicting Taylor from house and school. He wanted no legal blunders that would allow Taylor to take action against them, for example Taylor's expulsion from French of the Brewster boys, was cause for reproof, not dismissal.

Mr Taylor was allowed to attend the meeting of the Trustees, held at the National School, on Friday 29 January 1875 and Taylor's letter of the 28 January was read at the meeting.[22] Mr Walker, the secretary, told the Trustees that there were now only six day boys at the school, and the headmaster had only two boarders, which reflected a further decline in the number of scholars since the last meeting. There also continued to be complaints from the parents that the headmaster was refusing to teach French for the fee demanded by the Trustees. A correspondence on the subject of Edward Brewster's dismissal was laid before the Trustees and it was decided that, even after Mr Taylor's explanations, the school was in a very unsatisfactory state. Taylor now claimed that he had thought that Edward Brewster was a year older than he really was, so he would be willing to reinstate the boy at the school, which he did.[23]

George Selwyn, Bishop of Lichfield, proposed that a letter should be written to the Charity Commissioners to examine why Brewood School had ceased to have any advantage to the inhabitants of the neighbourhood, as were the wishes of the founder. This was seconded by Thomas George Anson, Earl of Lichfield.

Following Mr Rushton's death, Taylor believed he had the right to appoint Mr Rushton's successor, not the Trustees, as the scheme clearly stated that the headmaster should have the sole power of appointment and dismissal of all future assistant masters and teachers. As Mr Rushton was an Endowed master, not an assistant master, and was paid by the provision of the original Trust and his office had not been abolished by the scheme, the Trustees believed that they had the authority to advertise the post, not Taylor. Mr Reusch, the French master at the school, wanted to apply for the vacancy as he had been doing Mr Rushton's duties for some time.[24]

The Trustees then received another long letter of complaints about the curriculum and the examination system from Taylor who claimed that the school numbers had been declining for years. Three years before his appointment there had been over 100 boys, but when he came to office there were only 45 of which six were about to leave but others, Taylor believed, were not qualified to be at the school. He had not been aware, when he was appointed, that Wall had initially brought most of his boarders from Birkenhead and so there had been no attempt to form local connections for new pupils. Taylor believed that if he and the other candidates who had applied for the headmastership had been told that fact, they would have quickly realised that the school "was not in repute" and a further decrease in numbers of students was inevitable. This was Taylor's opinion which is not supported by the statistics that are available, nor by the reports in the local newspapers for years afterwards.

In Taylor's view there had been active hostility towards the school before he started teaching there. He had advertised the opening of the school in local papers for several weeks as soon as he arrived, and during the Christmas holidays of 1872 but received no applications for boarders. He blamed the Trustees for fostering a feeling of hostility which had contributed, either consciously or unconsciously to the decline of the school. In addition, the scheme of work was hurriedly passed, imperfect and clearly needed amending.

Mr Taylor added that the Reverend Kempson, who had been a headmaster at the school for 30 years, had also clearly felt that the school needed an input into its welfare and had bequeathed money for improvements: money for exhibitions to the universities and the requirement of more frequent and regular meetings of the Trustees. Whilst the Trustees had met more regularly there had often not been a quorum. Mr Taylor argued that a scheme of work should set down the regulations for the management and discipline of the school and this had not happened. At his interview, Taylor believed that he would be working under a new scheme issued by the Charity Commissioners and approved by the Endowed Schools Commission, which would classify the school as Classical. He would not have applied for the post of headmaster if he had known otherwise. The letter was signed James Heber Taylor, M.A. Trinity College Cambridge, M.A. Queen's College Oxford, B.Sc. London.

Mr Stanton from the Schools Inquiries Commission came to Brewood on 23 March to inspect the school and agreed that Taylor could be dismissed. Lord Hatherton wanted Taylor to be offered £100 as an incentive for him to leave, subject to the Charity Commissioners' approval.

Mr Higham, the builder, was asked to repair to second master's house and the adjoining school room, over a period of two years. The cost was £308 but Higham would only undertake the work on condition that he was paid immediately on completion. The builders were to collect the keys from Michael Machin, the blacksmith, who lived at the cottage near to the school in School House Lane, now known as School Road. Lord Hatherton then had the task of writing to Taylor informing him that his salary would be much diminished over the next two years, due to the extensive repairs needed to the second master's house. The new school scheme, that was due to be issued, continued to have the headmaster responsible to the Trustees. Mr Taylor resigned with effect from 29 September 1875, and Lord Hatherton accepted his resignation on behalf of the Trustees.

In spite of all the trouble with Taylor, there were over 20 applicants for the post and some written enquiries. Mr Thomas England Rhodes, headmaster of Alleynes School, Uttoxeter was unanimously appointed as the new headmaster of Brewood School.

Mr Taylor leaves Brewood

Mr Taylor left Brewood on Wednesday 29 September 1875. Mr Walker went to Brewood Grammar School and consulted with Mr Rhodes, Taylor's successor, about the state of the school. There was a serious problem with the water supply and the drains. Walker went to inspect the situation and he was not happy. Taylor would be required to restore the items that he had altered or removed, and bear the cost. The window that Mr Taylor had put into the boys' dining room was not properly filled in, neither were the passage and study doors. The boys' toilets had been removed, the casing taken from the boys' bath and some water pipes and taps taken away. The pig sty wall and doors had also been removed. Walker said that the repairs would be made good, finished to standard and the cost deducted from monies owing to Mr Taylor.

Taylor moved to Cambridge but whilst at Brewood he had also been on the electoral register for Wakefield, along with his brothers, Henry Martin Taylor and William Wilberforce Taylor. James Heber Taylor, and his wife and children eventually settled at Little Trinity House, 16 Jesus Lane, Cambridge, now a grade 1 listed building, where he became a private tutor and an examiner at Girton College, the first women's college in Cambridge. In 1879 he was appointed Deputy Proctor, Trinity, in the absence of the Junior Proctor.[25]

On the 1881 census at Jesus Lane, Cambridge, James was living with his wife and children and, his mother-in-law, Susannah Pearce. He had two students lodging at the house too: 21-year-old Frederick Mortimer Young from Leeds and 18-year-old Henry Sutton Timmis who was to become a member of the Mersey Docks and Harbour Board, and deputy chairman of the Building Committee for Liverpool Cathedral, amongst a great many other things. Ten years later, the students had left and James' brother William Wilberforce was staying with the family and, like his brother, was a private tutor and school examiner.

On Sunday 2 April 1888, Mr Taylor's son, John Charles, died suddenly at King William's College, Castletown on the Isle of Man. He had been a senior pupil at the college, described as amiable and kind. He had only been ill for a week, suffering from inflammation of the lungs. He was buried on 12 April at Malew Churchyard, Isle of Man.[26] Taylor was devastated by his son's death.

Taylor continued to teach and in 1890 was advertising that he was able to prepare students for Entrance or Scholarship Examinations and as he was in the unique position of being a graduate from three universities, he could advise students, to their advantage, on their choice of university.[27] The 1891 census reveals that Taylor continued to work as a private tutor and examiner.

However, in May 1902 Taylor was in court complaining of the incessant noise that Carmino Como, an organ grinder was making 100 yards from his home. Carmino Como was fined 2/6d and his employer, Antonio Rosso was also fined 1/- for failing to have his name painted on the cart. Mr Taylor though, was not alone in his complaint of the noise, day and night, of organ grinders, it caused a nuisance for many people.

Taylor had been very keen on photography since childhood and, after he left Brewood, became a member of the Cambridge Photographic Club, exhibiting photographs and lantern slides. He became President of the Club in 1911 and in the same year, gave a lecture at Hartlepool Photographic Society entitled "Stereoscopic photography". The newspaper described the lecture as extremely interesting and the reporter was impressed with Taylor's stereo-photographs which illustrated the talk.[28] Taylor also made a complete photographic survey of Trinity College. When this was finished it comprised of 300 photographs.[29]

Taylor registered the copyright of other photographs at Stationers' Company, the copyright office in London. These registered photographs included buildings such as King's College Chapel and also Ely Cathedral, but he diversified by registering a photograph of a peregrine falcon and a photograph of Archdeacon Emery, his daughter's father-in-law.[30] There are no known photographs that Taylor took at Brewood, although there is a photograph that he took whilst at Mill Hill School. In his obituary Mr Taylor was described as a perfectionist in his photography and his work was of a semi-professional standard. He was always willing to help his fellow members of the Cambridge Photographic Club.[31]

At Cambridge, Taylor also became involved in the Antiquarian Society. At their meeting on 3 March 1890, Taylor exhibited some Bactrian and Hindu coins from Varanasi on the banks of the river Ganges, as well as a pendant dial.[32] It is not known where he was able to find these coins, but possibly from his father, Reverend Taylor, who travelled the world after his retirement from Wakefield Grammar School in 1875.

James Heber Taylor died suddenly on Palm Sunday, 5 April 1914. His funeral was at Trinity College chapel where the flag flew at half-mast above Trinity College gateway, and he was buried at Huntingdon Road cemetery. The funeral was very well attended and he was described as a dearly loved husband, father and grandfather. As well as his family, masters of the Cambridge Colleges, many clergy and members of the Photographic Club were amongst the mourners. His detailed obituary in the papers emphasised Taylor's intelligence and academic ability.[33]

Taylor had clearly not been happy at Brewood and settled far more easily into Cambridge life, with his siblings. In 1876 a new scheme for governing Brewood Grammar School was put into effect by the Charity Commissioners under the Endowed Schools Act. The school again grew and developed under the new headmaster, T. E. Rhodes, but the happy memories in Brewood were of Taylor's predecessor, Reverend Wall.

Notes

1 Wall had not been officially allowed such a high number of boarders.
2 William Wilberforce Taylor was born at Wakefield in 1849. He was very academic and followed a teaching career becoming master of Rossall School between 1879–80, a mathematics master at Ripon Grammar School 1880–86 and finally a private tutor and examiner. In 1883 he applied for a patent for improvements in printing machines and later became a "Demonstrator of Physics".
3 Henry Martin Taylor achieved fame for his mathematical work, as well as becoming a barrister. He became a senior Fellow of Trinity College, Cambridge, a Fellow of the Royal Society and also Mayor of Cambridge. Henry Martin became blind when he was 51 years old, but continued with his research work and finding that there were no scientific books available at that time in braille he helped to devise a braille notation and remedied the situation.
4 SRO, CEG/2/1, Letter from Walker to Taylor, 12 September 1872.
5 SRO, D1416/4/2/14, Letter from Taylor to Walker, address 57 Moray Road, Tollington Park, 29 August 1872.
6 SRO, CEG/2/1, Letter from Walker to Taylor, 19 September 1872.
7 Augustus Leveson Vernon was the son of Henry Charles Vernon of Hilton Park. He married Selina Giffard, daughter of Walter Giffard of Chillington at Brewood parish church.
8 SRO, D1416/4/2/14, Letter from Wall to Walker, 5 October 1872.
9 SRO, D1416/4/2/14, Letter from Wall to Walker, 29 March 1873.
10 SRO, D1416/4/2/14, Letter from Taylor to Hatherton, 6 June 1873.
11 SRO, CEG/2/1, Letter from Walker to Taylor, 23 April 1873.
12 SRO, D1416/4/2/14.
13 SRO, D1416/4/2/8.
14 SRO, CEG/2/1, Trustees Meeting, 15 April 1873.
15 Douglas Thompson, *A History of Brewood Grammar School, 1553–1953* (Brewood Grammar School, 1953), p. 66.
16 SRO, D1416/4/2/13, Letter from James Heatley, 9 May 1873.

17 Edward Fernie was an accountant, like his father Edward Fernie. The elder Fernie had, for many years, though been working as a draper in Brewood. On the 1871 census, Edward Fernie the elder, and his family, including Edward junior, were living at 19 Eastgate Street, Stafford, later the premises of the William Salt Library. The family by the time of the 1881 census had moved to Wolverhampton Road, Stafford.

18 SRO, D1416/3/2/2, Letter from Walker to R.N. Hearne, 9 June 1873.

19 *Staffordshire Advertiser*, 8 November 1873, p. 2.

20 SRO, D1416/4/2/15, Letter from Taylor to Hatherton, 16 December 1874.

21 John Taylor was born in 1857 at Tinker's Lane, Brewood and was very likely one of Mr Rushton's pupils. He carved the stone pulpit at St Mary's Roman Catholic church, Brewood, as well as many buildings in Wolverhampton and Lichfield. He tragically died at the age of 30, 1887, after some scaffolding collapsed. He is buried in the parish churchyard at Brewood.

22 SRO, CEG/2/1.

23 Edward John Brewster of Stretton became a government civil servant and married Cicely Anne Griffin, daughter of Thomas Griffin of Preston Vale on 27 September 1887 at Stretton church.

24 Probably Julius Reusch from Germany who was a language teacher.

25 *Cambridge Independent Press*, 22 November 1879, p. 5.

26 *Cambridge Chronicle and Journal,* 20 April 1888, p. 4.

27 *Surrey Comet*, 11 January 1890, p. 8.

28 *Northern Daily Mail,* 14 December 1911, p. 4.

29 www.worldwar1schoolarchives.org *The Savilian*, Summer Term, 1914, p.18.

30 On 30 March 1894 there was an article in the *Cambridge Chronicle and University Journal* for the wedding at All Saints church, Cambridge, of Mary Ethel Taylor, the daughter of James and Mary Taylor to George Frederick Emery, of Trinity College Cambridge, Barrister at Law, and eldest son of Venerable Archdeacon Emery of The College, Ely. George Frederick Emery was an author of many books including *People's Guide to the Parish Councils Act so far as it effects rural parishes,* which was in its 7th edition in 1894, *Handy Guide to Patent Law and Practice,* 2nd edition 1904, *The People's Guide to the Workmen's Compensation Act,* 1906, *People's Guide to Free Trade,* 1924.

31 www.fadingimages.co.uk: *Cambridge and District Photography Society minutes,* 14 April 1914. *Cambridge and District Photographic Society* was initially known as *Cambridge and District Photographic Club.*

32 *Cambridge Chronicle and Journal,* 7 March 1890, p. 7.

33 *Cambridge Independent Press*, 10 April 1914, p. 4.

Addendum

Dr Matthew Knightley

Dr Matthew Knightley of Cossington, Leicestershire and Fowlmere, Cambridgeshire played a major role in the provision of education in Brewood, but who was this person, and why had he taken such a keen interest in the area?

Matthew Knightley and his career

Matthew Knightley stated in his will, written in 1560, that he was born in Brewood, and from the dates that he was at university, this was probably between 1477 and 1484. Matthew Knightley attended both Cambridge and Oxford Universities. He obtained his B.A. degree in March 1498/9 and his M.A. degree in 1502/3.[1] Knightley then continued his education qualifying as Bachelor of Canon Law in 1509 and his Bachelor of Civil Law in 1510. He also obtained his Master of Canon Law and then became a Doctor of Civil Law at Oxford in 1513, along with only four other students in that year. Knightley continued his studies at a foreign university, possibly Paris, where he obtained a doctorate in theology before returning to his parish of Cossington.[2] He was rector at Cossington in Leicestershire, from 1508, and also rector of Fowlmere, Cambridgeshire, from 1517 until his death in 1561, but spent most of his time at All Saints' parish, Cossington, where he is buried.

In his will, Matthew Knightley bequeathed money to his parishes as well as other deserving charities, including the Bede Houses of Leicester. Knightley also bequeathed four pounds to the poor people of the town and parish of Bruyde. [Brewood] where he was born, six shillings and eight pence to the vicar of Brewood and the same amount to the schoolmaster, again reinforcing his connection with Brewood Free School.

Matthew Knightley had a farm at Cossington which, at the time of his death, included livestock: 200 sheep and lambs, 28 cattle, pigs, geese, hens, ducks and bees. The farm provided milk, honey, cheese, meat, bacon, beer and plenty of wool. Dr Knightley enjoyed reading his large collection of books, and realised the importance of education. He owned a copy of Ludolph of Saxony's work *Vita Christi*, the *Life of Christ*, which he bequeathed to Sir Thomas Thorpe, along with two shillings.[3] To Thomas Babington of Rothley, Knightley bequeathed his best "Romlett of Malvessy" which amounted to 18 gallons of best Malvesey wine.[4]

Matthew Knightley became rector at Fowlmere in 1517, probably receiving help from his uncle, John Danyell of Felstead, Essex who was an employee of John de Vere, 13th Earl of Oxford, benefactor of the church at Fowlmere.[5] John Danyell was one of the executors of the Earl's will at his death in 1513, and had been bequeathed an annuity of £10. In his own will, dated 1 May 1518, and proved 22 January 1519, John Danyell requested that his nephews, Doctor Matthew Knightley and his brother William, were the executors, along with his cousin John Danyell of Messing. This John Danyell had married Grace, the daughter of Sir Edmund Denny, Chief Baron of the Exchequer. [6]

The churchwardens at Fowlmere were unhappy that Matthew Knightley rarely visited the church and were complaining, in 1554, that the church needed repairing and had still not been levelled by 1561.[7]

Matthew Knightley died at Cossington on the 9 July 1561 and was buried in an alabaster tomb within the church. It has been moved from its original position, but still remains in the church, on the north side of the chancel in a 14th century tomb recess and the inscription reads: Here lyethe Matthew Knyghtley, Doctore in Divinitye, and some tyme parson of Cossington, who departed thys worlde the 9th daye of July, in the year of oure Lord MDLXI.

Matthew Knightley's family

Matthew Knightley, wrote two key documents which help to give an insight into his family. There are also original documents relating to the family held in archives across the country.

The first reliable document is the will of Matthew Knightley, which he wrote on the 21 June 1560.[8] The second document is a letter that

Matthew Knightley wrote on 6 November 1557 to Robert Coke of Lincoln's Inn, London, and Mileham, Norfolk. Robert Coke had married Knightley's niece and Coke was enquiring about the family history of his wife, Winifred, the daughter of Matthew Knightley's brother, William.[9] Robert Coke and Winifred were the parents of Sir Edward Coke, the great barrister and a politician, who believed in the supremacy of the Common Law over the monarchy.[10] Using these and other original and secondary resources from county archives, a picture of Matthew Knightley's family emerges.

The Knightley family had lived at Knightley, Gnosall, from the thirteenth century and increased their property holding and influence in Staffordshire and other counties. They owned property in Brewood parish at Engleton, Broom Hall, [Bremhale], and the town of Brewood. John de Knightley, his son Richard and John Purcell leased Broom Hall to Hugh and Edith Parker of Patshull for one hundred years in 1410.[11] However, Richard Knightley, in 1422, was suing William Wooley, yeoman and several others in Brewood parish, for allowing their cattle to graze on his grass at Bromhaste, [Broom Hall].[12]

Matthew Knightley states that "John Knightley my father and Dame Cassandra Jefforde' (Giffard), were germaine cousins".[13] Cassandra, daughter of Thomas Humphreston of Humphreston Hall, near Albrighton, Shropshire, married Robert Giffard of Chillington Hall.

John Venn and his son, who edited *Alumni Cantabrigienses,* believed Matthew Knightley's father to be John of Norfolk. *The Visitations of Essex of 1558,* clearly states that Thomas Knightley of Bent [Bentley] in Staffordshire married a daughter of a Giffard, and they had three children, Thomas, who was the eldest and the heir, William Knightley of Marsham, Norfolk and Matthew Knightley.[14] The Hyde, Brewood, and Bentley Hall, Walsall, were homes of the Lane family. There were only a few named Trustees when the school was first formed, but John Lane was one of the earliest known Trustees of the new Brewood Free Grammer School.

There is much confusion about Matthew Knightley's family history within published sources. In his letter to Robert Coke, Matthew states that he was descended from the Staffordshire Knightley's and that "I was the youngeste & laste of that name". Matthew's father appears to have died when Matthew Knightley was a child as his uncle, John Danyell, [also spelt Daniell] of Felstead, Essex, supported him throughout his university education and gave him his "promotions".

It seems likely that Matthew's ancestors were the Knightley's of Broom Hall and Engleton. Matthew Knightley believed his grandfather Knightley, had died before 1457. He had been told by his relative, Richard Knightley of Fawsley, Northamptonshire, that their grandfathers had been "bretheren".[15] As brothers, these mentioned grandfathers would have been the children of Richard Knightley of Gnosall and his wife, Joan Giffard. In the early fifteenth century, Richard, son of Richard and Joan Knightley of Gnosall, purchased with his wife Elizabeth, and their eldest son John, land in Northamptonshire and a small estate in "Browode" [Brewood].[16]

In 1467 a Robert Knightley had leased the mill at Engleton from the Bishop of Lichfield for ten years at a rent of £2 13s 4d and in 1473 a fish pond within the manor of Brewood was leased to a Thomas Knightley for 20d.[17] Robert Knightley of Engleton and his wife Alice, also owned a house in Brewood town which they bought from William Blakemore on 2 January 1467 when Thomas Aron was vicar of Brewood.[18]

Robert Knightley had died by March 1478 when his widow, Alice Knightley of Engleton, was involved in a court case regarding trespassing.[19] The house at Engleton became the marital home of their daughter, Isabella, when she became the wife of Matthew Moreton of Moreton and Wilbrighton, Staffordshire. They had two sons: James Moreton, who later inherited the house at Moreton and Wilbrighton from his father, and Thomas who lived at Engleton. Matthew Moreton was the godfather of Matthew Knightley and, in his letter to Robert Coke, Knightley assumed that the family were still alive, and knew that they "keepethe a good howse". The Moreton family continued to have an interest in Brewood Grammar School through the centuries.

William Knightley

Matthew Knightley had two elder brothers, one of whom was William Knightley, a highly respected attorney who lived at Norwich and also owned property and rights over the lands in parts of Norfolk around the Hickling Broads, North Walsham and Wroxham, including Morgrave Knightley, near Martham, as well as rights over land at Clippesby and Rollesby.[20]

William Knightley, the eldest son, had been a lawyer from about 1495 and had married Margaret Pawe, daughter of Andrew Pawe, an attorney in Norwich, who had also been town clerk and clerk of the peace for Norfolk. Their daughter, Winifred married Robert Coke on 22 December 1543 at St Peter Parmentergate church, Norwich and were the parents of Sir Edward Coke. Sir Edward Coke was given two law books by his mother which began his library.[21] William and Margaret's daughter Audrey married Sir Thomas Gawdy, a lawyer and Justice of the Court of the King's Bench in 1548. Audrey was bequeathed 20 shillings by Matthew Knightley. Their daughter Letitia married William Clippesby of Clippesby, Norfolk, and, after his death, William Cardinall of North Bromley, Essex. She was also bequeathed 20 shillings by Matthew Knightley.[22] Another daughter Katherine had married Reginald Rowse of Badingham, Suffolk.

William Knightley's second wife was Agnes Hare, the sister of Sir Nicholas Hare, Knight and Master of the Rolls, Lord Keeper of the Great Seal.[23] They had a son George who married Katherine Pyrton. Agnes had two daughters from a previous marriage, Mary and Margaret.

Matthew Knightley had bequeathed 5 shillings and 4 pence to William Knightley in his will, "if he still be alive". In fact, if he is referring to his brother, and no relationship is mentioned, William had died in 1548, wishing to be buried at the church of St Peter Parmentergate at Norwich. He bequeathed money for food and drink to the prisoners in Norwich Greater Hall and Castle but made no mention of Matthew Knightley in his will.

Thomas Knightley

Very little is known about Thomas. He may have lived in London as in Matthew Knightley's letter to Robert Coke, Matthew Knightley mentioned that a tailor in Southwick, London, claimed to be the illegitimate son of his brother Thomas, but Matthew Knightley denied any truth in the rumour. A strong possibility is that Thomas is the Thomas Knyghtley, chaplain, who granted lands to John Giffard at Chillington in 1507. This Thomas Knightley obtained his Bachelor of Canon Law on 18 June 1505, and, at the same time became rector of St James' church, Colchester, Essex with the title Bachelor of Divinity.[24] It is possible that this living was obtained for Thomas Knightley by John Danyell of Messing, Colchester, cousin of John Danyell of Felstead and one of the executors of the latter's will along with his nephews, William and Matthew Knightley. Matthew Knightley did not bequeath anything to his brother Thomas which could imply that Thomas had died.

Other relatives

It is unknown whether Dr Knightley ever returned to Brewood, once he had settled in Cossington but he remembered his cousin Dorothy Shirley of Staunton and her family in his will. Dorothy Shirley, was the daughter of John Gifford and sister of Sir Thomas Giffard. She had married John Congreve of Stretton then, after his death, Francis Shirley of Staunton Harold and Ettingham. Francis Shirley was High Sheriff of Leicestershire and Matthew Knightley named him as overseer of his will. Ralph Shirley, one of Dorothy's sons, kept two gelding horses at Thomas Congreve's home at Stretton Hall, near Brewood, paying £20 per annum for their keep so that he could ride them at his leisure.[25] Matthew Knightley bequeathed his cousin Dorothy ten wedders, or male sheep, a high-quality linen tablecloth patterned in diamonds and two 'great' cushions. To his goddaughter, Ann Shirley, Dr Knightley bequeathed his greatest pan, a pair of flaxen sheets and twenty more wedders. To Dorothy Brokesby, wife of Robert Brokesby of Shoby, Leicestershire, and daughter of Dorothy and John Congreve, he bequeathed his great charger or horse.

The Shirley family were related to Sir Francis Pulteney of Misterton, Leicestershire, who had been Sheriff of Leicestershire and Warwickshire. He specifically requested in his will of 1541, probate 1544, that Dr Matthew Knightley, if he was still alive, preached a sermon at his funeral, for which he would be paid ten shillings.

The Danyells and Howards of Norfolk, Suffolk and Ireland

Whilst Matthew Knightley never refers to his mother by her christian name, she was the daughter of Sir Thomas Danyell or Daniell, Baron of Rathware and Lord Deputy of Ireland. Thomas Danyell died between 1478 and 1482. Her mother, Margaret, was the daughter of Sir Robert Howard, who had died in 1436, and sister of Sir John Howard, first Duke of Norfolk, who has been seen by historians as one of the most important men of the time. Sir John Howard was killed at the Battle of Bosworth in 1485, supporting Richard III. Margaret's cousin, was Elizabeth Howard, wife of John de Vere, 12th Earl of Oxford. As Matthew Knightley states in his will that he was born in Brewood, his mother must have obviously been living at Brewood at the time of his birth.

The Danyell's of Felstead, Essex, also lived at Brewood at some point. This is known because when John Danyell's wife, Margery, wrote her will in July 1520, proved in April 1523, she bequeathed ten pounds for repairs and adornments to the church at Brewood and also gave the church her household implements which were in the custody of Matthew Moreton of Engleton, indicating that the Danyell family knew Brewood quite well. Note that amongst the executors that Margery Danyell requested were her cousins John Danyell of Messing and Master Edward Fowke, clerk, who may have been the son of William Fowke of Brewood and his wife Jane Streethay.[26] William Fowke had lived at The Woolley, Brewood, in 1478 before moving to Brewood Hall.[27]

To Robert Coke, who had sent Matthew Knightley some gloves in his correspondence about the family, Matthew Knightley bequeathed a down bed, two pillows of down, a bolster of down all covered with white fustian, a pair of fustian blankets and 20 shillings in money.

Notes

1 The later date of 1484 for the birth of Knightley is possible as Thomas Wolsey graduated from Magdalen College Oxford in 1486, aged 15. *see ODNB:* Sybil M. Jack, *Thomas Wolsey.*

2 *Venn Alumni Cantabrigienses* iii. 30; *SHC 1931* p. 192 *and* Dr A.B. Emden to J.F. Fuggles in footnote 26 of *The Parish Clergy in the Archdeaconry of Leicester 1520–1540: Leicestershire Archaeological and Historical Society.*

3 A Thomas Thorpe was confrater at Wigston's hospital, Leicester, during the early and mid-sixteenth century and helped to ensure a good school on the premises, with two masters, retiring in 1566. Another possibility is Sir Thomas Thorpe, yeoman and merchant, who was buried 11 March 1574 at Sileby, Leicestershire, one of Matthew Knightley's parishes.

4 S.H. Skillington, *Medieval Cossington, a narrative based upon the researches of the late George Francis Farnham,* Chapter V.

5 Fowlmere had been inherited by Elizabeth Howard, through her grandmother Margaret de Plaiz, wife of John Howard, 1366–1437, and passed to Elizabeth's husband, John de Vere, 12th Earl of Oxford.

6 www.oxford-shakespeare.com National Archives Prob 11/19 f 102, *copyright* Nina Green.

7 *VCH Cambridgeshire.*

8 Will of Matthew Knightley, Leicestershire, Leicester and Rutland Record Office, written 21 June 1560, proved 19 July 1561.

9 Norfolk Record Office, EVL 584, 463X6 1466–1467. In this volume is a letter from Matthew Knightley to his nephew Robert Coke regarding the Knightley genealogy, dated 1557.

10 Robert Coke's wrote his will on 18 March 1560. His daughters Winifred, Dorothy, Elizabeth, Anne, Ursula, Margaret and son Edward Coke were all unmarried and at the time were under 21. The executors were Coke's wife, Winifred, and brother-in-law Thomas Gawdy, Esquire.

11 Northampton Archives K(C)142 1st November 1410.

12 SHC, *Volume XVII, 1896, Extracts from the Plea Rolls, De Banco Trinity 1 Henry VI,* pp. 90-91.

13 Letter from Matthew Knightley to Robert Coke: EVL 584 463 X6 Norfolk Record Office.

14 William Hervey, *Visitations of Essex 1558*, Harleian MS 1137 (The Harleian Society, Volume XIII, 1878).

15 This Richard Knightley died 1534.

16 www.historyofparliamentonliine.org Richard Knightley of Fawsley and Gnosall died 1442.

17 *VCH Brewood* and WSL, S.MS 335 (1) m 17.

18 *VCH Brewood* and WSL, S.MS 335 (1) m 17.

19 *SHC VI, New Series, Part I,* Extracts from the plea rolls 1478, Easter 18 Edward IV, p.113.

20 Norfolk Record Office, MC268/46/1-8 694x1, *A quitclaim by Thomas le Straunge, son of Robert to William Knyghtley, John Danyell and others dated 12 November 1515 relates to Morgrave Knightley, Norfolk the home of William Knightley.*

21 Kath Lynn Emerson, *A Who's Who of Tudor Women* [Internet].

22 Norfolk Record Office, *Blomefield XI* f 95–96, <u>and</u> *Will of William Knightley*, 1548, NCC Will register 55.

23 John A Burke, *Genealogical and heraldic history of the extinct and dormant baronetcies <u>and also</u>* Allen D Boyer, *Sir Edward Coke and the Elizabethan Age* pp. 2–3.

24 A.B. Emden, *Alumni Oxonienses 1500–1714.*

25 SRO, D1057/0/1 A – B folio 50.

26 www.oxford-shakespeare.com/Probate/PROB_11-65_ff_218-19.pdf

27 *SHC VI New Series Part 1,* Extracts from the plea rolls 1478, 18 Edward IV, p. 113.

TRUSTEES OF BREWOOD
GRAMMAR SCHOOL, 1780

George Anson, Shugborough

Nathaniel Lister, Armitage

Reverend William Inge, Canon of Lichfield

John Turton, Sugnall

Francis Eld, Seighford

John Williamson, Stafford

Nathaniel Barrett, Oaken [Codsall]

William Childe, Kinlett, near Bewdley, Shropshire

John Lane, Lincolns Inn

Fisher Littleton, Pipe Ridware, Lichfield

Walter Sneyd, Keele

John Sneyd, Belmont, Cheadle

George Chetwynd, Brockton

Sir Robert Lawley, Baronet, Canwall near Tamworth

Henry Vernon, Hilton near Wolverhampton

Richard Gildart, Norton, near Lichfield

John Dolphin, Shenstone

John Gough, Perry Hall near Birmingham

Source: *SRO, D1416/4/2/1.*

TRUSTEES OF BREWOOD
GRAMMAR SCHOOL, 1850

Source: Charles Dunkley, *Brewood Grammar School and the old Grammar Schools,* (D.McGill, Cannock, 1936), pp. 25-26.

Index

Stafford, 16, 45, 54-5, 72, 165, 166n15, 198, 207, 239, 263, 265

Stafford, Henry (1st Baron Stafford), 1-2, 4n2, 9

Stafford, Revd, 74

Standiford/Standeford, 153-4

Stanstead Abbots (Herts), 53, 58, 62

Stanton, Mr, 244, 270

Stevenson and Salt Bank, 72

Stoker's Croft, 127

Stone, 13, 56

Stowell, Lord see Scott, William

Stratford-le-Bow (London), 119, 131, 133-4

Stretton, 9, 10, 13, 195, 207, 242, 258, 264, 280

Sugnall Hall, 61

Talbot, Chetwynd-, family see Chetwynd-Talbot

Talbot, George (Revd), 120

Talbot, Richard (cordwainer), 40, 46, 114

Talbot, Richard (teacher), 112

Talbot, Robert, 71

Taunton Commission Report, 237-241, 253

Taylor, family of headmaster
   James Heber (headmaster), 151, 253-274
   Mary (wife née Pearce), 254
   James (Revd and father), 254-5, 272
   John Charles, 254, 271
   Mary Ethel see Emery, Mary Ethel
   Henry Martin (sibling), 254, 271, 273n3
   William Wilberforce (sibling), 254, 271, 273n2

Taylor, Benjamin, 129

Taylor, Edwin, 257-8

Taylor, John, 267

Taylor, Paul, 192

Teddesley Hall, 51, 211, 219

Telford, Thomas, 150

Temple, Frederick (Dr), 234-5

Thomas, John, 114

Thomas, William, 114

Thompson, John (Captain), 239-40

Thompson, Richard, 240

Thorneycroft, George Benjamin, 196

Thurstans, John, 193

Till, Mr, 122

Tixall, 16

Tollet, George, 55-6, 61-2

Toncks, John, 114

Tong (Salop), 2, 11, 13, 96

Trysull/Treesle, 15, 69, 231, 233, 239

Turner, Henry, 193, 197-201, 203, 217n40

Turner, John (elder), 75 91

Turner, John (younger), 91

Turner, William, 91

Turton, Mr (John), 61

Tysoe (Warks.), 4n2, 9

Underhill, Henry, 206

Underhill, James, 173, 206

Unett, Thomas (Revd), 54, 56-8, 61-2

Vane, Henry (Charity Commissioner), 207, 227-8

Vaughan, Elizabeth, 39-40 see also Newton, Elizabeth; Hand, Elizabeth

Vaughan, John (2nd Viscount Lisburne), 39, 44n37

Vaughan, Mrs, 39

Vaughton family, 117

Vauxhall see Brook House

Venables, Mr, 199-200

Vernon, Augustus Leverson, 256, 264 267, 273n7

Vernon, Henry Charles, 253

Virginia (America), 62-4

Wade, Charles, 153, 155, 158

Wakefield (Yorks), 254, 271-2

Walhouse, Edward see Littleton, Edward John (1st Baron Hatherton)

Wright, Mr, 55

Wrottesley Hall, 54

Wrottesley family

   E.J. (Revd), 242

   Richard (Revd), 54

Wrottesley, John, (9th Baronet and 1st Baron), 120

Wrottesley, John (2nd Baron), 169-70, 187, 205, 207-209, 211-2, 220, 225, 227-9, 239, 246n4

Wrottesley, Arthur (3rd Baron), 256, 259, 262, 264

Yorke, Philip (1st Earl of Hardwicke), 37-8